PATTERN RECOGNITION AND IMAGE ANALYSIS

Selected Papers from the IVth Spanish Symposium

T0320617

SERIES IN MACHINE PERCEPTION AND ARTIFICIAL INTELLIGENCE

Editors: **H. Bunke** (Univ. Bern, Switzerland) and
P. S. P. Wang (Northeastern Univ., USA)

Vol. 1: Pattern Recognition and Image Analysis: Selected Papers
from the IVth Spanish Symposium (Eds. *N. Pérez de la Blanca,
A. Sanfeliu and E. Vidal*)

Forthcoming

Vol. 2: Theory and Applications of Image Analysis: Selected Papers
from the 7th Scandinavian Conference on Image Analysis
(Eds. *P. Johansen and S. I. Olsen*)

Series in Machine Perception and Artificial Intelligence – Vol. 1

PATTERN RECOGNITION AND IMAGE ANALYSIS

Selected Papers from the IVth Spanish Symposium

Edited by

N. Pérez de la Blanca
Universidad de Granada, Granada

A. Sanfeliu
Universidad Politécnica de Cataluña, Barcelona

E. Vidal
Universidad Politécnica de Valencia, Valencia

World Scientific
Singapore • New Jersey • London • Hong Kong

Published by

World Scientific Publishing Co. Pte. Ltd.
P O Box 128, Farrer Road, Singapore 9128
USA office: Suite 1B, 1060 Main Street, River Edge, NJ 07661
UK office: 73 Lynton Mead, Totteridge, London N20 8DH

Library of Congress Cataloging-in-Publication Data

Pattern recognition and image analysis : selected papers from the IVth
   Spanish Symposium / edited by N. Pérez de la Blanca, A. Sanfeliu, E.
   Vidal.
      p.   cm. -- (Series in machine perception and artificial
   intelligence ; vol. 1)
      IVth National Symposium in Pattern Recognition and Image Analysis,
   held September 1990, Granada)
      Includes bibliographical references.
      ISBN 9810208812
      1. Image processing -- Congresses.   2. Pattern recognition systems -
   - Congresses.   3. Computer vision -- Congresses.   4. Automatic speech
   recognition -- Congresses.   I. Pérez de la Blanca, N.   II. Sanfeliu,
   Alberto.   III. Vidal, E.   IV. National Symposium in Pattern
   Recognition and Image Analysis (4th ; 1990 : Granada)   V. Series.
   TA1632.P39   1992   91-40583
   006.4--dc20   CIP

Printed in Singapore by Utopia Press.

PREFACE

Pattern Recognition, Image Analysis and Automatic Speech Recognition have been research areas of interest for a long time in Spain. Until 1982, the Spanish research groups which worked in these areas were spread in several scientific associations and their works seemed not to be sufficiently well known by the scientific community.

In order to join together and share the works related to Pattern Recognition, in 1982, a group of researchers from the universities and scientific institutions decided to create a national association. As a first step, it was originated as a Technical Group inside the CEA-IFAC (Spanish Committee for Automation — International Federation of Automatic Control), under the name "Grupo Técnico de Reconocimiento de Formas -GTRF- (Working Group for Pattern Recognition)". In the same year the incipient association became a member of the International Association for Pattern Recognition -IAPR-.

From 1982 to 1991 the GTRF has organized four national symposiums and has collaborated to coordinate research efforts in the Spanish scientific community. Now, in 1991, the growing interest in so many Pattern Recognition-related fields has made it convenient for the GTRF to be an independent association. The GTRF has thus become an association that enlists people mainly interested in Pattern Recognition, Image Analysis and Automatic Speech Recognition, as well as from other diverse fields such as engineering, computer science, medicine, biology, astronomy, optics, geology, etc.

The new association is denominated "Associación Española de Reconocimiento de Formas y Análisis de Imágenes -AERFAI- (Spanish Association for Pattern Recognition and Image Analysis)".

The AERFAI has assumed new aims, one of them being the dissemination of scientific work that is developed by Spanish research groups. As the last national symposium generated a number of interesting works, we decided to publish a selection of the corresponding papers, with a double purpose: to show the topics which the Spanish research groups are interested in and to make known who is working in each topic.

This book thus contains a selection of eighteen works presented at the IV National Symposium in Pattern Recognition and Image Analysis, held in September 1990 in Granada. The book is structured into four different subareas which more or less reflect the different research works:

1. *Pattern Recognition*
2. *Image Analysis and Computer Vision*
3. *Speech Recognition*
4. *Applications in Image Analysis and Computer Vision*

We hope that this selection of papers will be of interest to the scientific community and that it will help open new contacts between international research groups.

We are thankful to the Spanish colleagues who have contributed to this book with their efforts to translate and enhance the contents of their papers, as well as to the Editor in charge of this series, Prof. Horst Bunke, for his encouragement. We also want to thank Mr. Christopher Glennie of World Scientific Publ. Co., Singapore for his cooperation in the project.

N. Pérez de la Blanca
Universidad de Granada, Granada

A. Sanfeliu
Universidad Politécnica de Cataluña, Barcelona

E. Vidal
Universidad Politécnica de Valencia, Valencia

CONTENTS

PATTERN RECOGNITION

RELAXATION LABELING ALGORITHM BASED ON LEARNING AUTOMATA

E. Fernández

Grupo Avanzado de Control y Visión Artificial
Universidad Politécnica de Madrid, Madrid, Spain

ABSTRACT

Relaxation labeling processes resolve the problem of assigning labels to objects in a manner which is consistent with respect to some specific constraints (or compatibilities). This problem is resolved here by a team of learning automata interacting with an environment that gives responses as to the consistency of labeling selected by the automata. In the environment model proposed here, consistency includes not only compatibilities based on binary relations, but also the tertiary type. An analysis of the proposed relaxation process is given here, by using an explicit definition of consistency.

Afterwards, these processes are applied to the stereoscopic matching of edge points from constraints previously defined. The algorithm is very good in real-time applications, since parallel processing is able, and it is fairly robust to the noise component in the environment. In this application noise may be due to changes in both images, which are acquired from different perspectives.

1. Introduction

Relaxation labeling processes resolve the problem of assigning labels to objects in a manner which is consistent with respect to some domain-specific constraints (world model). Many problems in image processing and artificial intelligence can be formulated in these terms. These processes were initially proposed in vision systems to reduce ambiguity and noise [1]. Here, these processes are applied to solve the matching problem in stereopsis [5]. This problem consists in establishing correspondence between edge points from each image of the stereoscopic pair, in order to obtain a tridimensional structure of a scene. Ambiguity can arise in stereo matching, since each image was initially acquired

4

from a different perspective.

In a labeling problem, one is given [4]:

1) a set of objects, $U = \{1, 2, \ldots, n\}$,
2) a set of labels for each object, $\Lambda = \{1, \ldots, m\}$,
3) a neighbour relation over the objects that specifies which pairs (or N-tuples) of objects constrain each other, and
4) a set of constraints over labels at pairs (or N-tuples) of neighbouring objects.

Objects and labels sets are understood here like edge points belonging to both images of the stereoscopic pair. A probability vector $\underline{P}_i^k = (P_i^k(1), \ldots, P_i^k(m))'$ is associated to each object, where $P_i^k(\alpha)$ expresses the probability of assigning label α to node i at the kth stage of the iterative proccess ($P_i(\alpha)$ value is one if α is always assigned to i, otherwise it is zero). Initial value of the process P_i^0 is obtained through some low-level noisy measurements (for stereo matching, comparing features of two edge points, each one from a different stereo image). As $\underline{P}_i^k$ can take values for a continuous range, then a continuous labeling problem is concerned.

In relaxation labeling, constraints are expressed by real-valued functions $r_{ij}(\alpha, \beta)$ that specify the compatibility degree of assigning α to i, whether β is assigned to j. Here, we consider that these functions can take real values in a continuous range. Most of the compatibility functions are based on relations of binary order, since they add the least computation. However, there are some situations which require the use of tertiary order constraints. In a stereo matching when occlusion problems occur, a label can be assigned to objects in an image without correspondence in the other image (*null* label). Here, tertiary order constraints, like $r_{ijk}(m, \alpha, \beta)$, are involved for *null* labels (in this work, label m always represents these labels), due to the impossibility of defining binary order type.

Several continuous relaxation labeling methods were applied to vision systems. The first method was proposed by Rosenfeld et al. [1] which is a non-linear scheme based on heuristic considerations. In [2] another non-linear one based on a bayesian analysis is shown, where compabilities are understood as conditional probabilities. Faugeras and Berthod [3] propose an objective function whose minimum value is reached by a projected gradient algorithm. The final result for [3] depends on the initial values of probabilities. Hummel and Zucher [4] give a definition of consistency to be satisfied by consistent labelings, and an optimization algorithm to maximize a local medium consistency function.

Here, an algorithm based on learning automata is used, that includes not only binary type compatibilities like in [12], but also tertiary type. The same analysis method of the iterative process proposed in [12] is used here to obtain the identical local convergence results. This is a proof that relaxation labeling based on learning automata is extendable to higher order compatibilities also. Afterwards, these processes are applied to the stereoscopic matching of edge points from the constraints previously defined in [14]. Although, compatibility functions can take values in a continuous range, they were intended for the stereo matching algorithms to be of the "all of none" type that express relations of each edge point with respect to its neighbours. It was possible to define constraints of that type, and an increase of speed was noticed. For this case, relaxation labeling consists of a team of automata (as many automata as objects) where each automation selects a tentative labeling according to its label probability vector. The response of the environment to each automata depends upon the consistency of the labelings chosen by the automata team. Afterwards, automata update its probabilities vectors and the cycle is repeated until the convergency is reached.

Learning-automata relaxation labeling actually uses a probabilistic iterative scheme that becomes fairly robust to noise components in the environment. In stereo vision noise is due to changes in both images, since they are acquired from different perspectives. Stochastic relaxation was also used in [8] for vision at which intensity values of pixels belonging to an image neighbourhood are related as couplings of atoms in a chemical system. Annealing processes are simulated which guarantee convergence to the global maxima of the posterior distribution. In [9] an expression of potential energy for stereo matching is proposed from the energy analysis of a spring model, and the problem is to find a disparity map with minimal energy. Although a coarse-to-fine strategy is used in [9] a large computational cost is required to reach convergency. A model based on learning automata better accepts local parallel operations.

2. Consistency and Unambiguity

The definition of consistency given above is the same as in [4]. The variables α, β, Γ and γ will be used in the sequel as notation for labels, and variables i, j and k for objects. An unambiguous labeling assignment is a function mapping from U, the set of objects, to $\wedge$, the set of labels. This can be represented by an m-vector $\underline{P}_i = (P_i(1),...,P_i(m))'$ for each object i. The space of unambiguous labelings is defined by

$$K^* = \{\underline{P} \in \Re^{mn} / P = (\underline{P}'_1,...,\underline{P}'_n)'$$

$$\underline{P}_i = (P_i(1),...,P_i(m))' \in \Re^m$$

$$P_i(\alpha) = 0 \text{ ó } 1, \forall \alpha, i; \sum_{\alpha=1}^{m} P_i(\alpha) = 1, \forall i\} \tag{1}$$

Given a vector $\underline{P}$ in K^*, the corresponding unambiguous assignment is determined exactly, i.e., the set of vectors in K* is in one-to-one correspondence with the set of mappings from objects to labels. The space K* can be extended to the space of weighted labeling assignments by

$$K = \{P \in \Re^{mn} \,/\, \underline{P} = (\underline{P}'_1,\ldots,\underline{P}'_n)'$$

$$\underline{P}_i = (P_i(1),\ldots,P_i(m))' \in \Re^m$$

$$0 \le P_i(\alpha) \le 1, \; \sum_{\alpha=1}^{m} P_i(\alpha) = 1, \; \forall\, i\} \tag{2}$$

The space K^* can represent ambiguous labelings, and expresses the probability values previous to convergence in the process. The label m is considered when compatibility functions $r_{ijk}(m,\alpha,\beta)$ take place, since they could not be expressed by binary order relations (cases like $r_{ijj}(m,\alpha,\alpha)$ are also considered). Compatibility function values belong to the interval [0,1] (where value one means maximum compatibility). Cases like $r_{ii}(\alpha,\alpha)$ are always zero. Symmetry always exists for the tertiary case $r_{ijk}(m, \alpha, \beta) = r_{ijk}(m,\beta,\alpha)$, but this is not true for the binary case.

Definition 1) The support for labels α and m at object i by the label assignment $\underline{P}$ is given by

$$S_i(\alpha,\underline{P}) = \sum_{j=1}^{n} \sum_{\beta=1}^{m} r_{ij}(\alpha,\beta) \,.\, P_j(\beta) \tag{3}$$

$$S_i(m,\underline{P}) = \sum_{j=1}^{n} \sum_{\beta=1}^{n-1} \sum_{k=1}^{n} \sum_{\Gamma=1}^{m-1} r_{ijk}(m,\beta,\Gamma) \,.\, P_j(\beta) \,.\, P_k(\Gamma) \tag{4}$$

Definition 2) Let us suppose $\underline{P} \in K$ is a weighted labeling assignment, then $\underline{P}$ is consistent if

$$\sum_{\alpha=1}^{m} P_i(\alpha) \,.\, S_i(\alpha,\underline{P}) \ge \sum_{\alpha=1}^{m} v_i(\alpha) \,.\, S_i(\alpha,\underline{P}), \; \forall\, i, \; \forall\, \underline{v} \in K \tag{5}$$

Consistency is strict in Eq. 5, if inequality intervenes only.

3. Learning Automaton

A learning automaton is a stochastic automaton connected in a feedback loop with a random environment. A stochastic automaton is defined by a sextuple

$<I,O,Q,P,h,A>$, where I, O and Q are the inputs, outputs and states alphabets of the stochastic automaton. Output function h: $Q \rightarrow S$ sets up a mapping from each state to one output, and P is the transition probabilities function $IxQ \rightarrow [0,1]^n$. The function P is usually simplified by an action probability vector $\underline{P}$, where a probability value is assigned to each state. Vector $\underline{P}$ can be expressed as $\underline{P}^k=(P_1^k,...,P_n^k)$, where P_i^k is the election probability of the q_i state at the stage k. Values of P_i^k follow

$$0 \leq P_i^k \leq 1, i=1,..,n \quad \text{and} \quad \sum_{i=1}^{n} P_i^k=1 \tag{6}$$

Updating scheme A can be expressed at the stage k by $\underline{P}^{k+1} = A(\underline{P}^k,q^k,e^k)$ (e^k is the the automaton input at the stage k). A updates the probability vector for the next stage.

The operation of a learning automaton at the stage k consists of choosing an action i (i= 1,...,n, $q_i \in Q$) according to the probability vector $\underline{P}^k$. For this choice the environment responds with a random reward C_i. Then, the automaton updates the probability vector for the stage k+1, according to the updating scheme A. The cycle is repeated by choosing another action at k+1.

The environment is defined by the probabilities C_i (i=1,..,n), where each C_i is a constant value for a stationary environment. Three types of environment models exist [11], depending on the reactions of the environment. The P-model of an environment is for I = {0,1}, the Q-model is for I = {e_i,...,e_p}, and the S-model for I = [0,1].

4. Relaxation Labeling with Learning Automata including Tertiary Compatibilities

This relaxation labeling method consists of several learning automata, one for each object, at which each automation interacts with an environment. In Fig. 1 the relaxation labeling model is represented. Automata actions are associated with the possible labels of the considered object. If it is supposed that the automation A_i has chosen label α, according to its action probability vector $\underline{P}_i$, the environment response to the automaton A_i is symbolizied as $\beta_{i\alpha}$. This variable depends on the consistency of the labeling chosen by the automata team. If label ß is chosen by A_j, the contribution of A_j to A_i is one with probability $r_{ij}(\alpha,\beta)$. If α is equal to m (or *null*) label, then compatibilities of the type $r_{ijk}(m,\beta,\Gamma)$ are involved and a second automaton A_k is considered. A_i will use a simple average of all these as the environment reward. Then, environment responses are defined by

8

$$\beta_{i\alpha} = 1/A(r) . \sum_{j=1}^{n} X_{ij}^{\alpha} , \quad \alpha < m \tag{7}$$

$$\beta_{im} = 1/A'(r) . \sum_{j=1}^{n} \sum_{k=1}^{n} X_{ijk}^{m} , \quad 0 \leq r < n-1 \tag{8}$$

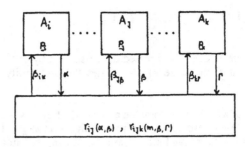

Fig. 1. Relaxation labeling with learning automata.

In Eqs. 7 and 8 X_{ij}^{α} and X_{ijk}^{m} are both random variables that can take 0 or 1 with the following distributions

$$\text{Prob } [X_{ij}^{\alpha}=1] = \sum_{\beta=1}^{m-1} r_{ij}(\alpha,\beta) . P_j(\beta) \tag{9}$$

$$\text{Prob } [X_{ijk}^{m}=1] = \sum_{\beta=1}^{m-1} \sum_{\Gamma=1}^{m-1} r_{ijk}(m,\beta,\Gamma) . P_j(\beta) . P_k(\Gamma) \tag{10}$$

A(r) and A'(r) in Eqs. 7 and 8 mean the number of binary and tertiary relations of each object with respect to the remainder of the objects. Variables A(r) and A'(r) depend on the number r of objects that have chosen label m, since X_{ij}^{α} always takes zero provided that label m has been chosen by A_j. It is the same for X_{ijk}^{m}, whether A_j and/ or A_k have chosen label m.

It is easy to see that $\beta_{i\alpha}$ can take a finite set of values belonging to the interval [0,1]. Also, the distribution of $\beta_{i\alpha}$ is time varying because it depends on $\underline{P}$. Thus, we have a nonstationary Q-model environment for each automaton.

Let us rewrite X_{ij}^{α} and X_{ijk}^{m} by the following mass functions

$$\text{Prob } [X_{ij}{}^{\alpha} = r_{ij}(\alpha,\beta)] = P_j(\beta) \tag{11}$$

$$\text{Prob } [X_{ijk}{}^{m} = r_{ijk}(m,\beta,\Gamma)] = P_j(\beta) \cdot P_k(\Gamma) \tag{12}$$

Then, the expressions of the environment responses enter into the analysis as

$$E[\beta_{i\alpha}/\underline{P}] = E[\Phi] \cdot \sum_{j=1}^{n} \sum_{\beta=1}^{m-1} r_{ij}(\alpha,\beta) \cdot P_j(\beta), \ \alpha < m \tag{13}$$

$$E[\beta_{im}/\underline{P}] = E[\Psi] \cdot \sum_{j,k=1}^{n} \sum_{\beta,\Gamma=1}^{m-1} r_{ijk}(m,\beta,\Gamma) \cdot P_j(\beta) \cdot P_k(\Gamma) \tag{14}$$

In Eqs. 13 and 14 the expressions of $E[\Phi]$ and $E[\Psi]$ are

$$E[\Phi] = \sum_{r=0}^{n-1} 1/A(r) \cdot P_r[X=r]$$

$$= 1/V_n \cdot \sum_{i=0}^{n} [1-P_i(m)] + \sum_{r=1}^{n-1} 1/A(r) \cdot P_r[X=r] \tag{15}$$

$$E[\Psi] = \sum_{r=0}^{n-1} 1/A(r) \cdot P_r[X=r]$$

$$= 1/V'_n \cdot \sum_{i=0}^{n} [1-P_i(m)] + \sum_{r=1}^{n-1} 1/A(r) \cdot P_r[X=r] \tag{16}$$

In Eqs. 15 and 16, $P_r[X=r]$ indicates the probability of r objects choosing label m from the total number V_n (V'_n represents in Eq. 16 the total number for binary relations). $P_r[X=r]$ depends only on $P_i(m)$, $i=1,...,n$. A classical updating scheme in learning automata theory, called Linear Reward Inaction (denoted by L_{R-I}), is used in this case as the updating scheme. If the automaton A_i has chosen the label α at the kth stage, updating of probabilities at the next stage from the environment response $\beta_{i\alpha}(k)$ is

$$P_{i\alpha}(k+1) = P_{i\alpha}(k) + a \cdot [1 - P_{i\alpha}(k)] \cdot \beta_{i\alpha}(k) \tag{17}$$

$$P_{i\beta}(k+1) = P_{i\beta}(k) - a \cdot P_{i\beta}(k) \cdot \beta_{i\alpha}(k), \ \beta \neq \alpha \tag{18}$$

5. Analysis of the Proposed Relaxation Process

Let us express the ordinary differential equation ODE of the proposed process as

$$\Delta \underline{P}(k) = E[\underline{P}(k+1)-\underline{P}(k)/\underline{P}(k)]. \tag{19}$$

Let

$$\Delta \underline{P}(k) = (\Delta \underline{P}_1(k),\dots,\Delta \underline{P}_n(k)) \tag{20}$$

and

$$\Delta \underline{P}_i(k) = (\Delta P_{i1}(k),\dots,\Delta P_{im}(k)) \tag{21}$$

Since $\underline{P}_i(k)$ is a Markovian process, the ODE in Eq. 19 can be expressed as $\underline{\dot{P}}=\underline{f}(\underline{P})$. Now, using Eqs. 11-16, we get the expression of each element in Eq. 21

$$\Delta P_{i\alpha}(k) = E[\Phi] \cdot a\, P_{i\alpha} \cdot \{\sum_{\beta=\alpha}^{m-1} P_{i\beta} \cdot [\sum_{j=1}^{n}\sum_{\Gamma=1}^{m-1} \{r_{ij}(\alpha,\Gamma)-r_{ij}(\beta,\Gamma)\} \cdot P_{j\Gamma}]$$

$$+ a\, P_{i\alpha}\, P_{im} \cdot [\sum_{j=1}^{n}\sum_{\Gamma=1}^{m-1} \{E[\Phi] \cdot r_{ij}(\alpha,\Gamma) - \sum_{k=1}^{n}\sum_{\gamma=1}^{m-1} E[\Psi] \cdot r_{ijk}(m,\Gamma,\gamma)$$

$$\cdot P_{k\gamma}\} \cdot P_{j\Gamma}]\} = a\, f_{i\alpha}(\underline{P}),\ \alpha \neq m \tag{22}$$

$$\Delta P_{im}(k) = a\, P_{im} \cdot \{\sum_{\beta=1}^{m-1} P_{i\beta} \cdot [\sum_{j=1}^{n}\sum_{\Gamma=1}^{m-1} \{\sum_{k=1}^{n}\sum_{\gamma=1}^{m-1} E[\Psi] \cdot r_{ijk}(\alpha,\Gamma,\gamma) \cdot P_{k\gamma}$$

$$- E[\Phi] \cdot r_{ij}(\beta,\Gamma)\} \cdot P_{j\Gamma}]\} = a\, f_{im}(\underline{P}) \tag{23}$$

Let us suppose that we are considering a labeling with unambiguous and strictly consistent solutions of the type $\underline{P}^0=(e'_{\alpha1},\dots,e'_{\alpha l},e'_m,\dots,e'_m)'$, where each $e'_{\alpha i}$ $(i=1,\dots,l)$ is an m-dimensional unit vector with the α_i-th unity component. Vectors of $\underline{P}^0$ from $1+1$ $(1<1\leq n)$ to n have the mth unity component (there is no special significance for considering these elements the last components). Vectors of the type $\underline{P}^0$ belong to the K^* space (Eq. 1), since they represent the unambiguous labelings. Vectors like $\underline{P}^0$ will be referred to subsequently as *corners*. The first step for the analysis of the ODE in Eq. 19 is the study of the zeros of f (Eqs. 22-23), and then to investigate if solutions like $\underline{P}^0$ are also zeros of $\underline{f}$. This is demonstrated by the following lemma (its proof appears in Appendix A).

Lemma 1

All the solutions of $\underline{P}^0$ are zeros of $\underline{f}$. Others zeros $\underline{P}$ of $\underline{f}$ satisfy

If $P_{im} = 0$, then

$$\sum_{j=1}^{n} \sum_{\beta=1}^{m-1} \{r_{ij}(1,\beta) - r_{ij}(\alpha,\beta)\} \cdot P_{j\beta} = 0, \quad \alpha < m, \ P_{i\alpha} \neq 0 \tag{24}$$

and

If $P_{im} \neq 0$, besides Eq. 24 they also satisfy

$$\sum_{j=1}^{n} \sum_{\beta=1}^{m-1} [E[\Phi] \cdot r_{ij}(1,\beta) - \{\sum_{j=1}^{n} \sum_{\beta=1}^{m-1} E[\Psi] \cdot r_{ijk}(m,\beta,\Gamma) \cdot P_{kr}\}] \cdot P_{j\beta} = 0 \tag{25}$$

Consider the ordinary differential equation (ODE) given by

$$\dot{\underline{P}} = \underline{f}(\underline{P}) \tag{26}$$

From Lemma 1 we know all the stationary points of Eq. 26. The following lemma is concerned with its stability properties (its proof appears in Appendix B). The stability analysis of a *corner* vector $\underline{P}^0 = (e'_{t1},...,e'_{tl},e'_{m},...,e'_{m})'$ is made in a local zone of $\underline{P}^0$, as the function $\underline{f}(\underline{P})$ is non-linear. The function $\underline{f}(\underline{P})$ is approximated in the local zone of $\underline{P}^0$ by a linear function in order to analyse the stability of the linear function. The analysis method used in this case is by Lyapunov.

Lemma 2

1) If the vector $\underline{P}$ is a *corner* which represents a strictly consistent labeling, then it is an asymptotically stable stationary point of Eq. 26.

2) Each *corner* that is a stable stationary point of Eq. 26 represents a consistent labeling.

3) Each nonconsistent *corner* and each interior zero of $\underline{f}$ (Eq. 26) is an unstable stationary point of Eq. 26.

Now that the solutions to Eq. 26 are well characterized, the next step in the analysis is to show that the algorithm converges to the solution of Eq. 26. It was proved in [12] that the sequence of interpolated processes $\{\underline{P}^a(.)\}$ converges weakly to the process

12

$\underline{X}$ (.), which satisfies the ODE $\underline{\dot{X}} = \underline{f}(X)$, as $\underline{P}^a(0) = \underline{X}(0)$ and a → 0. The same proof given in [12] has application for the process proposed here, since the environment responses $\beta_{i\alpha}$ ($\alpha < m$) and β_{im} have the same properties as in [12] to follow this Theorem.

6. Experimental Results

The so-called block scenes have been used in the experiments. The images were taken by applying a linear shift to the cameras and the digitized images were processed by a spatial resolution of 128x128 pixels. For the first stereoscopic pair, we have included in the scene objects of repeated shapes, with the purpose of testing the way in which the algorithms solve the ambiguity problem. In Fig. 2 it is shown results of stereo matching for edge points and edges. Correspondence for edge points is pointed out by the same number in both images of Fig. 2, whereas for edges it is pointed out by the same number included in a cycle.

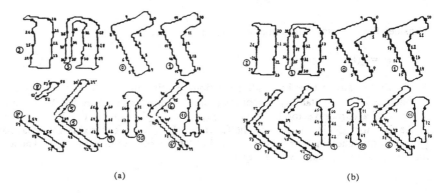

(a)   (b)

Fig. 2. Matching of edge points and edges of images. (a) Object points and object edges. (b) Label points and label edges.

If there appears wrong matching (like those corresponding to the object edges 3, 3' and 8 in Fig. 2) it is due to the fact that the characteristics obtained from these points differ from those of their equivalent points 3' and 8 is the edge break. Points in edge 11 appear without correspondence. This last problem has rather no significance, since labeling algorithms get the *null* label when the consistency value is small. Tables 1 and 2 show

0 (1.00)	3 (1.00)	6 (0.75)	8'(1.00)	11 (1.00)
1 (1.00)	3'(1.00)	6'(1.00)	9 (1.00)	
2 (1.00)	5 (0.75)	8 (1.00)	10 (0.88)	

Table 1. Correspondences in one per cent between edges shown in Fig. 2.

the average in one per cent of correspondences for edge points and edges, when relaxation processes were run eight times.

0 (1.00)	17 (1.00)	32 (0.88)	48 (1.00)	63 (1.00)
1 (1.00)	18 (1.00)	33 (0.63)	49 (1.00)	64 (1.00)
2 (1.00)	19 (1.00)	34 (0.63)	50 (1.00)	65 (0.88)
3 (1.00)	20 (0.50)	35 (0.63)	51 (1.00)	66 (1.00)
4 (1.00)	21 (1.00)	36 (0.63)	52 (0.50)	67 (1.00)
5 (1.00)	22 (1.00)	37 (0.63)	52'(0.50)	68 (1.00)
6 (1.00)	23 (1.00)	38 (0.50)	53 (0.50)	69 (1.00)
7 (1.00)	24 (1.00)	39 (0.75)	53'(0.50)	70 (1.00)
8 (1.00)	25 (1.00)	40 (0.75)	54 (0.63)	71 (0.88)
9 (0.88)	26 (1.00)	41 (0.75)	55 (0.63)	72 (0.38)
10 (1.00)	27 (0.75)	42 (0.63)	56 (0.50)	73 (0.38)
11 (1.00)	28 (0.88)	43 (0.75)	57 (0.63)	
12 (1.00)	29 (0.88)	44 (0.88)	58 (0.63)	
13 (1.00)	29'(1.00)	45 (0.63)	59 (0.63)	
14 (1.00)	30 (0.88)	46 (0.50)	60 (1.00)	
15 (1.00)	30'(1.00)	47 (0.75)	61 (1.00)	
16 (1.00)	31 (0.88)	47'(1.00)	62 (1.00)	

Table 2. Correspondences in one per cent between edge points shown in Fig. 2.

A second stereoscopic pair is shown with the purpose of testing the way in which the algorithms detect occlusion. Note that total occlusion is detected in all the cases as it is shown in Fig. 3. Tables 3 and 4 show the average in one per cent of correspondences for edge points and edges, when relaxation processes were also run eight times.

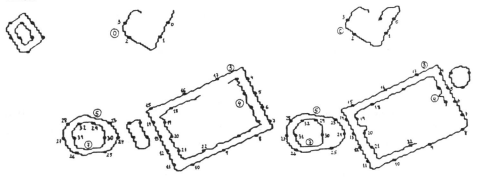

Fig. 3. Matching of edge points and edges of images. (a) Object points and object edges. (b) Label points and label edges.

7. Conclusions

A relaxation algorithm based on learning automata has been proposed. Automata

14

interact with an environment which includes besides binary order compatibilities also tertiary order. After the analysis of the algorithm, we get the same conclusions as the environment that included only compatibilities of binary type. Then, this relaxation algorithm was applied to obtain stereoscopic matching. Deductions made in the process analysis were confirmed by the good experimental results that were obtained. The type of environment used was a P-model (responses all or none), not a Q-model, in order to decrease the interactions number that reached the convergence.

0 (1.00)	3 (1.00)	4 (1.00)	5 (1.00)	7 (1.00)

Table 3. Correspondences in one per cent between edges shown in Fig. 3.

0 (1.00)	8 (1.00)	17 (1.00)	25 (1.00)
1 (1.00)	9 (1.00)	18 (1.00)	26 (1.00)
2 (1.00)	10 (1.00)	19 (1.00)	27 (1.00)
3 (1.00)	12 (1.00)	20 (1.00)	28 (1.00)
4 (1.00)	13 (1.00)	21 (0.88)	29 (0.63)
5 (1.00)	14 (1.00)	22 (1.00)	30 (1.00)
6 (1.00)	15 (1.00)	23 (0.63)	31 (1.00)
7 (1.00)	16 (1.00)	24 (1.00)	32 (0.88)

Table 4. Correspondences in one per cent between edge points shown in Fig. 3.

Appendix A

By inspection from Eqs. 22 and 23 it is obvious that for a *corner* $\underline{P}^0$, $f_{i\alpha}(\underline{P}^0) = 0$, $\alpha \neq m$ and $f_{im}(\underline{P}^0) = 0$. In the case of $P_{im} \neq 0$ we will analyse other zeros of $\underline{f}$. The following expressions are defined, since they allow more simplification after

$$C_{i\alpha} = E[\Phi] \cdot \sum_{j=1}^{n} \sum_{\beta=1}^{m-1} r_{ij}(\alpha,\beta) \cdot P_{j\beta} \tag{27}$$

and

$$g_{i\alpha} = \sum_{\beta \neq \alpha}^{m-1} P_{i\beta} \cdot [\sum_{j=1}^{n} \sum_{\Gamma=1}^{m-1} \{ E[\Psi] \cdot r_{ij}(\alpha,\Gamma) - E[\Phi] \cdot r_{ij}(\beta,\Gamma) \} \cdot P_{j\Gamma}]$$

$$= \sum_{\beta \neq \alpha}^{m-1} P_{i\beta} \cdot [C_{i\alpha} - C_{i\beta}] \tag{28}$$

Let us suppose that for the first 1 labels ($1 \leq$ m-1) probability is distinct of zero (there is no significance considering $P_{i\alpha} \neq 0$, for $\alpha \neq 1$), and the rest of the probabilities are zeroes. Then, we must have $g_{i\alpha} = 0$, $\alpha \leq 1$. Operating with $g_{i1} - g_{i\beta}$ in Eqs. 27 and 28, it follows

$$\sum_{\alpha=1}^{1} P_{i\alpha} = 1, \ i=1, \dots ,n \tag{29}$$

We notice

$$g_{i1} - g_{i\alpha} = C_{i1} - C_{i\alpha} \tag{30}$$

Let us consider Eqs. 22 and 23. From Eq. 30 we see that the zeros of $\underline{f}$ in this case follow the lemma.

The next step is the analysis of $\underline{f}$ zeros when $P_{im} \neq 0$, $P_{i\alpha} \neq 0$, $\alpha \leq 1$ ($1 \leq$ m-1) and the remainder of the probabilities are zero. Besides Eqs. 27 and 28, other functions in this case are defined

$$C_{im} = E[\Psi] \cdot \sum_{j=1}^{n} \sum_{\beta=1}^{m-1} \sum_{k=1}^{n} \sum_{\Gamma=1}^{m-1} r_{ijk}(m,\beta,\Gamma) \cdot P_{j\beta} \cdot P_{k\Gamma} \tag{31}$$

and

$$g_{im} = \sum_{\beta=1}^{m-1} P_{i\beta} \cdot [\sum_{j=1}^{n} \sum_{\Gamma=1}^{m-1} \sum_{k=1}^{n} \sum_{\gamma=1}^{m-1} \{E[\Psi] \cdot r_{ijk}(m,\Gamma,\gamma) P_{k\gamma} - E[\Phi]$$

$$\cdot r_{ij}(\alpha,\Gamma)\} \cdot P_{j\Gamma}] = \sum_{\beta=\alpha}^{m-1} P_{i\beta} \cdot [C_{im} - C_{i\beta}] \tag{32}$$

From Eqs. 31 and 32, we get

$$g_{i\alpha} + P_{im} [C_{i\alpha} - C_{im}] = 0 \tag{33}$$

and

$$g_{i\alpha} = 0, \ \alpha \leq 1, \ \alpha \neq m \tag{34}$$

Let us operate the following expressions

$$g_{i1} + P_{im} \ [C_{i1}-C_{im}] - g_{i2} - P_{im} \ [C_{i2}-C_{im}]$$

$$\cdot$$
$$\cdot$$

$$g_{i1} + P_{im} \ [C_{i1}-C_{im}] - g_{i1} - P_{im} \ [C_{i1}-C_{im}]$$
$$g_{i1} + P_{im} \ [C_{i1}-C_{im}] - g_{im} \tag{35}$$

If each expression in Eq. 35 is equalized to zero, we infer

$$C_{i1} - C_{i\alpha} = 0, \ \forall \ \alpha \leq 1 \tag{36}$$

and

$$C_{i1} - C_{im} = 0 \tag{37}$$

From Eq. 37, and considering Eqs. 22 and 23, we see that the zeros of f satisfy the lemma for this case.

Remark 1): Lemma 1 is general, although label 1 has been considered. Let us suppose label ß with $P_{i\beta} \neq 0$ (and $\beta \leq 1$), then we have

$$C_{i1}-C_{i\alpha} = C_{i1}-C_{i\beta} + C_{i\beta}-C_{i\alpha} = C_{i\beta}-C_{i\alpha}$$
$$C_{i1}-C_{im} = C_{i1}-C_{i\beta} + C_{i\beta}-C_{im} = C_{i\beta}-C_{im} \tag{38}$$

Equalities obtained from the above lemma are transformed into others at which label β is concerned instead of label 1, since $C_{i1}-C_{i\beta}=0$ in Lemma 1.

Appendix B

We notice that the function f(P) in Eqs. 22 and 23 is non-linear. Therefore, the stability analysis of a *corner* $\underline{P}^0=(e'_{\alpha 1},...,e'_{\alpha 1},e'_m,...,e'_m)'$ (where, e'_{ti}, i=1,...,1, $t_i \leq m-1$ is a unit vector) will be in a local zone of $\underline{P}^0$. The function $\underline{f}(\underline{P})$ is approximated by a linear one in the local zone of $\underline{P}^0$ in order to analyse the stability of the linear function. After applying the linear approximation of $\underline{f}(\underline{P})$ the components of $\underline{f}(\underline{P})$ have the following expressions

$$f_{i\alpha} = 1/V_n \cdot P_{i\alpha} \sum_{j=1}^{l} \{ r_{ij}(\alpha,\alpha_{tj}) - r_{ij}(\alpha_{ti},\alpha_{tj}) \} + T.O.S.,$$

$$\alpha \neq t_i \ (\alpha < m) \tag{39}$$

$$f_{im} = P_{im} \cdot \sum_{j=1}^{l} [\sum_{k=1}^{l} \{r_{ijk}(m,\alpha_{tj},\alpha_{tk})/V'_n\} - r_{ij}(\alpha_{ti},\alpha_{tj})/V_n]$$

$$+ T.O.S. \tag{40}$$

After applying the linear approximation of $\underline{P}^0$, other unit vectors of $\underline{P}^0$, e'_m, have the following expression

$$f_{i\alpha} = P_{i\alpha} \cdot \sum_{j=1}^{l} [r_{ij}(\alpha,\alpha_{tj})/V_n - \sum_{k=1}^{l} \{r_{ijk}(m,\alpha_{tj},\alpha_{tk})/V'_n\}] + T.O.S. \tag{41}$$

The following transformation allows us to change the origin to the vector $\underline{P}^0$

$$\begin{aligned} \tilde{P}_{i\alpha} &= P_{i\alpha}, \ \alpha \neq t_i \\ &= 1 - P_{iti}, \ \alpha = t_i, \ i = 1,...,l \end{aligned} \tag{42}$$

$$\begin{aligned} \tilde{P}_{i\alpha} &= P_{i\alpha}, \ \alpha \neq m \\ &= 1 - P_{im}, \ \alpha = m, \ i = l+1,...,n \end{aligned} \tag{43}$$

After applying the transformation of Eqs. 42 and 43, the components of $\underline{f}$ have the following expressions

$$f_{i\alpha} = 1/V_n \cdot \tilde{P}_{i\alpha} \sum_{j=1}^{l} [r_{ij}(\alpha,\alpha_{tj}) - r_{ij}(\alpha_{ti},\alpha_{tj})] + T.O.S., \ \alpha < m \tag{44}$$

$$f_{im} = \tilde{P}_{im} \cdot \sum_{j=1}^{l} [\sum_{k=1}^{l} \{r_{ijk}(m,\alpha_{tj},\alpha_{tk})/V'_n\} - r_{ij}(\alpha_{ti},\alpha_{tj})/V_n] + T.O.S.,$$

$$i = 1,...,l \tag{45}$$

$$f_{i\alpha} = \tilde{P}_{i\alpha} \cdot \sum_{k=1}^{l} [r_{ij}(\alpha,\alpha_{tj})/V_n - \sum_{j=1}^{l} \{r_{ijk}(m,\alpha_{tj},\alpha_{tk})/V'_n\}] + T.O.S.,$$

$$\forall \alpha, \ i = l+1,...,n \tag{46}$$

1) Let us define the positive definite function $\forall\, \widetilde{\underline{P}} \in K,\ \widetilde{\underline{P}} \neq \widetilde{\underline{P}}^0$

$$U_1(\widetilde{\underline{P}}) = \sum_{i=1}^{n} \left[\sum_{\alpha=1}^{m-1} \widetilde{P}_{i\alpha} + \widetilde{P}_{im} \right] \tag{47}$$

Derivative function of $U_1(\widetilde{\underline{P}}^0)$ in Eq. 47 from the linear function has the expression

$$\dot{U}_1(\widetilde{\underline{P}}) = \text{diag}\,(a_{i\beta}, a_{im})\ \text{x diag}\,(P_{i\alpha}, P_{im}), \ \alpha < m \tag{48}$$

where

$$a_{i\alpha} = 1/V_n \sum_{j=1}^{l} [r_{ij}(\alpha, \alpha_{tj}) - r_{ij}(\alpha_{ti}, \alpha_{tj})], \ \alpha < m \tag{49}$$

$$a_{im} = \sum_{j=1}^{l} \left[\sum_{k=1}^{l} \{r_{ijk}(m, \alpha_{tj}, \alpha_{tk})/V'_n\} - r_{ij}(\alpha_{ti}, \alpha_{tj})/V_n \right]$$
$$i = 1, \dots, l \tag{50}$$

$$a_{i\alpha} = \sum_{k=1}^{l} [r_{ij}(\alpha, \alpha_{tj})/V_n - \sum_{j=1}^{l} r_{ijk}(m, \alpha_{tj}, \alpha_{tk})/V'_n], \ i = l+1, \dots, n \tag{51}$$

As $\widetilde{\underline{P}}$ is a strictly consistent labeling, we infer $a_{i\alpha} < 0,\ \forall\,\alpha,\ 1=1, \dots, n$. Then, $\dot{U}_1(\widetilde{\underline{P}})$ is negative definite except in the origin.

2) The EDO $\dot{\widetilde{\underline{P}}} = \underline{f}(\widetilde{\underline{P}})$ can be expressed as $\dot{\widetilde{\underline{P}}} = A\widetilde{\underline{P}}$, where $a = \text{diag}(a_{i\alpha})$. If $\widetilde{\underline{P}}$ is a stable stationary point, the eigenvalues have nonpositive real parts and hence $a_{i\alpha} < 0,\ \forall\,\alpha$, $1=1, \dots, n$. This implies $\widetilde{\underline{P}}$ is consistent.

3) Let us suppose that $\underline{P}^0$ is a nonconsistent *corner*. Then, at least for one unit vector $e'_{\alpha ti}$ (or e'_m) of $\underline{P}^0$, say e', we must have

$$\sum_{j=1}^{l} [r_{ij}(\alpha, \alpha_{tj}) - r_{ij}(\alpha_{ti}, \alpha_{tj})] > 0, \ i = 1, \dots, l \tag{52}$$

$$\sum_{j=1}^{l} \left[\sum_{k=1}^{l} \{r_{ijk}(m, \alpha_{tj}, \alpha_{tk})/V'_n\} - r_{ij}(\alpha_{ti}, \alpha_{tj})/V_n \right] > 0,$$

$$i = l+1, \dots, n \tag{53}$$

Consider the positive definite function (except in $\underline{P}^0$)

$$U_2(\widetilde{\underline{P}}) = P_{i\alpha i} \; , \; i = 1,\ldots,l$$

$$= P_{i\alpha m}, \; i = l+1,\ldots,n \tag{54}$$

Then

$$\dot{U}_2(\widetilde{\underline{P}}) = f_{i\alpha i} \; , \; i = 1,\ldots,l$$

$$= f_{i\alpha m} \quad , \; i = l+1,\ldots,n \tag{55}$$

Eq. 55 is unstable in $\underline{P}^0$ as Lyapunov, since $\dot{U}_2(\widetilde{\underline{P}})$ is positive except in $\underline{P}^0$ (Eqs. 44-46).

Consider $\bar{\underline{P}} = (\bar{\underline{P}}'_1, \ldots, \bar{\underline{P}}'_n)'$ as an interior zero of $\underline{f}$ with $P_{i\alpha} \neq 0$, and the following transformation of $\bar{\underline{P}}$ to the origin

$$\widetilde{P}_{i\alpha} = P_{i\alpha} - \bar{P}_{i\alpha} \; , \quad \alpha < m$$

$$\widetilde{P}_{im} = P_{im} - \bar{P}_{im} \; , \quad i = 1,\ldots,n \tag{56}$$

We can express the linear transformation of Eq. 56 as $\dot{\widetilde{\underline{P}}} = A\widetilde{\underline{P}}$, where all the diagonal elements of A are zero. Hence, at least one eigenvalue of A must have a positive real part and P is unstable. Even the rare case of all eigenvalues being purely imaginary can be excluded if A is made to be odd by adding a few extra objects or labels.

Remark 2): As non-linear terms in Eqs. 22 and 23 were not considered in detail, necessary and sufficient conditions are not inferred for asymptotic stability which has been until now a difficult problem.

8. References

1. A. Rosenfeld, R.A. Hummel, and S.W. Zucker, *Scene labeling by relaxation operations*, IEEE Trans. Syst., Man, Cybern. **SMC-6** (1976) pp. 420-443.

2. S. Peleg, *A new probabilistic relaxation scheme*, IEEE Trans. on Pattern Anal. Machine Intell. **PAMI-2** (1979) pp. 362-369.

3. O.D. Faugeras and M. Berthod, *Improving consistency and reducing*

20

ambiguity in stochastic labeling: An optimization approach, IEEE Trans. Pattern Anal. Machine Intell. **PAMI-3** (1981) pp. 412-424.

4. R.A. Hummel, and S.W. Zucker, *On the foundations of relaxation labeling processes*, IEEE Trans. Pattern Anal. Machine Intell. **PAMI-5** (1983) pp. 267-287.

5. S.T. Barnard and M.A. Fischler, *Computational stereo*, ACM Computing Surveys, **vol. 14** (1982), pp. 553-572.

6. D. Marr and T. Poggio, *Cooperative computation of stereo disparity*, (Science, N.Y., 1976) pp. 283-287.

7. R.O. Duda and P.E. Hart, *Pattern clasification and scene analysis*, (Wiley, N.Y., 1973).

8. S. Geman and D. Geman, *Stochastic relaxation, Gibbs distributions, and the Bayesian restoration of images*, IEEE Trans. Pattern Anal. Machine Intell. **PAMI-6** (1984) pp. 721-741.

9. S. T. Barnard, *Stochastic stereo matching over scale*, Int. Journal of Computer Vision, **vol. 3** (1989) pp. 17-32.

10. S. Lakshmivarahan and M.A.L. Thathachar, *Absolutely expedient learning algorithms for stochastic automata*, IEEE Trans. Syst., Man, Cybern. **SMC-3** (1973) pp. 281-286.

11. K.S. Narendra and M.A.L. Thathachar, *Learning automata: A survey*, IEEE Trans. Syst., Man, Cybern. **SMC-4** (1974) pp. 323-334.

12. M.A.L. Thathachar and P.S. Sastry, *Relaxation labeling with learning automata*, IEEE Trans. Pattern Anal. Machine Intell. **PAMI-6** (1986) pp. 137-156.

13. E. Fernández, *Resolution of occlusion and correspondence in stereopsis by a relaxation labeling of images*, PhD. dissertation (E.T.S.I. de Telecomunicación de Madrid, 1989)

14. D. Maravall and E. Fernández, *Contributions to the range computation and correspondence problems in stereoscopic vision*, IV Simposio Internacional del Conocimiento y su Ingeniería, (Barcelona, 1990).

PARALLEL ALGORITHMS FOR PATTERN RECOGNITION

F. F. Rivera

Departamento de Electrónica. Facultad de Física
Universidad de Santiago, 15076 Santiago, Spain

J. M. Carazo

Centro Nacional de Biotecnología, C.S.I.C.
Universidad Autónoma de Madrid, Spain

J. I. Benavides

Departamento de Electrónica. E.U. Politécnica de Córdoba, Spain

E. L. Zapata

Departamento de Electrónica. Facultad de Física
Universidad de Santiago, 15076 Santiago, Spain

ABSTRACT

In this work we present a partition and mapping methodology to implement sequential algorithms on synchronous parallel computers with hypercube topology. This procedure is specifically applicable to data set classification algorithms in the field of pattern recognition. By using this methodology and because of the regularity properties of the classification algorithms, optimum execution time results are obtained in the parallel algorithm. Finally, as an example, we present the parallelization of the fuzzy covariance algorithm.

1. Introduction

One of the most challenging tasks in parallel computing at present is the development of efficient software strategies that made possible the simultaneous use of all the processors. In this work we present how we have approached this problem in the implementation of some of the most significative algorithms in pattern recognition on hypercube parallel computers, achieving order-of-magnitude increase in computational capacity.

The field of pattern recognition is founded on a series of techniques aimed at structuring a data set into groups defined by certain preestablished patterns. The software tools needed in this field are computationally very costly, as they require operations to be performed in sets with large amounts of data. This computational cost makes the parallelization of pattern recognition algorithms specially attractive and profitable. In fact, in the last few years, parallel algorithms have been proposed for the purpose of solving several problems in pattern recognition, both on the software and hardware levels.

Ni and Jain[1] have proposed a systolic architecture for classification with a potential performance of about 1300 times the one achieved by a sequential processor. Other systolic solutions[2,3] for classification algorithms are presented in the references.

On the other hand, the software implementation of this type of algorithms on SIMD systems is also appropriate, specifically, Li and Fang[4] have developed a classification algorithm for a very restricted type of problems on hypercube systems assuming that the number of processors is larger than the product of the number of data items and the number of their properties and that these two values are integer powers of 2. The proposal we present in this work can be considered a generalization of these results, not only with respect to the algorithms but also with respect to the parallelization methodology.

One of the properties which determine the future of a parallel architecture is the spectrum of problems to which it can be efficiently adapted. In this line, hypercube computers are very versatile due to the fact that, topologically, they offer a good compromise between node connectivity and diameter of interprocessor communications, they can be reconfigured as other topologies, such as rings, trees or meshes, and they are easy to program.

Specifically, a multiprocessor system with a q-dimensional hypercube topology is made up of $Q = 2^q$ processors interconnected as the vertex of a q-dimensional binary cube. A generic processor of index r $(0 \leq r < Q)$ possesses bidirectional communication links with the q processors of index $r^{(b)}$ $(0 \leq b < q)$, where $r^{(b)}$ is the integer whose binary representation differs from r only in the b-th bit. A system whose topology presents this configuration can be structured in different ways as a function of several factors such as memory organization (shared or distributed), concurrence (fine or coarse grained), programming model (SIMD or MIMD), etc.

In principle, each processor can run a different process on different data in an asynchronous mode, leading to potentially very powerful, although very complex, algorithmic designs. In an effort to avoid the complexity associated with this latter approach, we have oriented our researches towards synchronous programming modes, that is, modes that keep all processors performing the same operation on different data (SIMD mode). Indeed we have found that this simpler programming mode allows for very efficient implementations of the operations we are interested on. When programming this mode it is often found useful to introduce some way to select those processors that are to remain active/inactive during the execution of a given step of the process, this is usually accomplished by introducing a special processors variable that tells the processors their working state. In addition, we will consider a SIMD hypercube computer with distributed memory, fine grained concurrence and synchronous operating mode.

In the field of pattern recognition, there are three methods to solve the problem of classification analysis of data[5]: hierarchical, based on graph theory and optimization of objective functions. The usual input to this type of algorithms is a data matrix X, and the usual output is some index representing the membership of each data item to each class. In order to specify the analysis we will now perform, we will call X the set of N data items corresponding to the same number of observations of some physical process. We will denote this set as $X = \{X_0, X_1, ..., X_{N-1}\}$.

The problem consists in obtaining a partition of X into C disjoint classes, where C is an integer such that $2 \leq C \leq N$, so that the members of each class have a higher similarity degree among them than to members of the rest of the classes.

In this work we present the parallel implementation of some of the best known classification algorithms. The study is focused on synchronous SIMD parallel computers with distributed memory and hypercube interconnection topology. The mapping methodology is based on a partition of the hypercube dimensions that depends on those of the problem space.

The paper is divided into the following parts: First we introduce pattern recognition and its bases from the viewpoint of parallel computing on hypercube computers, we then study the parallelization of some of these algorithms. Finally, we present, as an example, the parallelization of the fuzzy covariance classification algorithm.

2. Classification algorithms on hypercube systems

The basic operation for the conversion of sequential into parallel algorithms on architectures such as the one we have just described is the fragmentation of vector operations or of the nested loops of the type DO or FOR. So, different iterations are executed by different processors[6]. Consequently, both the data with which they operate and the results produced by the iterations must be distributed among the processors. The processing structure, that is, the nested loops, is what determines the distribution of the data structures. In general, pattern recognition algorithms are adequate for the spatial distribution of the nested loops. Usually one of those loops goes through the set of N data items being processed.

Let us suppose that the original sequential algorithm has the following not restrictive nested loop structure:

$$\textbf{for } (l_0 = 0; l_0 < D_0; l_0 + +)$$
$$\textbf{for } (l_1 = 0; l_1 < D_1; l_1 + +)$$
$$\text{........}$$
$$\textbf{for } (l_{k-1} = 0; l_{k-1} < D_{k-1}; l_{k-1} + +)\{$$
$$s(l_{k-1}, ..., l_1, l_0); \}$$

Where $s(l_{k-1}, ..., l_1, l_0)$ is a block of assignment operations. Each step of the process (iteration) can be considered as a vector $(l_{k-1}, ..., l_1, l_0)$ in a k-dimensional space S of loop indexes made up of $D = D_0 * D_1 * ... * D_{k-1}$ points, where some of the loops go through the set of data items N.

On the other hand, from a practical viewpoint, a parallel algorithm must be flexible enough to adapt to problems whose size is independent from the number of processors available. In particular, when the index space of the loops of the sequential algorithm is smaller than the hypercube dimension, there will be a set of processors which will remain inactive. And when the index space of the loops is larger than the hypercube dimension, each processor will have to operate sequentially with subsets of the index space of the loops instead of operating with individual points. There is not a unique way of defining and assigning the subsets, and a study of each sequential nested loop set must be carried out in order to determine the distribution scheme which optimizes its parallelization.

The design procedure we use for converting a sequential algorithm into its parallel counterpart on an hypercube system follows the following five steps[7]:

1) Analysis of the sequential algorithm, identifying the dimensions of its nested loops and their dependencies.

2) Partitioning the dimensions of the hypercube into subsets associated with the iterations of the loops in the sequential algorithm.

3) Distribution of the data structures used in the algorithm among the processors following the indexing schemes of the processors and the data.

4) Construction of the parallel algorithm.

5) Optimization of the parallel algorithm by modifying the partition of step 2 and the distribution of step 3.

Some of the features which make this methodology appropriate for the parallelization of classification problems are:

(i) Its optimum results on algorithms with a high degree of loop concurrence.

(ii) The fact that it is based on modularity properties (that is, capacity of division of processors into new hypercubes) of this type of interconnection scheme.

(iii) Its generality due to its independence from the number of loops, the number of iterations of each loop and the dimension of the hypercube (in fact, the number of iterations and the dimension of the hypercube are considered as variable parameters within the parallel algorithm).

(iv) It is a methodology which exploits the large scale and fine grained parallelism.

The first stage of the methodology consists in the study of the properties of the sequential algorithm. It includes dependence problems, numerical stability and algorithmic complexity. The task in the second step is the distribution of the assignation statements $(l_{k-1}, ..., l_1, l_0)$ and their corresponding data structures among the processors of a generic q-dimensional hypercube.

The partition of the q dimensions of the hypercube into k subsets of q_i dimensions each in such a way that $q = q_0 + q_1 + ... + q_{k-1}$ and that their order is consecutive according to the indexing scheme of the processors. Each of these partitions is called a subcube. If we denote the index of each processor as $r(0 \leq r < 2^q)$, it can be represented by a k-dimensional vector $(r_{k-1}, ..., r_1, r_0)$ in which r_i is the value of the bits from position $q_i - 1$ to q_i of the binary representation of r, where we assume $q_{-1} = 0$. Therefore: $r = r_0 + r_1 2^{q_0} + r_2 2^{q_0 + q_1} + ... + r_{k-1} 2^{q - q_{k-1}}$. The value of the index vector of each processor will be used to assign the corresponding part of block $s(l_{k-1}, ..., l_1, l_0)$.

In the third stage of the methodology, the D points of the k-dimensional loop index space are distributed among the processors according to the partitioning of the hypercube. This way, the processors will execute equally sized subsets of the sentence block $s(l_{k-1}, ..., l_1, l_0)$. More precisely, each processor is assigned only d of the D points in the index space, where $d = d_{k-1} * ... * d_1 * d_0$, where $d_i = \lceil D_i / 2^{q_i} \rceil$.

In other words, d_i is the size of the i-th dimension of the "sub-block" of sentences $ls(p_{k-1}, ..., p_1, p_0)$ belonging to each processor, the control variable p_i of this sub-block has the variability range $[0, di)$.

We have used two types of distribution schemes[8] because of their simplicity and performance, they will be referred as "consecutive" and "cyclic". In the consecutive distribution scheme, sentence block $s(l_{k-1}, ..., l_1, l_0)$ is executed in the local sentence block $ls(p_{k-1}, ..., p_1, p_0)$ by the processor whose index vector $(r_{k-1}, ..., r_1, r_0)$ is given by $r_i = \lfloor li/di \rfloor$, and where $p_i = l_i \mathbf{mod} d_i$ are the local loop control indexes of the corresponding local iteration, for $i = 0, 1, ..., k-1$. In the cyclic distribution, $s(l_{k-1}, ..., l_1, l_0)$ is executed in the sentence block $ls(p_{k-1}, ..., p_1, p_0)$ by the processor whose index vector is given by expression $r_i = l_i \mathbf{mod} 2^{q_i}$, and where $p_i = \lfloor l_i / 2^{q_i} \rfloor$ represent the local loop parameters, with i varying from 0 to $k-1$.

At this point we followed the idea of writing our programs in a machineindependent way, the aim being to be able to run the same code in different platforms as well as easily accommodating hardware up-grades and changes.

Once the computations have been distributed, the implementation stage of the parallel algorithm will not differ much from that of the sequential one in the operations each processor is going to carry out. In fact, the sentences will be the same. The part that is different occurs when either results or data need to be output or input. In this case, the necessary communications and the manner of effectively implementing them must be carefully studied.

The data classification algorithms that we have implemented are designed using fine grained programming, so that only communications between pairs of processors which are physical neighbors are used. We do not take advantage of special functions allowing for communications between any pair of nodes. Moreover, we do not use the possibility of multinode communications in which the processor can send a data item to several neighbors at the same time either. These facilities are available in some systems found in the market, but the analysis of the algorithms that use them depends to a great extent on the efficiency of these facilities and not on the algorithm itself.

3. FC algorithm

The example we present belongs to the type of classification methods which are aimed at the optimization of an objective function. These methods are based on the assumption that the classifications for which local extremes of a certain objective function occur are the prefered ones. In this work we present one of those optimizational methods (this is called G-K method). We have presented other classification methods in previous works[9,10].

Gustafson and Kessel[11] have proposed a modification for the group of FCM algorithms in order to consider the possibility of assigning different classes for the same data set X presenting different geometric shapes. As the norm or distance adopted for establishing a measure of the dissimilarity between elements is what imposes a certain topological structure to the classes, a local variation of this measure is proposed so that it changes dynamically with the evolution of the classification algorithm and with each particular class. The algorithms based on this type of functions are called fuzzy covariance algorithms FC.

We will consider a Mahalanobis norm on R^P induced by positively defined symmetric matrices of $P*P$ elements. We will denote $\vec{A}$ as a vector containing C of these matrices $\vec{A} = (A_0, A_1, ..., A_{C-1})$ and we will consider the norm induced by the inner product induced on R^P by this matrix A_K given by:

$$< X_I, X_I >_{A_K} = X_I^T * A_K * X_I = (\| X_I \|_{A_K})^{1/2}$$

The distance between any two points X_I and X_E that belong to the space R^P is defined by the norm $\| X_I - X_E \|_{A_K}$. The objective function that must be minimized in order to obtain the final classification of the data is given by the following expressions:

$$f(U, V, \vec{A}) = \sum_{I=0}^{N-1} \sum_{K=0}^{C-1} U_{IK}^m * (\| X_I - V_K \|_{A_K})^2 \qquad (1)$$

$$V_{KJ} = \sum_{I=0}^{N-1} U_{IK}^m * X_{IJ} / \sum_{I=0}^{N-1} U_{IK}^m \qquad (2)$$

Where U is the matrix that contains the membership of each point to each class, V is the center of each class and $m \in [1, \infty)$ is a preestablished fuzziness parameter.

Graphically, we can consider that the application of the Euclidean norm favors the generation of classes with spherical shapes in R^P. Whereas the use of matrices A_K is aimed at adapting each class to the geometric shape to which it is better suited, making the distances between the components of each dimension of the space R^P contribute with a different weight to the measure of the distance.

In order to make the minimization problem computable, it is necessary to introduce the restriction that the determinant of matrices A_K must have a given finite value[5]. Considering the restriction that $\det(A_K) = \sigma_K > 0$ for each integer $K \in [0, C-1]$ we obtain a volume limitation on R^P in the K-th class. This is, the larger the value of σ_K the larger the volume "encompassed" by its associated class in the space R^P. Therefore, matrices A_K vary but maintain a fixed determinant, which graphically has the search of the optimum topological shape for the K-th class associated to it by restricting the possible membership of each point to a fixed volume in this class.

The expression for the calculation of the C matrices $A_K (K = 0, 1, ..., C-1)$, which induce the norm on R^P from the elements of the membership matrix and the centers of the classes, is as follows:

$$A_K = (\sigma_K * \det(S_{J_K}))^{1/P} * S_{J_K}^{-1} \qquad (3)$$

Where $S_{J_K}^{-1}$ is the inverse of the dispersion matrix S_{J_K} of the K-th class, which is symmetric and defined positive. Its calculation is given by the expression[11]:

$$S_{J_K} = \sum_{I=0}^{N-1} U_{IK}^m * (X_I - V_K)(X_I - V_K)^T \tag{4}$$

Using the concepts we have just defined, we can introduce the following iterative algorithm which evaluates a local minimum of the objective function proposed in[11]:

FC1: Establish the convergence criterium and an initial value for the elements of the membership matrix U. Assign values to the fuzziness parameter m and to the volume limits of each class σ_k.

do

> **FC2:** Calculate the centers of the C classes from the membership matrix.
>
> **FC3:** Calculate the dispersion matrices S_{J_k} using the membership matrices and the centers of the classes according to Eq. 4.
>
> **FC4:** Evaluate matrices A_k, which induce the norm on each class, using the inverse matrices and the determinants of the dispersion matrices following Eq. 3.
>
> **FC5:** Calculate the elements of the membership matrices U from the measurements of dissimilarity between each point and each center of the classes according with the norm imposed by matrix A_k.

while The convergence criterium is not verified.

The sequential algorithmic complexity of each iteration is of order $O(C * P^2 * (N + P))$. The total algorithm will have the same order of complexity multiplied by the number of iterations of the do-while loop. More specifically, the complexity of the FC2 and FC5 stages is $O(N * P * C)$. Stage FC3, for the calculation of C dispersion matrices with $P * P$ elements each, goes through the memberships of the N elements in the data set, therefore its complexity is $O(C * P^2 * N)$. Finally, the algorithmic complexity of stage FC4 is $O(C * P^3)$, as it requires the calculation of the inverse matrices of the C dispersion matrices with $P * P$ elements each.

The deepest loops of the sequential implementation of this algorithm occur in the calculation of the dispersion matrices, the level of nesting is four, with dimensions C, P, P and N; This is the reason why we will consider a 4-partition.

This 4-partition of the q dimensions of the hypercube is such that $q = q_0 + q_1 + q_2 + q_3$. Where q_0 is associated with the number of data items N of the set X, q_1 with the number of classes C, and q_2 and q_3 with the number of components P. They will represent, respectively, the rows and the columns of the dispersion and the norm matrices.

We have used a cyclic distribution scheme for the data in the matrices intervening in the implementation of the parallel algorithm, they will be stored as follows:

X: The J-th component of the I-th point X_{IJ} will be stored in position x_{ij} of the local submatrix x of the $Q_1 * Q_2$ processors for which

$r_0 = I \bmod Q_0$, $0 \le r_1 \le Q_1$, $0 \le r_2 \le Q_2$ and $r_3 = J \bmod Q_3$. Where $i = \lfloor I/Q_0 \rfloor$ and $j = \lfloor J/Q_3 \rfloor$.

V: The J-th component of the center of the K-th class V_{KJ} will be stored in position v_{kj} of the local submatrix v of all the $Q_0 * Q_2$ processors in which $0 \le r_0 \le Q_0$, $r_1 = K \bmod Q_1$, $0 \le r_2 \le Q_2$ and $r_3 = J \bmod Q_3$. Where $k = \lfloor K/Q_1 \rfloor$ and $j = \lfloor J/Q_3 \rfloor$.

U: The membership of the I-th point to the K-th class U_{IK} will be stored in position u_{ik} of the local submatrix u of the $Q_2 * Q_3$ processors in which $r_0 = I \bmod Q_0$, $r_1 = K \bmod Q_1$, $0 \le r_2 \le Q_2$ and $0 \le r_3 \le Q_3$. Where $i = \lfloor I/Q_0 \rfloor$ and $k = \lfloor K/Q_1 \rfloor$.

S: Element S_{LJ} of the diffusion matrix of the K-th class S_{J_K} will be stored in position s_{klj} of the three dimensional submatrix s of the Q_0 processors in which $0 \le r_0 \le Q_0$, $r_1 = K \bmod Q_1$, $r_2 = L \bmod Q_2$ and $r_3 = J \bmod Q_3$. Where $k = \lfloor K/Q_1 \rfloor$, $l = \lfloor L/Q_2 \rfloor$ and $j = \lfloor J/Q_3 \rfloor$.

A: Each element A_{LJ} of the matrix A_K which induces the norm of the K-th class, will be stored in position a_{klj} of the local three dimensional matrix a of the Q_0 processors for which $0 \le r_0 \le Q_0$, $r_1 = K \bmod Q_1$, $r_2 = L \bmod Q_2$ and $r_3 = J \bmod Q_3$. Where $k = \lfloor K/Q_1 \rfloor$, $l = \lfloor L/Q_2 \rfloor$ and $j = \lfloor J/Q_3 \rfloor$.

σ: Element σ_K which fixes the determinant of matrix A_K will be stored in position d_k of subvector d in the $Q_0 * Q_2 * Q_3$ processors which verify $0 \le r_0 \le Q_0$, $r_1 = K \bmod Q_1$, $0 \le r_2 \le Q_2$ $0 \le r_3 \le Q_3$. Where $k = \lfloor K/Q_1 \rfloor$.

As an example we present the ACLAN code of the function that evaluates the centers of the classes for each iteration of the resulting parallel algorithm. ACLAN is a parallel programming language based on the C language[12,13], its main features of which are shown in Table 1.

In this code the real vectors $su[\,]$ and $sup[\,][\,]$ store, respectively, the partial results of the sums of the numerator and denominator of the Eq. 2 that we use for obtaining the class centers.

```
void class centers()
{
1    for(k = 0; k < c; k + +){
2        su[k] := 0;
3        for(j = 0; j < p2; j + +){
4            sup[k][j] := 0;
5            for(i = 0; i < n; i + +){
6                MASK := ((k * Q1 + r1 < C)&&(i * Q0 + r0 < N));
7                su[k] := su[k] + u[i][k]    {MASK&&!j};
8                sup[k][j] := sup[k][j] + u[i][k] * x[i][j]    {MASK&&(j * Q3 + r3 < P)};}}}
9    for(t = 0; t < q0; t + +){
10        su2[*](neigh[t]) < - - su[*];
11        sup2[*][*](neigh[t]) < - - sup[*][*];
12        su[*] := su[*] + su2[*];
13        sup[*][*] := sup[*][*] + sup2[*][*]; }
14    for(k = 0; k < c; k + +)
```

```
15      for(j = 0; j < p2; j + +){
16          MASK := ((k * Q1 + r1 < C)&&(j * Q3 + r3 < P));
17          v[k][j] := sup[k][j]/su[k]    {MASK}; }
        }
```

$su2[\ ]$ and $sup2[\ ][\ ]$ are vectors analogous to $su[\ ]$ and $sup[\ ][\ ]$, and they are used as receivers of the messages between processors.

In this ACLAN function, variables n, c, $p1$ and $p2$ are the local dimensions associated with the data of the problem, and hence associated with the global dimensions N, C, P and P respectively.

Symbol	Meaning	Explanation
: =	Local assignment	Data transfer from one register to another in the same PE.
: = :	Local exchange	Data swap between two registers of the same PE.
< --	Remote assignment	Data transfer from one register to another in a different PE.
< -- >	Remote exchange	Data swap between two registers in directly connected PEs.
< = =	Central assignment	Data transfer from PE to CU or viceversa.
. /:/	Bit operator	Extract a bit or a range of bits. (/ / means optional)
in : /:/	Set operator	Check if a value is in a certain range. (/ / means optional).
#	Parallel register	Identify the index of the PE.
neigh[]	Keyword	Identify the interconnection functions.

Table 1. Basic parallel structures of ACLAN.

The total algorithmic complexity of each iteration of the parallel FC algorithm is

$$O(n(c(p_2(Q_1Q_3 + p_1) + p_1q_3 + q_2) + P(p_2(q_2 + p_1 + Q_2Q_3) + P(p_2 + q_2 + q_3) + p_1q_3) + p_1p_2(q_0 + Q_2Q_3) + q_1))$$

Which is obtained from the combination of the complexities of each of the outlined steps of each iteration.

More specifically, stage FC1 has a complexity of $O(n * c)$, but as it is external to the main loop it does not participate in the total complexity. Stage FC2 presents a complexity of $O(c * p_2 * (n + q_0) + q_1 + q_3)$ as can be easily seen from the analysis of the code shown as an example. Furthermore, the complexity of stage FC3 is $O(c * p_2 * (n * Q_2 * Q_3) + p_1 * q_0)$.

Stage FC4 is made up of several matrix calculation functions[14] with the following complexities: Cholesky decomposition: $O(P * (p_2 * q_2 + p_1 * (p_2 + q_3)))$; calculation of the determinant: $O(p_2 + q_3)$; data exchange[14]: $O(p_1 * p_2 * Q_2 * Q_3)$ and $O(p_2 * P * Q_2 * Q_3)$; calculation of the inverse of a triangular matrix: $O(P^2 * (p_2 + q_2 + q_3))$; and, finally, the matrix product: $O(p_1 * p_2 * P)$. All these terms must be multiplied by the complexity of the most external loop which goes through all the classes of order $O(c)$, and as a result, we obtain a total complexity for this stage of $O(c * (P * (p_2 * q_2 + p_1 * (p_2 + q_3) + P * (p_2 + q_2 + q_3)) + p_2 * Q_2 * Q_3 * (p_1 + P)))$. Finally, the complexity of stage FC5 is $O(n * (c * (p_1 * (p_2 + q_3) + q_2) + q_1))$.

From the analysis of this expression for the complexity we observe that it is convenient to make $q_2 = q_3 = 0$, because in this way we avoid the communications associated with the data exchange that is needed for the calculation of the inverse of the dispersion matrices. This particular case does not mean an increase in either the computational or memory cost, as the parameter of the problem associated with these partitions, P is not the dominant factor in the data sets to which this algorithm is usually applied.

q_0	q_1	q_2	q_3	Q	FC1	FC2	FC3	FC4	FC5	TOTAL
0	0	0	0	1	NC	NPC	NCP	CP^3	NCP^2	$CP_2(N+P)$
0	0	0	p_3	P	NC	$CN+p_3$	NCP	$CP^2 p_3$	$NCPp_3$	$CPp_3(P+N)$
0	0	p_3	0	P	NC	NPC	NCP^2	CP^3	$NC(P+p_3)$	$CP^2(P+N)$
0	c_2	0	0	C	N	$NP+c_2$	PN	P^3	$N(P^2+c_2)$	$P^2(N+P)+Nc_2$
n_2	0	0	0	N	C	CPn_2	$P(C+n_2)$	CP^3	CP^2	$CP(n_2+P^2)$
0	0	p_3	p_3	P^2	NC	$NC+p_3$	NCP^2	CP^3	NCp_3	$C(P^2(N+P)+Np_3)$
0	c_2	0	p_3	CP	N	$N+c_2+p_3$	NP	$P^2 p_3$	$N(Pp_3+c_2)$	$Pp_3(P+N)+Nc_2$
0	c_2	p_3	0	CP	N	$NP+c_2$	NP^2	CP^3	$N(P+c_2)$	$P^3(C+N)+Nc_2$
n_2	0	0	p_3	NP	C	Cn_2+p_3	$P(C+n_2)$	$CP^2 p_3$	CPp_3	$CP^2 p_3+n_2(C+P)$
n_2	0	p_3	0	NP	C	CPn_2	CP^2+n_2	CP^3	CP	$CP(P^2+n_2)$
n_2	c_2	0	0	NC	1	Pn_2+c_2	Pn_2	P^3	P^2+c_2	$P(P^2+n_2)+c_2$
0	c_2	p_3	p_3	CP^2	N	$N+c_2+p_3$	NP^2	P^3	$N(c_2+p_3)$	$P^2(P+N)+Nc_2$
n_2	0	p_3	p_3	NP^2	C	Cn_2+p_3	CP^2+n_2	CP^3	Cp_3	$C(P^3+n_2)$
n_2	c_2	0	p_3	NPC	1	$n_2+c_2+p_3$	$P+n_2$	$P^2 p_3$	Pp_3+c_2	$P^2 p_3+c_2+n_2$
n_2	c_2	p_3	0	NPC	1	Pn_2+c_2	P^2+n_2	P^3	$P+c_2$	$P^3+c_2+Pn_2$
n_2	c_2	p_3	p_3	NCP^2	1	$n_2+c_2+p_3$	P^2+n_2	P^3	c_2+p_3	$P^3+c_2+n_2$

Table 2. Algorithmic complexity of the parallel FC algorithm.

Table 2 shows the results of the complexities of these functions for some specific instances of the partition of the hypercube. Where $n_2 = \lceil log_2 N \rceil$, $c_2 = \lceil log_2 C \rceil$ and $p_3 = \lceil log_2 P \rceil$. It can be seen that the complexity for the case of a single processor coincides with that of the sequential algorithm, and that the minimum complexity

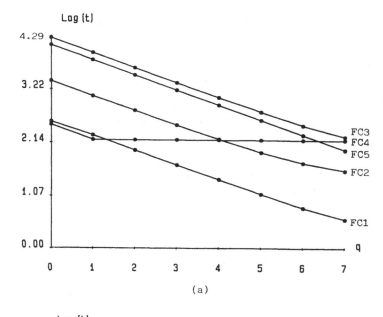

(a)

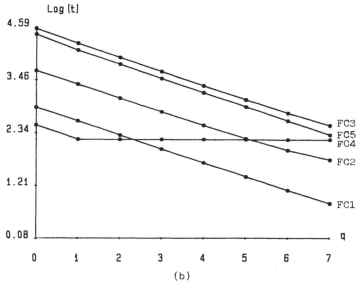

(b)

Figure 1. Runtime of the parallel FC algorithm versus hypercube dimensions.

is obtained for a partition where $q_0 = \lceil log_2 N \rceil$, $q_1 = \lceil log_2 C \rceil$, $q_2 = 0$ and $q_3 = 0$ and its value is $O(P * (P^2 + n_2) + c_2)$. Observe that stage FC4 presents a complexity which is independent from N and, also, the large influence of communications on q_2 and q_3 due to the terms Q_2 and Q_3 of the storage changes.

Figure 1 represents the execution times on a logarithmic scale with respect to q for each of the functions in an iteration of the parallel FC algorithm on the hypercube NCUBE/10^{15} for problems where (a) $N = 800$, $C = 6$ and $P = 6$ and (b) $N = 1600$, $C = 6$ and $P = 6$. We have considered a partition where $q_0 = q - 1$, $q_1 = 1$ and $q_2 = q_3 = 0$, which is the one that obtains the best results for each value of q. Observe that in both graphs all the execution times decrease almost linearly with q except for stage FC4, as it is only affected by the changes in q_1, and this value only changes when going from $q = 0$ to $q = 1$ with the partitions chosen in this case.

Figure 2 shows the efficiency of the algorithm with the same restrictions as in the previous figures.

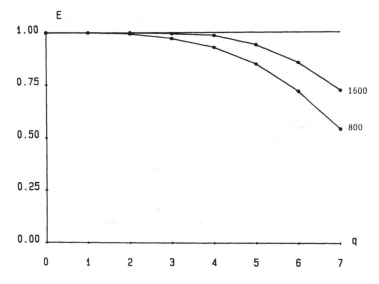

Figure 2. Efficiency of the parallel FC algorithm.

The redundance, that is, the number of data items repeated in the storage of the submatrices in different processors, is

$$np_2(Q_1 Q_2 - 1) + cp_2(Q_0 Q_2 - 1) + nc(Q_2 Q_3 - 1) + cp_1 p_2(Q_0 - 1) + cp_1 p_2(Q_0 - 1) + c(Q_0 Q_2 Q_3 - 1)$$

Each of the terms of this expression is associated with submatrices x, v, u, a, s and σ, respectively. The total memory used for the elements of the local submatrices on each processor is $n * p_2 + c * p_2 + n * c + c * p_1 * p_2 + c * p_1 * p_2 + c$ positions.

4. Conclusions

The procedure for the parallelization of classification algorithms that we present in this work allows for the parallel implementation of programs for SIMD hypercube computers from the corresponding optimum sequential algorithms. The parallelism obtained is maximum when the nested loops of the sequential code are distributed in topologically equivalent subcubes. The key to the efficiency of the design rests on a good distribution of the data in such a way that each subcube can operate on data stored on their processors with a minimum of interprocessor communications.

The main conclusions resulting from this work are the following:

(i)   The methodology does not introduce any restriction on the size of the data, except for the limitation of the local memories or the number of processors available.

(ii)   The degree of parallelism is increased when the number of processors in the system increases.

(iii)   The performance can be optimized by means of an adequate selection of the partitions of the hypercube and the data distribution.

A large amount of classification algorithms have been developed using this methodology, and the results obtained corroborate the aforementioned conclusions, confirming this procedure as an adequate tool for the parallelization of sequential algorithms in the field of pattern recognition.

5. Acknowledgements

This work was supported by the Ministry of Education and Science (CICYT) of Spain under contracts TIC88-0094, MIC88-0549, the Xunta de Galicia XUGA-80406488, and the Spanihs institution Fundación Ramón Areces.

6. References

1. L. Ni and A. Jain, *A VLSI systolic architecture for pattern clustering.* IEEE Trans. Pattern Anal. Machine Intell. **7(1)** (1985) p. 80.

2. K. Hwang ans S.P. Su, *VLSI architectures for feature extraction and pattern classification.* Comput. Vision. Graph Image Process. **24** (1983) p. 215.

3. E.L. Zapata, R. Doallo, F.F. Rivera and M.A. Ismail, *A VLSI systolic architecture for fuzzy clustering.* Microprocessing and Microprogramming. **18** (1988) p. 647.

4. X. Li and Z. Fang, *Parallel algorithms for clustering on hypercube SIMD computers.* Proc. IEEE Conf. on Computer Vision and Pattern Recognition. (1986) p. 130.

5. J.C. Bezdek, *Pattern recognition with fuzzy objective function algorithms.* Plenum Press. (1981).

6. C.D. Polychronopoulus, D.J. Kuck and D.A. Padua, *Utilizing multidimensional loop parallelism on large-scale parallel processor systems.* IEEE Trans. on Comput. **38 - 9** (1989) p. 1285.

7. E.L. Zapata, F.F. Rivera, and O.G. Plata, *On the partition of algorithms into*

34

hypercubes. In *Advances on Parallel Computing.* D.J. Evans Ed. London. JAI Press. (1990) p. 149.

8. S.L. Johnsson, *Communication efficient basic linear algebra computations on hypercube architectures.* J. Parallel and Distributed Computing, 4 (1987) p. 133.

9. F.F. Rivera, M.A. Ismail and E.L. Zapata, *Parallel squared error clustering on hypercube arrays* J. Parallel and Distributed Computing. 8 (1990) p. 292.

10. E.L. Zapata, F.F. Rivera and M.A. Ismail, *Parallel fuzzy clustering on fixed size hypercube SIMD computers.* Parallel Computing 11 (1989) p. 291.

11. D.E. Gustafson and N. Kessel, *Fuzzy clustering with a fuzzy covariance matrix.* Proc. IEEE-CDC. 2 K.S. Fu Ed. IEEE Press. New Jersey. (1979) p. 761.

12. O.G. Plata, F.F. Rivera, J.I. Benavides and E.L. Zapata, *ACLAN, A parallel programming language for signal processing.* IEEE MELECON'89. (1989) p. 261.

13. O.G. Plata, F. Argello, J.D. Bruguera and E.L. Zapata, *An array processing language for real time programming of hypercube concurrent computers.* Proc. Int. Conf. on Software Engineering for Real Time Systems. (IEE Press, London) (1989) p. 141.

14. F.F. Rivera, *Partición y proyección de algoritmos en computadores hipercubo: Reconocimiento de formas.* Ph.D. Dissertation. Dept. Electrnica. Fac. Fsica. Univ. Santiago. (1990)

15. *NCUBE Handbook and Programer's Manual,* NCUBE, Beaverton, OR. (1988)

SYNTHESIS AND CLASSIFICATION OF 2-D SHAPES FROM THEIR LANDMARK POINTS

N. Pérez de la Blanca, J. Fdez-Valdivia and R. Molina

Departamento de Ciencias de la Computación e I.A.
Universidad de Granada. 18071 Granada. Spain.

ABSTRACT

This paper presents new contributions to the problem of synthesis and classification of boundaries based on their landmark set. The approach is invariant not only to global transformation groups but also to local deformations. The main points of this approach are, the characterization of a shape using as landmark a subset of points of its curve of curvatures and the use of certain specific splines to interpolate between these points. We define the pattern curves as the mean of the probability distribution defining the shape classes. Simulating this distribution of probabilities we reproduce a realistic representation of the shape.

1 Introduction

Invariant characterization of shapes with respect to transformation groups is one of the most challenging problems in pattern recognition theory. A first approach in solving this problem is to apply multivariate statistical techniques on vectors of features obtained from the original data. This approach has two main drawbacks: first the impossibility of obtaining coherent graphical representations of the shape from the resulting mean vector and second the impossibility of giving an order to the variables of the feature vector[2]. An alternative in overcoming these difficulties is to use the shape boundary directly. In this case there are general procedures obtaining invariant estimation with respect to the classical geometry groups, such as euclidean, similarities and affine group. However, as Grenander[7,8] shows there are shapes for which these transformation groups can not represent all their possible variations, but if we use a more general group such as the diffeomorphism group, we obtain a grade of variability rather higher than required. Therefore, it is necessary to develop new methods that are not only invariant to global transformations but also allow local changes without affecting our assumption on the type of shape we have.

Among the different approaches for characterizing shapes from their boundaries that given by Bookstein[2], based on their curvature values, have several advantages. First, it reduces by one the dimensionality of the problem; second, the characterization is invariant to similarities, and third it allows estimation of the landmark points defining the global behaviour of the curve.

The main aim of this paper is to present a new way of using the information provided by the curve of curvatures and particularly by the landmark points to obtain an invariant characterization of two dimensional shapes using Grenander's methodology[5,6,7,8] to synthesize shapes. Section 2 describes a type of biological image on which we have applied this methodology. In section 3 we discuss the concept of landmark point and its estimation. Section 4 presents a model for synthesizing boundaries from its landmark points. Section 5 shows some experiments on shape classifications based on landmark set. Section 6 shows some results of applying the techniques described in section 5 to our test images.

2 The Test Images

The test problem we have is the characterization of the different shapes associated to the head and tail of certain microorganisms called nematodes. Figure 1 shows some examples of these shapes. The images have been captured by transmission using a CCD video camera attached to a Fotomicroscope Zeiss III. All the images have 512x512 pixels in size and 256 grey levels.

According to the three-dimensional structure of the nematodes, biologists move the microscope focus two dimensional through the nematode body looking for the features that determine the nematode specie. That means each focus two dimensional does not contain all the information about a determined feature by itself . Since using a block of images for estimation purposes implies a lot of computation, we decided to choose the particular focus plane that we believed represented in the best way the feature that we wanted to detect.

There are several sources of distortion which influence our observed images. Apart from the limited number of pixels of our video camera and frame grabber, the lack of uniformity in the light distribution on the field of observation and the possible dirty spots present on the lenses are also sources of noise when we are trying to identify features in a image from the grey level of the pixels.

In order to remove all these distortions we observed a background image together with each data image. By background image we mean an image taken in the same conditions but putting a clean slide in the microscope. Using both data and background images, we calculated a new image from the following equation on the pixels

$$\text{transform\_image}_i = 255 \text{ x } min(1, \lambda \text{ x } A_i/B_i) \tag{1}$$

A being the raw data image, B the background image and λ a constant less than one. By trial and error we chose $\lambda = 0.75$.

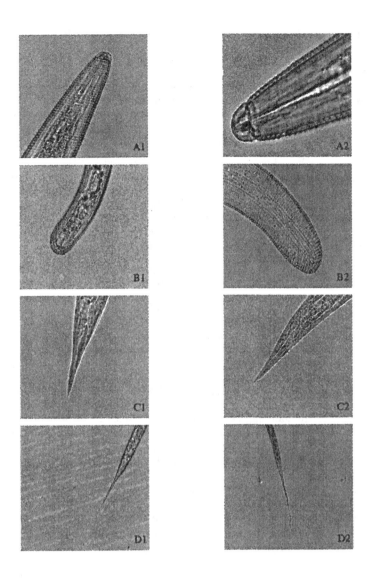

Figure 1: A_i, B_i, C_i and D_i, i=1,2 show different shapes of head, rounded tail, conic Tail and filiform tail respectively.

3 Landmark Set and Template Estimations

We now suppose that all the information necessary to characterize a two dimensional shape is on its boundary. Then the first step is to get a boundary estimation without gaps and one pixel width. To do this we use a simple procedure. We start estimating a threshold for binarizing the image using an iterative algorithm [10]. After cleaning the binarized image from isolated noisy pixels we estimate the boundary using the morphological expression[13],

$$\partial B = (B \oplus E) - B \qquad (2)$$

B being the set whose border we want to estimate, and E a three by three square.

The landmark concept such as it was introduced in Bookstein[2] is associated to those points being local maximum or minimum of the curve of curvatures. The most appealing point of this concept is the support given to it by some psychological experiments, Attneave et col[1]. However, and as we later show, this landmark point concept is dependent on the interpolation procedure used to join them. Therefore it is necessary to introduce a more precise definition.

Definition 1 *A finite set of points on a two dimensional boundary can be defined as a landmark point set for the shape represented by such boundary, if an interpolation procedure exists which, based on this set, make up a new curve representing the same shape.*

This definition clarifies the relationship between landmark points and interpolation procedure. In Bookstein's definition this relationship wasn't clear becouse a direct linear interpolation was implied.

We start estimating the curve of curvatures of the boundary and from it we estimate the landmark set. The main problem when we try to estimate curvatures on a discrete curve is the noise from the discretization process. To avoid this effect we have estimated the gaussian curvature at each point of the curve using the method proposed in[9].This method estimates the curvature value at a point P from the angle formed by the orthogonal regression fitted tangent lines in sample points at equal distances to the left and right of the point P. The number of points to be used for fitting the tangent lines depend on the amount of smoothing we want to impose on the results. A value between 10 and 25 can be chosen. Figure 2 shows estimations with different parameter values.

Once we have estimated an adequately smooth curve of curvatures a straightforward way of estimating the landmark points is to choose those with absolute value of curvature above a threshold. Although this procedure is simple and works in a lot of cases, it is quite dependent on the smoothness of the vector C and it does not guarantee that all the points we get are true landmarks. The number of landmarks identifying a shape will depend on the amount of roughness we consider important to define that shape.

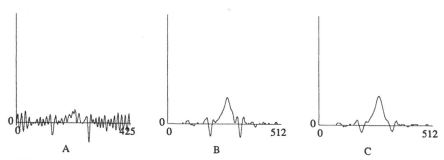

Figure 2: Graphs of curvatures curve using 5,15 and 25 points (A,B,C) respectively

A procedure for estimating landmarks is given by Knoerr[9]. There, the landmark point concept is again dependent on the interpolation procedure. It look for the landmark set fitting a new curve made up of contiguous alternate monotone sections to the estimated curve of curvature. The transition points between sections are the landmarks, that is if $C = (c_i, i = 0, \cdots, n - 1)$ denotes the n values defining the curvature in a boundary we fit to this vector another one $C^* = (c_i^*, i = 0, \cdots, n - 1)$ verifying the above condition, and from this we estimate the landmarks. The estimation procedure, for values of m and p fixed, can be defined in the following way

$$\min_{\{(l_i, c_i^*)\}} Q_p = \sum_i |c_i - c_i^*|^p, \ p > 0 \qquad (3)$$

with

$$l_0 = 0, \ 0 \le l_i - l_{i-1} \le 1, \ l_{n-1} = m - 1 \qquad (4)$$

$$c_{i+1}^* \ge c_i^* \ if \ sign(l_{i+1}) > 0 \quad and \quad c_{i+1}^* \le c_i^* \ if \ sign(l_{i+1}) < 0 \qquad (5)$$

where the c_i^* take values in a finite set verifying $\min_j c_j \le c_i^* \le \max_j c_j$. l_i and $sign(l_i)$ being the label and curvature sign of each section respectively. Eq.4 and Eq.5 express continuity and monotony conditions respectively. This optimization problem can be solved through the following expression using dynamic programming

$$Q_{p,i}(l_{i-1}, c_{i-1}^*) = \min_{\{(l_i, c_i^*)\}} \{|c_i - c_i^*|^p + Q_{p,i}(l_{i+1}, c_{i+1}^*)\} \qquad (6)$$

Since the only condition on the behaviour of the curve of curvatures is piecewise monotony the set of estimated landmark point is useful for many of the interpolation procedures. Figure 3 shows the results of applying this procedures to our test images where $p = 2$.

40

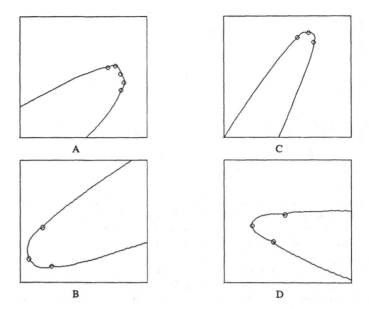

Figure 3: Head countour estimations toguether with the estimated landmak points using Knoerr's method

3.1 *Template Estimation*

We define a template S^* as an average vector

$$S^* = \frac{1}{n} \sum_{i=1,..,n} s_i \qquad (7)$$

$\{s_i\}$ being different vectors representing the same shape.

Once the landmark point set is determined, the idea is to use a boundary sample set to estimate a template of the shape. To do this an interpolation procedure between landmarks have to be specified.

A very direct interpolation procedure is to join the landmarks with segments, giving a raw polygonal approach to the boundary. In this case the template is defined by the vector whose components are the lengths of the segments and the angle between adjacent segments. It is easy to show situations in which this approach it is inappropiate. Figure 6 shows one of these situations. It is clear from this example that the distance between adjacent landmarks and the behaviour of the curve between them are the main factors influencing our interpolation procedure.

An alternative to the interpolation by straight lines is to approach the curve between landmarks using a polygonal. It is evident that the bigger the number of points the closer approximation to the boundary. However to define a template we have to fix a number of points. Knoerr[9] estimated this number from the mean value of the number of points given by a sample set of raw contours.

In order to get a smoother interpolation procedure we have look for a parametric class of functions fitting the behaviour of the curve between landmarks and verifying conditions of regularity on the landmark points. In this case the landmark set we consider contain strictly that given by Knoerr's estimation method. A new point, having zero curvature variation, between each two adjacent maximum and minimum of curvature is taken. We assume that the regularity of the curve of curvatures allows us to suppose the existence of at least one point verifying this condition. In those situations where there are more than one of these points we choose that more equidistant from the extremities. Now the number of landmark points is $2m$, m being the number the local maximum and minimum considered. In this case we have two different templates. A *polygonal template* which is estimated as in the raw approach and a *shape template* that is the average of the interpolated curves.

The biggest landmark set we could get is given by all the points verifying

$$\frac{dC(s)}{ds} = 0 \qquad (8)$$

C(s) being the estimated curve of curvatures.

3.2 Interpolation Procedure

The interpolation procedure we use is based on the belief that in between two adjacent landmark points the behaviour of the curve of curvatures has to verify the following equation for some $\rho > 0$ value

$$\frac{d^2C(s)}{ds^2} - \rho^2 C(s) = 0 \qquad (9)$$

$C(s)$ and ds being the curve of curvatures and arc element respectively. The curve solution of this equation is called local spline curve in tension[14]. This equation for $\rho = 0$ expresses a linear behaviour of the curvature in terms of the arc and for ρ increasing C(s) tend to zero. This means that for high values of ρ the interpolated curve tend to fit a straight line and for $\rho = 0$ we get geometric splines. Consequently, this model allows us to fit a wide range of curves having the same landmark points. The regularity condition to be verified by the whole interpolated curve is that the tangent line and curvature are continuous at the joints. Eq.11 below reflects this condition. Now the vector defining the shape template will also contain a ρ value for each segment.

The solution of the Eq.9 in terms of an orthogonal coordinate system is[14]

$$y(x) = \frac{1}{\rho_i^2} \left(c_{i-1} \frac{sh\rho_i(d_i - x)}{sh\rho_i d_i} + c_i \frac{sh\rho_i x}{sh\rho_i d_i} + x \frac{c_{i-1} - c_i}{d_i} - c_{i-1} \right) \qquad (10)$$

where c_i is the curvature value in the landmark point i, d_i the distance from the (i-1)-th to the i-th points and ρ_i the value of the tension parameter on the interval i-th.

The coefficients c_i are the solutions of the continuity equation systems[14]

$$\alpha_i c_{i-1} + (\beta_i + \beta_{i-1})c_i + \alpha_{i+1}c_{i+1} = \phi_i \qquad i = 1, 2, ..., n-1 \qquad (11)$$

in which

$$\alpha_i = \frac{1}{\rho_i^2}\left(\frac{1}{d_i} - \frac{\rho_i}{sh\rho_i d_i}\right) \qquad \beta_i = \frac{1}{\rho_i^2}\left(\frac{\rho_i ch\rho_i d_i}{sh\rho_i d_i} - \frac{1}{d_i}\right) \qquad (12)$$

ϕ_i measure between -pi and pi being the angle rotated clockwise from the i-th to the (i+1)-th segments .

Since the equation systems given by Eq.11 has n-1 equation and n+1 unknown we have to impose border conditions to solve it. In our examples we choose $c_0 = c_n =$ constant.

4   Shape Synthesis Model

By shape synthesis we mean to find an invariant mathematical model with respect to transformation groups and local deformations, representing the shape of interest and such that by simulation of it we could have new representations of this shape. A complete methodology in this way has been given by Grenander[5,6,7]. The idea is to consider a big set of basic elements from which we could make up shape classes and to impose on it those constraints defining the possible configurations of a particular shape. For instance, let us consider the set of all the segments in R^2. It is evident that using segments we could approximate whatever shape as closely as desired, but not any finite set of segments approach a given shape. The basic elements of this approach are: a space of generators (G), a connector graph (σ), regularity conditions on σ (R) and a transformation group (T, T:G $\rightarrow$ G).

Let C be the configuration space, that is

$$C = \{c|c = \sigma(g_0, g_1, ..., g_{n-1}), (g_0, g_1, ..., g_{n-1})\epsilon G^n\} \qquad (13)$$

where g_i denote the generators, n is the number of landmark points and σ is the graph defining the connection between the generators. If C(R) denote the set of configurations verifying the regularity conditions (R), the goal in which we are interested in is to know what subset of C(R) represent the shape being considered. To generate possible elements of C(R) defining the shape of interest we start from a template $S\epsilon G^n$ and apply transformations $T_j \epsilon T$ to its generators requiring that the resulting configurations belong to C(R),

$$E(S) = \{c|c = \sigma(T_0 g^0, T_1 g^1, ..., T_{n-1} g^{n-1})\epsilon C(R), (T_0, T_1, ..., T_{n-1})\epsilon T^n\} \qquad (14)$$

It is clear that not all the vectors $(T_0, T_1, ..., T_{n-1})\epsilon T^n$ generate configurations equally well representing the same shape as the template. In order to properly constrain the set of possible configurations from a template, Grenander[7] introduces a probability measure on the space T of values defining the transformation group. Fixing T as the Euclidean group x Scale, a T-valued markov process on the edge graph is used such that the components of the matrices $T_0, T_1, ..., T_{n-1}$

$$T_i = \begin{pmatrix} 1 + t_{0i} & t_{1i} \\ -t_{1i} & 1 + t_{0i} \end{pmatrix} \tag{15}$$

be independent first order Markov process. This parametrization of the T_i elements is only a matter of analytical convenience to get linear dependence from the parameters[9]. Since we are interested only in small deformations, we assume that $\{(t_{0i}, t_{1i})\}$ are jointly gaussian. In this case, the distribution over the local deformations of the template is a $2n$-variate Gaussian distribution. In our examples, given that the number of landmark points is small, we simulate the conditional distribution to (R) directly[8]. For those cases where the size of the covariance matrix is too big to be simulated directly, iterative methods can be used using an extended version of the Gibbs sampler[7,9,11,12].

Now and according to the definition introduced on the concept of landmark point set we consider a fifth element, an interpolation procedure. Let us take into account that to fix a landmark point set is equivalent to accepting that the behaviour of the curve in between each two adjacent landmarks only has to verify certain smoothness conditions. So the model we propose is compose of the following vector of elements (G,σ,R,T,I) where: G = segments on the plane, σ = cyclic graph, R= polygons simple and closed, T = euclidean or scale and I= interpolation function reproducing the curve behaviour between landmarks under smoothness conditions. The simulation of this model is carried out in two steps. First we simulate the $2n$ gaussian distribution conditioned to (R) associated to the vectors joining the estimated landmark points. Second we interpolate the resulting points according to the procedure given in section 3.2.

5 Classification from curvature

Now we present some statistical classification experiments based on our images emphasizing the strength of the information contained in the landmark point set. We label the classes as follows: Head (CB), Rounded Tail (CR), Conical Tail (CC), Filiform Tail (CF).

For each type of shape we take a sample of thirty images and, using the method explained in section 3 we calculate thirty vectors $\{c_i\}$ from them. The pattern associated to each shape is calculated from the average of the c_i curves. Figure 4 show estimations from the shapes in Figure 1. Two different statistical multivariate methods were used to classify the observations as random samples from one of the patterns, Discriminant Analysis and Classification Trees[3]. Since the number of values defining each estimate vector of curvatures is too big (around 500) and we think the only important points are those defining landmarks, we have extracted a 25 length subsample of each vector including the landmark points.

We used the subroutine BMDP-7M to carry out the discriminant analysis of our data set. To validate the estimated classifier we split the data set into two equal

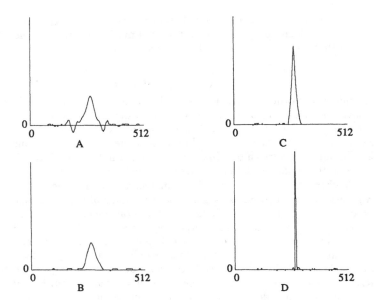

Figure 4: A,B,C,D show the curve of curvatures estimated patterns for the shapes show in figure.1

parts using one of them to estimate and the other to validate the estimation. Table 1 shows the estimations of the coefficients of the classification functions, and Table 2 shows that the most important variables in these functions are those associated to the landmarks. Using these functions we got a perfect classification of the other part of the sample .

TABLE 1	P9	P10	P11	P12	P13	P14	P18	Const.
CB	357.0	-788.8	-59.7	5.6	64.4	17.8	-269.5	-208.9
CR	100.2	150.9	26.1	6.8	102.0	11.9	-21.7	-73.8
CC	-73.7	133.8	-7.4	15.4	215.6	26.8	-63.8	-301.0
CF	-60.8	86.4	6.1	-0.4	264.7	0.9	-54.4	-408.6

TABLE 2	MOST SIGNIFICANT VARIABLES			
VAR	P13	P10	P14	P12
F.VALUE	2221.9	502.8	72.6	21.6

The intuitive meanings of these variables are P13: CR/CC/CF Maximum of Curvature, P10: CB Minimum of Curvature, P14: CB Maximum of Curvature, P12: CC Maximum of Curvature.

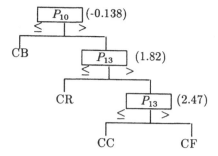

Figure 5:

Using CART package we built the classification tree shown in Figure 5. With this classifier we also got a 100% success classifying the other part of the sample. We used 10-fold cross-validation to calculate the cost of misclassification getting nil in all the classes.

6 Examples

Figure 6 shows four boundaries from four nematode head images together with the estimated polygonal template obtained from the estimate landmarks. Figure 7 shows the interpolated boundaries obtained from the polygonal templates shown in figure 6.

In these examples the ρ values are chosen by trial and error. We have also estimated these values using a step-by-step optimization procedure. We tried the quadratic and linear norms obtaining better results with the latter. Figure 8 shows the fit obtained with the estimated ρ values. For the ρ value associated to the segment joining the first and last landmark points we fix a high value.

7 Conclusions

We have presented a new method to synthesize and simulate boundaries based on the relationship between a landmark point set and the interpolation procedure associated to it. Although more simulation experiments have to be done to establish the true performances of the proposed method this shows to be efficient in terms of computing since to simulate new representations we only use the estimated landmark points. Another advantage of this method is the representation of the boundary by a function instead of a set of points. Some experiments with boundaries from biological shapes show that the most important information on the boundary is carried by the landmark points defined in terms of curvature.

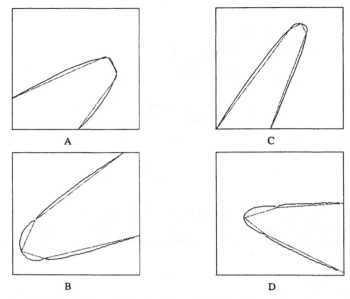

Figure 6: Estimated boundaries together with their polygonal templates

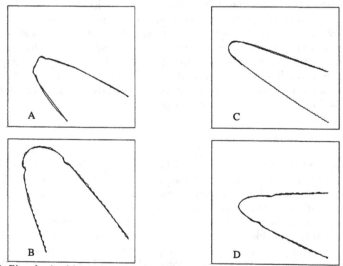

Figure 7: Fits obtained by trail and error of the ρ values for four head boundaries

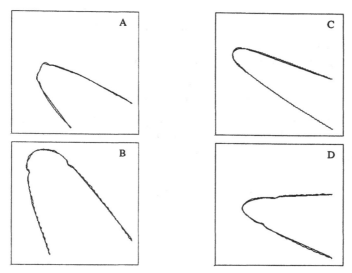

Figure 8: Fits obtained from estimated values of ρ for the same boundaries than figure.7

References

[1] F. Attneave and M. D. Arnoult. *The quantitative study of shape and pattern perception*. Psych. Bull. **53**, (1956) 452.

[2] Bookstein, F.L. (1978). *The Measurement of Biological Shape and Shape Change*. Lectures Notes in Biomathematics n.24, Springer-Verlag.

[3] Breiman,L., Friedman,J.H., Olshen,R.A. and Stone,C.J.. *Classification and Regression Trees*. (Wadsworth Inc. California 1984).

[4] Fdez-Valdivia, J., Pérez de la Blanca, N. *Characterization of shapes in microscopical digital images*, 7th SCIA, Alboorg. (1991).

[5] Grenander, U. *Pattern Synthesis. Lectures in Pattern Theory Vol. 1*. Applied Mathematical Sciences **vol 18**,(Springer Verlag. 1976).

[6] Grenander, U. *Tutorial on Pattern Theory*. Technical Report (Univ. of Brown. 1983).

[7] Grenander, U., Keenan, D.M. *Towards automated image understanding*. Journal of Applied Probability, **vol 16**, n.2, (1989), 207-221.

[8] Grenander, U., Chow, Y., Keenan, D.M. *HANDS. A Pattern Theoretic Study of Biological Shapes*. (Springer-Verlag. 1991)

[9] Knoerr, A. *Globals Models of Natural Boundaries: Theory and Applications.* Report in Pattern Theory 148. Brown University. (1988).

[10] Mardia,K.,V., Hainsworth,T.J. . A spatial thresholding method for image segmentation. *IEEE Trans. on PAMI.* **vol 10**,(1988), 919-927.

[11] Ripley,B.D. Recognizing organisms from their shape - a case study in image analysis. *Proc. XVth International Biometrics Conference*, Budapest, (1990), 259-263.

[12] Ripley,B.D. Classification and clustering in spatial and image data. 15 Jahrestagung von Gesellschaft fur Klassifikation, Salzburg. (1991).

[13] Serra, J. *Image Analysis and Mathematical Morphology.* (Academic Press, London, 1982).

[14] Su Bu-Qing, Liu Ding-Yuan *Computational Geometry. Curve and Surface Modeling.* (Academic Press, 1989).

INFERRING REGULAR LANGUAGES IN POLYNOMIAL UPDATED TIME

J. Oncina and P. García

Departamento Sistemas Informáticos y Computación
Universidad Politécnica de Valencia, Valencia, Spain

ABSTRACT*

An algorithm is described such that, given a set of positive data and a set of negative data of an unknown regular language, obtains a Deterministic Finite Automaton consistent with the data. The update time of this algorithm is $O(p^3 n)$ where p is the sum of the lengths of all the strings constituting the positive data and n is the sum of the lengths of those corresponding to the negative data. Moreover, this algorithm identifies any regular language in the limit.

1. Introduction

The inductive inference paradigm[1] is the basis of an approach to the automatic learning problem. In this framework there are a lot of theoretical results that tells us what is learnable by means of algorithmic strategies, and give us the general properties of the inference algorithms[2]. On the other hand, in connection with the Syntactical Pattern Recognition framework, many grammatical inference algorithms exist that can be used in the learning phase of pattern recognition tasks[3,4,5,6].

If we revise the (regular grammar) inference algorithms proposed in the last twenty years, we can immediately observe that only positive data is taken into account. This is

* Work partially supported by the Spanish CICYT under grant TIC-0448/89

rather a paradoxical situation. It is well known that the class of regular languages can not be correctly identified from only positive presentation; but any recursively enumerable class of languages is identifiable using a complete presentation (with positive and negative data)[7]. What is the reason for not making use of the negative information? Very often, when a new method is proposed, there is no explanation of the reason for this limitation and when this explanation exists, it is usually argued that the use of this information constitues an intactable problem. To support this last argument it is usual to resort to the Gold result establishingt hat the problem of finding a DFA with a minimum number of states and compatible with a complete presentation is NP-Hard[7]. The origin of this somewhat misleading relation between the minimum compatible DFA problem and the regular language inference problem is, however, rather clear. In fact, any algorithm that would construct a DFA with a minimum number of states compatible with all the data already processed, has the property of identifying any regular language in the limit . From the Gold result it follows that an inference method like this can not be efficient. However, using this result to conclude the intractability of the regular language inference problem is erroneous. This conclusion is particularly surprising if we observe that in the very same paper in wich the probable intractability of the minimum compatible DFA problem is established[4], Gold proposes a polynomial algorithm (that doesn't find a minimum DFA for each finite set of data) that allows us to identify any regular language in the limit.

In this paper we propose a new algorithm that can identify the class of regular languages from a complete presentation. Given an arbitrary sample, this method obtains a (non necessarily minimum) DFA compatible with the sample. Moreover, it this sample includes a "characteristic set", the algorithm is shown to supply the minimum DFA compatible with the sample. The proposed method is based on state clustering. It is well known that if S_+ is a "structurally complete" sample of a regular language L (all the transitions of the unknown source automaton $A(L)$ are used for the acceptation of the strings in S_+) there exists a partition π on the state set of the prefix tree acceptor of S_+, $PT(S_+)$, such that $PT(S_+)/\pi$ is isomorphic to $A(L)$. If we can take advantage of the words in Σ^*-L to reject some partitions, then the inference problem reduces to a guided search in the lattice of all the possible partitions. Unfortunately the search space grows exponentially with the size of the state set in $PT(S_+)$ and then with the size of S_+.

Instad of attempting exhaustive search, the proposed algorithm tries to merge pairs of states in $PT(S_+)$ according to an specific order and only does it if the automaton that the result rejects all the negative data. The algorithm obtains in polynomial time with the size of the sample, a DFA compatible with this sample, and when the sample is large enough the obtained automaton is the minimum DFA for the unknown language.

This algorithm, like the one proposed by Gold[4] has the disadvantage of not being incremental. However, while the Gold's algorithm has the additionaldisadvantage that it doesn' t generalize unless the sample has a characteristic set. On the other hand our algorithm is free of this inconvenience and then it is better for use in learning tasks.

2. Basic Concepts And Notation

Let Σ be a fixed finite alphabet of symbols. The set of all finite strings of symbols from Σ is denoted by Σ^*. The length of a string u is denoted by $|u|$. The unique string of length zero is denoted by λ. The concatenation of two strings u, w is denoted by uv. If a string $u = vw$ we say that v (w) is a prefix (suffix) of u. A language is any subset of Σ^*.

If L is a language over Σ, we define the set of prefixes over L as:

$$Pr(L) = \{\ u \in \Sigma^* \ | \ \exists\ v \in \Sigma^*, uv \in L\ \}$$

and the set of tails of u in L as:

$$T_L(u) = \{\ v \in \Sigma^* \ | \ uv \in L\ \}$$

A finite automaton (FA) A is defined by a five-tuple $(Q, \Sigma, \delta, q_0, F)$ where Q is a finite set of states, q_0 is the initial state, $F \subseteq Q$ is the set of final states and $\delta: Qx\Sigma \rightarrow 2^Q$ is the transition function. A is deterministic if for all $q \in Q$ and for all $a \in \Sigma$, $\delta(q,a)$ has at most one element. The language accepted by A is denoted by $L(A)$. A language is regular iff it is accepted by a FA. We say that q is an a-successor of p If $p \in \delta(q,a)$.

If $A = (Q, \Sigma, \delta, q_0, F)$ is a FA and π is a partition of Q, we denote by $B(q,\pi)$ the only block that contains q and we denote the quotient set $\{\ B(q,\pi)\ |\ q \in Q\ \}$ as Q/π. Given a FA A and a partition π over Q, we define the quotient automaton A/π as:

$$A/\pi = (Q/\pi, \Sigma, \delta', B(q_0,\pi), \{B \in Q/\pi\ |\ B \cap F \neq \varnothing\})$$

where δ' is defined as:

$$\forall B, B' \in Q/\pi,\ \forall a \in \Sigma,\ B' \in \delta'(B,a)\ \text{if}\ \exists q, q' \in Q,\ q \in B,\ q' \in B'\ :\ q' \in \delta(q,a).$$

Given A and π over Q, it is easyly seen that $L(A) \subseteq L(A/\pi)$.

Given $A = (Q, \Sigma, \delta, q_0, F)$, $L(A)=L$, the partition π_L defined as $B(q,\pi_L)=B(q',\pi_L)$ iff $\forall x \in \Sigma^*\ \delta(q,x) \cap F \neq \varnothing$ iff $\delta(q',x) \cap F \neq \varnothing$ produces a A/π_L that is the AFD that has the minimum number of states and accepts $L(A)$; this automaton is called the canonical automaton of the language L and we denote it by $A(L)$.

Given L, we can also define the canonical automaton $A(L) = (Q, \Sigma, \delta, q_0, F)$ as:

$$Q = \{\ T_L(u)\ |\ u \in Pr(L)\ \};\ q_0 = T_L(\lambda);\ F = \{\ T_L(u)\ |\ u \in L\ \};$$

$$\delta(T_L(u),a) = T_L(ua)\ \text{where}\ u, ua \in Pr(L)$$

A Sample S of a language L is a finite set of words that we can represent as $S=(S_+, S_-)$ where S_+ is a subset of L (positive sample) and S_- is included in the complementary language of L (Negative Sample).

Let S_+ be the positive sample from a regular language L, we say that S_+ is structurally complete if all the transitions of $A(L)$ are used in the acceptance of the strings in S_+.

Let S_+ be a positive sample from a regular language L, we can define the prefix tree acceptor of S_+ as $PT(S_+) = (Pr(S_+),\Sigma,,\delta,\lambda,S_+)$ where δ is defined as: $\delta(u,a) = ua$ where $u, ua \in Pr(S_+)$. This automaton only accepts the strings belonging to S_+.

It is well known that if S_+ is a structurally complete sample of a regular language L, then there exists a partition π on the states of $PT(S_+)$ such that $PT(S_+)/\pi$ is the $A(L)$.

3. Inference Algorithm

We denote as the lexicographic order in Σ^* as "$<$ ". Given a positive sample S_+ and a partition π over the set of all the prefixes of all the strings of the sample, the order "$<$" allows to define an order between the blocks of the partition.

<u>Definition 3.1</u>

Let S_+ be a positive sample, let π be a partition over $Pr(S_+)$ and let B_i,B_j be two blocks of π. We say that $B_i < B_j$ iff some $u \in B_i : \forall v \in B_j,\ u < v$ exists.

3.1 Operation Joint

Given a partition π over $Pr(S_+)$ and given $B_i,B_j \in \pi$ we define the set $J(\pi,B_i,B_j)$ as:

$$J(\pi,B_i,B_j) = \{ B \in \pi \mid B \neq B_i,\ B \neq B_j \} \cup \{ B_i \cup B_j \}$$

In the rest of the paper we assume that the subindex of a block is the same as the subindex of the smallest string belonging to the block. If a block has only one string we will represent it indistinctly as a block or as a string.

3.2 The Inference Algorithm

Given a sample $S = (S_+,S_-)$ of an unknown regular language L, this algorithm produces an automaton $PT(S_+)/\pi_r$ where π_r can be recursively obtained as follows:

$$\pi_0 = Pr(S_+) = \{\ u_0, \ .. \ , u_r\ \}$$

(we suppose that the the prefixes are indexed in lexicographical order, therefore $u_0=\lambda$)

$$\pi_n = J(\ \pi_{n-1},B,u_n)$$

if $\exists\ B,\ B' \in \pi_{n-1}$ such that both B and u_n are a-successors of B' and $B<u_n$ and is the first a-successor of B' that fulfill
$$S_-\cap L(A_0/J(\pi_{n-1},B,u_n)) = \varnothing.$$

$$\pi_n = J(\ \pi_{n-1},B,u_n\ )$$

if $B < u_n$ and is the first block in π_{n-1} such that
$$S_-\cap L(A_0/J(\pi_{n-1},B,u_n))=\varnothing.$$

$$\pi_n = \pi_{n-1}$$

otherwise

3.3 Example

Let $S_+ = \{\ 111,\ 000,\ 11101,\ 01\ \}$ be a positive sample and let $S_- = \{\ 0, 1, 00, 11\ \}$ be a negative sample. In this example we will show the automaton A_0/π_n for each step of the above algorithm.

The set of the prefixes of S_+ in lexicographical order is:

$$< \lambda, 0, 1, 00, 01, 11, 000, 111, 1110, 11101 >$$

The first step is to build $A_0=PT(S_+)$. Therefore the first automaton is the automaton of the Figure 3.1.

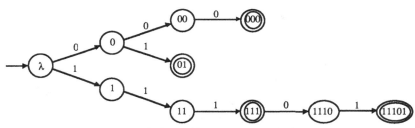

Fig.3.1. Initial Automaton: A_0/π_0

Obtaining π_1, $(u_1 = 0)$:

As λ has not any 0-successor smaller than 0,then we try to merge the state 0 with the state λ; in other words, we perform the operation $J(\pi_0,\lambda,0)$, and we show the automaton

54

$A_0/J(\pi_0,\lambda,0)$ shown in Figure 3.2. and we can see that this automaton doesn't fulfill $L(A_0/J(\pi_0,\lambda,0)) \cap S_- = \varnothing$ ($1 \in S_-$ is accepted by the automaton) .

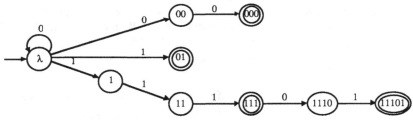

Fig.3.2. $A_0/J(\pi_0,\lambda,0)$ (not compatible with the sample)

Now there are no more states to try to merge with u_1 ($= 0$), and we have that $\pi_1 = \pi_0$.

Obtaining π_2, ($u_2 = 1$)

The algorithm obtains $A_0/J(\pi_1,\lambda,1)$ and accepts $11 \in S_-$. Next we try with $A_0/J(\pi_1,0,1)$ that also accepts 11. Then we have $\pi_2 = \pi_1$.

Obtaining A_3, ($u_3 = 00$)

$A_0/J(\pi_2,\lambda,00)$ accepts $0 \in S_-$

$A_0/J(\pi_2,0,00)$ accepts $00 \in S_-$

$A_0/J(\pi_2,1,00)$, shown in the figure Figure 3.3, rejects all the negative data. Thus $\pi_3 = J(\pi_2,1,00)$

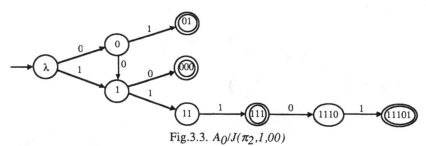

Fig.3.3. $A_0/J(\pi_2,1,00)$

The corresponding partition is:

$$\pi_3 = \{ \ \lambda, \ 0, \ \{ \ 1, \ 00 \ \}, \ 01, \ 11, \ 111, \ 1110, \ 11101 \ \}$$

The next automata for A_0/π_n, $n=4,...,9$ are shown in figures 3.4 to 3.9. The final automaton, A_0/π_9, recognizes the language over the alphabet $\{0,1\}$ of all the words where the difference between the number of 0's and the number of 1's is a multiple of 3.

55

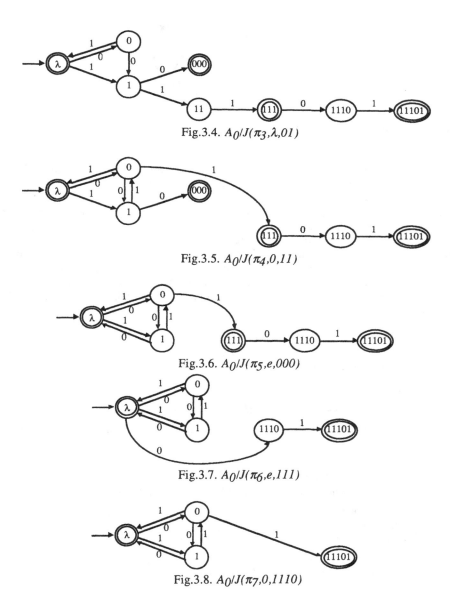

Fig.3.4. $A_0/J(\pi_3,\lambda,01)$

Fig.3.5. $A_0/J(\pi_4,0,11)$

Fig.3.6. $A_0/J(\pi_5,e,000)$

Fig.3.7. $A_0/J(\pi_6,e,111)$

Fig.3.8. $A_0/J(\pi_7,0,1110)$

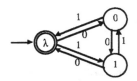

Fig.3.9. $A_0/J(\pi_8, e, 11101)$

4. Identification In The Limit

The concept of identification in the limit was introduced by Gold[1]. In this model, an algorithm $\mathcal{A}$ reads strings of a presentation and for each readln string it conjectures a DFA as the solution. We say that the algorithm $\mathcal{A}$ identifies the DFA A in the limit iff it for any presentation of $L(A)$ the infinite sequence of automata conjetured by $\mathcal{A}$ converges to a DFA that accepts the same language as the original A. It should be noted that the convergence point will depend on the presentation.

To show that the here proposed inference algorithm effectively identifies any regular language in the limit, we will see that for all possible DFA a finite sample (that grows polynomically with the size of the automaton) exists which, if it is included in the set of strings reads by the automaton, then the algorithm produces this DFA. Correspondingly, as for as a sample can be arbitrarily large we can guarantee that this sample is included in the sample that the algorithm reads.

4.1 Preliminary definitions

Short prefix (Sp):

$$Sp(L) = \{ w \mid w \in Pr(L) \text{ y } \neg \exists v \colon T_L(w) = T_L(v) \text{ and } v < w \}$$

We can observe that for a given language L there must be as many *short prefixes* as states in $A(L)$.

Nucleus:

$$N(L) = \{ ua \mid ua \in Pr(L) \text{ and } u \in Sp(L) \} \cup \{ \lambda \}$$

It is clear that if $ua \in N(L)$ then $u \in Sp(L)$. If we call n the number of states in $A(L)$, it is clear that, in the worst case, the number of strings in $N(L)$ is $n |\Sigma| + 1$.

Complete sample:

We say that a sample $S = (S_+, S_-)$ is complete if it fulfils the following two properties:

$\forall u \in N(L), \exists v \colon uv \in S_+;$ and if $u \in L$, then $v = \lambda$.

$\forall u \in Sp(L)$, $\forall v \in N(L)$: $\delta(q_0,u) \neq \delta(q_0,v)$ either $\exists uu' \in S_+$: $\exists vu' \in S_-$ or $\exists vv' \in S_+$: $\exists uv' \in S_-$.

The first rule is to guarantee that S_+ is a structurally complete sample. With the second rule we can assure that, if we try to merge two disctint states (respect to $A(L)$)belonging to $N(L)$, then a negative string exist that does not allow us do it. We can observe that in the worst case the number of samples that we need is:

$$|S_+| \text{ and } |S_-| < n^2 . |\Sigma|$$

Lemma 4.1

Let L be a regular language, let $S=(S_+,S_-)$ be a complete sample of L, let π a partition in $Sp(S_+)$, let $u \in N(L)$ and $v \in Sp(L)$ and suppose that $u,v \in B \in \pi$. Then

$$L(A_0/\pi) \cap S_- = \varnothing ==> T_L(u) = T_L(v).$$

Proof:

suppose that this is not true, then $\exists u,v$: $u \in N(L)$, $v \in Sp(L)$: $L(A_0/\pi) \cap S_- = \varnothing$ and $T_L(u) \neq T_L(v)$. Then from the construction of S_+ and S_- it is clear that either $\exists vv' \in S_+$: $uv' \in S_-$ or $\exists uu' \in S_+$: $vu' \in S_-$. If we suppose that the first is true (we can show the other in a similar way), and becouse both u and v belong to the same block of the partition, then in A_0/π all the tails for v must be tails for u, then as $vv' \in L(A_0/\pi)$, uv' must also belong to $L(A_0/\pi)$ but also $uv' \in S_-$, and this is in contradiction with $L(A_0/\pi) \cap S_- = \varnothing$

$\square$

Lemma 4.2

Let L be a regular language, let $S = (S_+, S_-)$ be a complete sample of L, let π a partition over $Pr(S_+)$ and let u,v be two strings such that $T_L(u) = T_L(v)$. Then

$$S_- \cap L(A_0/\pi) = \varnothing ==> S_- \cap L(A_0/J(\pi,u,v)) = \varnothing.$$

Proof:

Suppose that this is not true. Then $\exists u,v : T_L(u)=T_L(v)$, $S_- \cap L(A_0/\pi)=\varnothing$ but $S_- \cap L(A_0/J(\pi,u,v)) \neq \varnothing$. Let $x \in S_- \cap L(A_0/J(\pi,u,v))$, it is obvious that $x \in L(A_0/J(\pi,u,v)) - L(A_0/\pi)$. Then x can be written as $x=x_1x_2$ where either $u \in \delta(e,x_1)$ and $\delta(v,x_2) \cap F \neq \varnothing$ or $v \in \delta(e,x_1)$ and $\delta(u,x_2) \cap F \neq \varnothing$, because otherwise $x \in L(A_0/\pi)$. But since $T_L(u)=T_L(v)$ then $x \in L$ and this is contradictory with $x \in S_-$.

$\square$

Let π_i be the partition over $Pr(S_+)$ that is produced by the algorithm in the iteration i. In this partition the meger of states of A_0 only have affected the states $\{u_0,..,u_i\}$ (for the states larger than u_i, the automaon maintain with the tree shape of A_0). If $A_0/\pi_i=(Q_i,S,d_i,l,F_i)$ let $A'_i=(Q'_i,S,d'_i,l,F'_i)$ be the subacceptor of A_0/π_i induced for the elimination of the states $\{u_{i+1},...,u_r\}$. We will see that if S is a complete sample, in each step of the algorithm we obtain a quotient automaton $A_0/\pi_i)$ such as A'_i is isomorphic to a subacceptor of $A(L)$.

Theorem 4.1

Let S be a complete sample of a regular language L, let $A(L)=(\Sigma,Q,q_0,F,\delta)$ and let $A_0/\pi_i=(\Sigma,Q_i,q_0,F_i,\delta_i)$ then $Q'_i\subseteq Q$, $F'_i\subseteq F$, $\delta_i\subseteq\delta$.

Proof: (By induction)

If $i=0$ this is obvious, $A_0/\pi_0=PT(S_+)$ then:

$Q'_0=\{\lambda\}$ because $u_0 = \lambda$

$$F'_0= \begin{cases} \{\lambda\} \text{ if } \lambda \in S_+ \\ \varnothing \text{ otherwise} \end{cases}$$

$\delta'_i = \varnothing$

We suppose the theorem holds for $i-1$ and we will prove it will also hold for i. We will going to distinguish three cases, according to the three possibilities of the algorithm.

1) suppose that $\exists B, B' \in \pi_{i-1}: B < u_i$ and both B and u_i are a-successors of B' and also B is the first a-successor of B' that fullfil $S_-\cap L(A_0/J(\pi_{i-1},B,u_i))=\varnothing$

(the situation is represented in the figure 4.1)

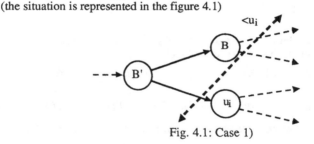

Fig. 4.1: Case 1)

Since B and u_i are a-successors of B' it is clear that, in $A(L)$, $T_L(u_i)=T_L(B)$ and since $S_-\cap L(A_0/\pi_{i-1})=\varnothing$ then from the Lemma 4.2 it is always true that $S_-\cap L(A_0/J(\pi_{i-1},B,u_i))=\varnothing$, then when we construct $\pi_i=J(\pi_{i-1},B,u_i)$ it is true that $u_i\in B$ and then $Q'_i=Q'_{i-1}\subseteq Q$. It is also clear that if $u_i\in F_i$ by construction of S_+ a string v in B must exist such that $v<u_i$ and $v\in F_i$, then $F'_i = F'_{i-1}\subseteq F$. And since both the transition (B',a,u_i) and (B',a,B) talso exist then $\delta'_i = \delta'_{i-1}\subseteq\delta$.

Note that, if $u_i \notin N(L)$ and if $B' < u_i$ is such that (B',a,u_i), then since $B' < u_i$, B' must belong to $Sp(L)$ and as since the positive sample we have for all the strings $xa \in N(L)$ a string xav, in particular we have a string such that $x = B'$ and since $xa \in L(N)$ then the transition (B',a,xa) must exist and it also is obvious that $xa < u_i$ and then xa must belong to a block $B < u_i$ and now we have the same conditions as at the beginning of this point. Then for the next points we can suppose that $u_i \in N(L)$.

2) Suppose now that the first condition is not true and the second condition holds, then: $\exists B < u_i$ and B is the first block of π_{i-1} that fullfil $S_- \cap L(A_0/J(\pi_{i-1},B,u_n)) = \varnothing$. (the situation is represented in the figure 4.2)

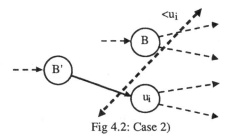

Fig 4.2: Case 2)

Since the first condition is not true u_i must belong to $N(L)$ and also if we call B' as the predecessor of u_i then u_i is the first a-successor of B'. Since $B < u_i$ then $B \in Pc(L)$ and since $u_i \in N(L)$ then from the Lemma 1 we have that $T_L(B) = T_L(u_i)$ and when we construct π_i it is clear that $u_i \in B$ and then $Q'_i = Q'_{i-1} \subseteq Q$ it is also clear that if $u_i \in F_i$, by the construction of S_+ a string v in B must exist such that $v < u_i$ and $v \in F_i$, then $F'_i = F'_{i-1} \subseteq F$. And since $\delta'_i = \delta'_{i-1} \cup \{(B',a,B)\}$ and as this transition comes from (B',a,u_i) and $T_L(u_i) = T_L(B)$ it is clear that $(B',a,B) \in \delta$ and then $\delta'_i \subseteq \delta$.

3) Suppose now that $\neg \exists B < u_i$ that satisfy $S_- \cap L(A_0/J(\pi_{n-1},B,u_n)) = \varnothing$ using Lemma 4.2 this is equivalent to $\neg \exists B < u_i$: $T(B) = T(u_i)$ then we have that $u_i \in Sp(L)$ and then and then $u_i \in Q$ and then $Q'_i = Q'_{i-1} \cup \{u_i\} \subseteq Q$. Moreover for the same reason it is also true that $F'_i \subseteq F$ and for ending, if B' is the predecessor of u_i and as $B' \in Sp(L)$ then it is clear that $(B',a,u_i) \in \delta$ and then $\delta'_i = \delta_{i-1} \cup \{(B',a,u_i)\} \subseteq \delta$.

$\square$

Theorem 4.2

This proposed algorithm identifies in the limit the class of regular languages.

Proof:

Since we are studying the inference in the limit we can suppose that the sample is complete. Let L be the regular language we are searching for. We call $A(L)=(\Sigma,Q,e,F,\delta)$, and let $A_r=(\Sigma,Q_r,e,F_r,\delta_r)$ be the automaton obtained from the algorithm. We must show that $Q_r=Q$, $F_r=F$ and $\delta_r=\delta$.

It is clear from Theorem 4.1 that $Q_r\subseteq Q$, $F_r\subseteq F$ and $\delta_r\subseteq\delta$. We go on to show that $Q\subseteq Q_r$. Suppose it is false; then $x\in Sp(L)$ and $x\in Q-Q_r$ must exist from the construction of S_+ then a block B in Q_r must exist such that $x\in B$ it is clear that $B\in Pc(L)$ and since $L(A_0/\pi_r)\cap S_-=\varnothing$ then for the Lemma 1 we have that $T_L(x)=T_L(B)$ and this is in contradiction with $x\in Q-Q_r$.

Since F contains also states and all the states are represented in S_+ then $F\subseteq F_r$. And in the same way, since S_+ is structurally complete then $\delta\subseteq\delta_r$. then we have what we wanted to show.

❑

We are going to determine the complexity of this algorithm in the worst case. This case is when we can not merge any state. In what follws we define p and n as:

$$p=\sum_{x\in S_-} |x| \quad \text{and} \quad n=\sum_{x\in S_+} |x|$$

To obtain the searched automaton we must compute all the series $A(S,r)$ of automata; that is a total of p automata. To compute $A(S,i)$ from $A(S,i-1)$, the worst case is when we try with all the previous states and we have only found it inadequate with the last string of the negative sample. Then we have tried i times, and since the time needed to know if the negative sample is accepted for a nondeterministic automaton is in the worst case proportional to $e \cdot n$ where e is the number of states. Then the time needed to build $A(S,n)$ must be $i \cdot e \cdot n$, consequently, since the worst case is when we can never merge any state, then the number of states is as large as p. Therefore, the overall complexity is

$$\sum_{i=1}^{p} i.p.n \in O(p^3.n)$$

5. References

[1]   E. M. Gold. "Language identification in the limit". *Information and Control,* 10: pp 447-474, 1967.

[2]   D. Angluin and C. H. Smith. "Inductive inference: theory and methods". *Computing Surveys,* 15(3), pp 237-269, 1983.

[3]   K. S. Fu and T. L. Booth. "Grammatical Inference: Introduction and Survey". parts 1 and 2. *IEEE Trans. Sys. Man and Cyber.,* SMC-5: 95-111, pp 409-423, 1975.

[4]   R. C. González and M. G. Thomason. "Syntactic Pattern Recognition, an introduction". *Addison-Wesley,* Reading Mass., 1978.

[5]   K. S. Fu. "Syntactic Pattern Recognition and Applications". *Prentice-Hall,* New York, 1982.

[6]   L. Miclet. "Grammatical Inference". In *Syntactic and Structural Pattern Recognition.* H. Bunke and A. San Feliu (eds.) *World Scientific,* pp 237-290, 1990.

[7]   E. M. Gold. "Complexity of automaton identification from given data". *Information and Control,* 37 pp 302-320, 1978.

IMAGE ANALYSIS AND COMPUTER VISION

PROJECTIVE INVARIANTS TO IDENTIFY POLYHEDRIC 3D OBJECTS *

A. Sanfeliu and A. Llorens

Instituto de Cibernética
Dept. Ingeniería de Sistemas, Automática e Inf. Ind.
Univ. Politécnica de Cataluña
Diagonal 647, 2 planta, 08028 Barcelona, Spain
e-mail (earn) : sanfeliu@ic.upc.es

Abstract

This article presents a method to represent and recognize 3D polyhedric scene objects from a set of 3D reference models by means of the projective invariants of each model faces. This method can be applied to identify partially occluded objects from a 2D projective view of the scene. The essence of the method consist of the use of invariants which do not depend on the perspective projection. The method can be applied to isolate and partially occluded objects since is based in the invariants of every face of the models. The method have low time and space complexity.

1 Introduction

The identification of objects in industrial tasks is one of the goals for the sensor based robots. The fact that the physical objects are 3D produces huge problems in the identification task since the perspective projection must be taken into account. Moreover the partial occlusion of the objects make worst the problem. The industrial vision processors are not prepared to solve this task however in some cases they can be applied to the 2D case.

There have been published some studies in the search for 3D invariants oriented to the identification of objects in scenes. The identification of 3D objects by means of invariants can be categorized into two groups: (1) the methods based on the depth map of the scene; and (2) the methods based on the gray leves (or color) of the reflected light of the scene. The first category presents the advantage that the information extracted from the scene image is very robust and that we can get the information of the surface orientation straightaway. Moreover the main invariant is the Euclidean distance which simplifies the search for the identification of objects. From the point of view of disadvantages it must be mentioned the high computing cost of extracting the depth by passive methods, the lost of some part of the image information due to the used sensors and the lost of the color information of the image. Examples of methods

---

*This work was partially supported by Fundación Areces

based on depth maps can be found in (Oshima and Shirai, 1983), (Grimson and Lozano-Perez, 1985), (Ikeuchi, 1987) and (Chen and Kak, 1989).

In the second category there are the methods based on 2D images of reflected light, gray level or color. There are several approaches used in this category which are based on invariants or pseudo-invariants. One of the most popular approaches is the use of a set of projective views of an object (named "aspect graphs") as reference models, from where the objects of the scene are identified. This approach is used when the features of the scene image can be controlled and the objects can be found in one of oriented projective views of the reference models. The advantage of this approach is that efficient algorithms can be found, however the constraints imposed to the objects in the scene reduces the number of applications to a few ones.

Another approach of the second category is based in projective invariants. In this case, the objects can be in any position and orientation as well as at different depths from the camera. Moreover, as in the previous cases, the objects must be identified although they are partially occluded. The advantage of this approach is that there are almost not constraints on the objects neither on the scene image which implies that the methods based on projective invariants will be able to be applied to general scene images. However the knowledge on these methods is very restrictive and the methods known have a huge time complexity as well as are quite sensibles to noise or segmentation process. There have been several works in this area for example ACRONYM (Brooks, 1981), the system developed by (Lowe, 1985) and the works developed by the author and colleagues (Sanfeliu 1987; Sanfeliu, Añaños and Dunjo, 1989).

In this article we will present a new way of representing 3D polyhedric models by means of projective invariants which will allow to identify 3D objects in a scene image from a 2D projective view. The identification could be done for isolate polyhedric objects as well as for partially occluded polyhedric objects.

In order to eliminate ambiguities we will use the following terminology: a *reference model* is a physical 3D object created in a 3D CAD generator system; a *face* is a planar surface of a 3D reference model (the surfaces of the models are planars since we are only working with polyhedric 3D reference models); an *object* is a perspective projection of a 3D reference model; and a *surface* is a closed contour before is identified by a reference model.

2 Representation of 3D polyhedric models by means of projective invariants

In this section we will explain the type of model representation. In the first subsection we will describe the vertex representation. In the second subsection we will explain the complete representation of models from the described vertex representation. In the last subsection we will explain the system of projective invariants which have been chosen to represent the surfaces of the models.

2.1 Representing a reference model by means of the face vertices

The focus of this work is based on representing reference models by their boundary faces and the faces by their vertices. The reference models can be described in this way without ambiguity since they are polyhedrics. This way of representing reference objects is not new and have been used by several research people in the past.

The essence of the work is the way how the vertices are represented. Each vertex is represented by the faces from where is generated and their spatial position is related to the geometric center and a set of orthonormal axes. The vertex V_i^q of a reference model (M_q) is described as follows:

$$V_i^q = f(g(S_j^q, S_{j+1}^q, ...), (X_i, Y_i, Z_i)) \tag{1}$$

where S_j^q is the face j, g is the function which relates the faces with the vertex and (X_i, Y_i, Z_i) are the coordinates of the vertex related to the coordinate axes of the reference model. We assume that the coordinates axes pass through the geometric center of the reference model.

In order to identify a face of a reference model from one of their perspective views, it is required to know at least one of the invariant systems of the face to the perspective projection. If we have such system and the system generates all the possible invariants we will able to use such representation in the identification. In this way a vertex V_i^q will be described as:

$$V_i^q = f(g(I(S_j^q), I(S_{j+1}^q), ...), (X_i, Y_i, Z_i)) \tag{2}$$

where $I(S_j^q)$ is the invariant system of the face S_j^q.

This representation has a double purpose. First it permits to identify the surface vertices of an object from the face vertices of a model. The identification is done without the knowledge of the complete reference model.

Second, the representation of a reference model is reduced to the representation of its vertices, the relation between them and the invariants of each face (however that this representation does not permits to optimize the search in the initial hypothesis step and in order to speed up this process is recommended to have additional information). The way of representing a reference model by their vertices permits to generate a compact and efficient structure from the point of view of recognition.

The selected representation structure is based on the *Extended Gaussian* proposed by Horn (Horn, 1984) and more specifically on the derivate structure proposed by Chen and Kak (Chen and Kak, 1989). The representation structure is a sphere of vertex-face features where the vertices are projected from the geometric center of the reference model. This structure is presented in the next subsection.

2.2 Representation of models based on a sphere of vertex-face features

In order to be efficient in the recognition process using the vertices and faces of a reference model it is required to have a structure from where we could access to the vertices and attributes

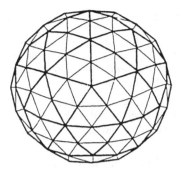

Fig. 1 *Tesseled sphere approximated by a geodesic polyhedron*

in low polynomial time.

From the structures proposed we have selected the one described by Chen and Kak which is based on the *Extended Gaussian* of Horn.

A reference model is represented by a sphere centered in its geometric center which coordinate axes are the ones defined in the model. The sphere is the minimum envelope which covers the model. The surface of the sphere contains the projection of the vertices of the model from the geometric center, created by the intersection of the rays that pass through the geometric center and the vertex, and the sphere. Figure 2 shows the sphere with the projected vertices of a model and figure 3 shows the sphere of vertex-face features where the connection of the model vertices are drawn.

Every projected vertex in the surface of the sphere is spatially oriented with respect to the coordinate axes. The vertices include as attributes the vertices and faces to which is connected and the real coordinates to the geometric center.

The sphere of features does not permits to develop efficient algorithms for the extraction the vertices if it is not transformed into another geometric shape. Chen and Kak proposed an efficient geometric shape for this purpose. They propose to transform the sphere in a geodesic polyhedron whose tesselation cells have the same attributes. Starting from an icosaedro they obtain a geodesic polyhedron whose cells are symmetrical, have the same area and the resolution can be modified (see figure 1).

By using this geodesic polyhedron some very efficient methods for extracting information of the reference models can be implemented. The functions which we have implemented are:

1. *Vertex-assignment function*: This function permits to assign a vertex of an object to model vertex, represented by the sphere of vertex-face features, by using the spatial inferred orientation. This function is used to select the points of the tesselation which are closer to the orientation of the object extracted vertex. As it can be deduced, the inferred orientation of the object vertices could not match exactly with a vertex of

69

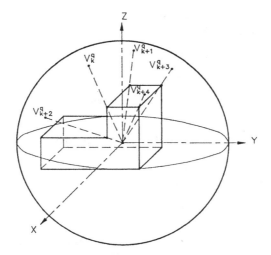

Fig. 2 *Vertices of the model projected into the sphere of vertex-face features*

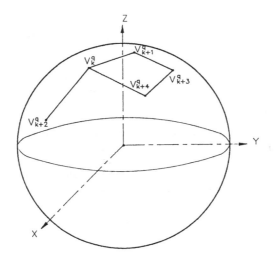

Fig. 3 *Sphere of vertex-face features*

the tesselation because of the resolution taken into account to construct the geodesic polyhedron, the errors of segmentation or due to the inference of the depth.

2. *Find-neighbourhood*: This function serves to find the nearest neighbourhood of a model vertex.

3. *Find-vertex*: This function finds the list of the model vertices which are closer to an object vertex by using the model invariants.

2.3 Projective invariant for a model face

In this work we have used a system of projective invariants which permits to characterized every model face by a set of ordered points which describe the face. These points can be the vertices of the contour of the face or any other group of ordered points which characterized the face. More generic projective invariants and their mathematical foundations can be seen in (Llorens, 1991).

The system of projective invariants considered in this work are based in the cross ratio between four areas built by five vertices of a face. The method requires to fix one of the vertices. For a polygon of n vertices the number of invariants is:

$$\binom{n}{5}$$

which implies that the number of invariants is $\frac{n!}{5!(n-5)!}$. Denoting by Δ_{ijk} the area formed by the vertices V_i^q, V_j^q, V_k^q, the mathematical formula of the projective invariant is:

$$I_{i,j,k,l,m} = \frac{\Delta_{ijk}\Delta_{ilm}}{\Delta_{ikl}\Delta_{ijm}} \tag{3}$$

where $\Delta_{ikl} \neq 0$ and $\Delta_{ijm} \neq 0$.

In order to clarify the method let us going to show the projective invariants of the polygon shown in figure 4. Since the polygon of figure 4 has 6 vertices the number of projective invariants is $\frac{n!}{5!(6-5)!} = \frac{6!}{5!} = 6$. The projective invariants are the six combinations of the indices in such way that no one is repeated (by permutation) and that every resultant index is greater than its predecessor. The projective invariants are:

$$I_{1,2,3,4,5} = \frac{\Delta_{123}\Delta_{145}}{\Delta_{134}\Delta_{125}} \tag{4}$$

$$I_{1,2,3,4,6} = \frac{\Delta_{123}\Delta_{146}}{\Delta_{134}\Delta_{126}} \tag{5}$$

$$I_{2,3,4,5,6} = \frac{\Delta_{234}\Delta_{256}}{\Delta_{245}\Delta_{236}} \tag{6}$$

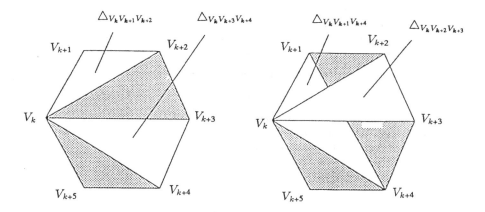

Fig. 4 *Areas taken into account to compute the projective invariants*

$$I_{3,4,5,6,1} = \frac{\Delta_{345}\Delta_{361}}{\Delta_{356}\Delta_{341}} \tag{7}$$

$$I_{4,5,6,1,2} = \frac{\Delta_{456}\Delta_{413}}{\Delta_{461}\Delta_{453}} \tag{8}$$

$$I_{5,6,1,2,3} = \frac{\Delta_{561}\Delta_{524}}{\Delta_{512}\Delta_{564}} \tag{9}$$

This type of projective invariants can be applied to the computation of any group of points which lay in a face, for example the vertices of the contour of every model face. The constraints of the method are:

1. The number of points must be at least of five. With less than five points can not be found projective invariants.

2. From the five vertices at least three of them can not be colinears since the area generated by them would be zero.

3. The projection of the face can not be a straight line which is a singularity in the projective space.

The projective invariants described in this work have the following advantages:

1. The calculation of the invariants is robust since the computation of an area is always more robust than many other features (distance of two points, etc...). However as we will see in the next subsection the sensibility of the projective invariant can be large and depends on the geometry of the projected vertices.

2. The value of every projective invariant is unique and the same for any projection view (except for the singularities) if the extracted points have the same relative theoretical value. However, as we will see later, due to the digitalization sampling and the segmentation process, these values can differ substantially.

3. The projective invariants can be applied to any group of ordered points.

4. The projective invariants are fast to obtain.

5. Since the invariants can be built from any group of five points, the method that we explain in this work can be used to recognize faces which are partially occluded. If the face have n vertices and t are occluded at least there will be

$$\left(\begin{array}{c} n - t \\ 5 \end{array} \right)$$

projective invariants available for recognizing the face.

The disadvantages of the projective invariants are:

1. If there are less than five points these invariants can not be used.

2. The number of perspective invariants can be very high if the number of points to consider is high. This implies that the vertices to generate invariants must be selected in advance to reduce the number of combinations. There are several solutions which reduce this problem to a linear one.

3. The sensibility of the invariant is a basic issue which must be taken into acount in the recognition process (see next subsection).

2.4 Sensibility of the projective invariants

One of the most important issues in representation is the sensibility of the selected features to errors produced at the different steps of the image processing. The preliminary processes of computer vision produce important distortions in the extraction of points and segments. The variation between the exact position of a vertex and the extracted vertex can make fail the process of recognition. For this reason it is essential to know how sensibles are the projective invariants before we procede to use them in the recognition process.

The sensibility of a projective invariant with respect to a parameter is is the percentage of change of the projective invariant with respect to the percentage of change of the parameter. The sensibility is computed for a specific *projective configuration*. A projective configuration is a selection of five vertices for which a projective invariant is computed.

A projective invariant, $I_{i,j,k,l,m}$, of five vertices can be rewritten as follows (see figure 5):

$$I_{i,j,k,l,m} = \frac{\Delta_{ijk}\Delta_{ilm}}{\Delta_{ilk}\Delta_{ijm}} = \frac{< u_{ik}, x_j >< u_{im}, x_l >}{< u_{ik}, x_l >< u_{im}, x_j >} \tag{10}$$

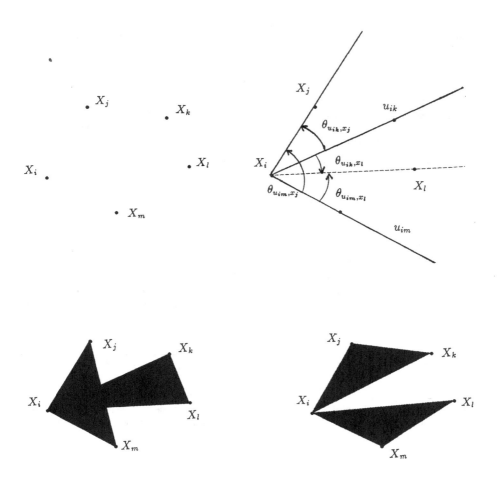

Fig. 5 *Projective configurations for five vertices*

Since $< u_{ik}, x_j >$ is nothing but the dot product between a straight line, u_{ik}, which pass through the vertives x_i and x_k, and the vertex x_j, then $I_{i,j,k,l,m}$ is transformed into (see (Llorens, 1991) for details):

$$I_{i,j,k,l,m} = \frac{sin\theta_{u_{ik},x_j} sin\theta_{u_{im},x_l}}{sin\theta_{u_{ik},x_l} sin\theta_{u_{im},x_j}} \quad (11)$$

The resulting invariant depends on the angles between two of the five vertices and the two straight lines formed by the other three vertices (see figure 5). For this reason the sensibility will be measured with respect to these angles θ.

The sensibility with respect to the parameter θ_{u_{ik},x_j} is

$$S_{I_{i,j,k,l,m}}(\theta_{u_{ik},x_j}) = \left| \frac{\frac{dI_{i,j,k,l,m}}{I_{i,j,k,l,m}}}{\frac{d\theta_{u_{ik},x_j}}{\theta_{u_{ik},x_j}}} \right| = \left| \frac{\theta_{u_{ik},x_j}}{tan\theta_{u_{ik},x_j}} \right| \quad (12)$$

For the other three angles the sensibility is the same except that for the two which are in the denominator there is a change in the sign.

The global sensibility is the gradient module of the four partial derivatives of the projective invariant with respect to the angles. However, these partial derivaties are the sensibilities of the projective invariant with respect to the angles, so the sensibility will be the gradient module of the sensibilities for each angle . The global sensibility ($S_{i,j,k,l,m}$) is computed as follows:

$$S_{I_{i,j,k,l,m}} = \sqrt{(S_{I_{i,j,k,l,m}}(\theta_{u_{ik},x_j})^2 + (S_{I_{i,j,k,l,m}}(\theta_{u_{im},x_l})^2 + (S_{I_{i,j,k,l,m}}(\theta_{u_{ik},x_l})^2 + (S_{I_{i,j,k,l,m}}(\theta_{u_{im},x_j})^2}$$
$$(13)$$

The range of $S_{i,j,k,l,m}(\theta_{u_{ik},x_j})$ goes from 0 to 1, where 0 means that the projective invariant is not sensible to the position of vertex x_j and 1 means that the projective invariant is completely sensible. The range of the global sensibility goes from 0 to 2 where the last value implies maximum sensibility.

The global sensibility give us an idea of how good will be the invariant for a specific projective configuration. However high sensibility does not necessarily imply a large error in the computation of the invariant.

The sensibility is not associated to the error extraction but there is a correlation between the probability of a wrong extraction and the sensibility. Due to this correlation we can use as a general rule the following: "high sensibility implies high probability in the error of the extracted projective invariant".

For the application of the recognition of 3D objects, the sensibility is obtained for the vertices of the projective projection. The invariants which sensibility is higher than a threshold are not considered for the matching with the invariants of the model vertices since they have a high probability of being wrong.

3   Method to identify 3D objects of a 2D scene

The procedure to identify 3D objects is based in the projective invariants described before and in the representation of 3D reference models. Given a set of reference 3D models, M_q with $1 \leq q \leq p$, which have been modelized by means of the invariants of very face, and a 2D scene where there are objects partially occluded the identification method is the following:

1. **Segmentation and extraction of features**

    (a) The contours are detected by means of convolution operators with a mask like the Sobel one. Once binarized the resulting image, there are applied several operations to extract the lines and vertices of the image contours (Añaños, Sanfeliu, 1988). The result is a list (LC) of the interior contours of the image, where LC_i contains the vertices and the attributes of contour i.

    (b) For every object vertex, V_j^E, it is generated a list ($LC_{V_j^E}$) of the image contours that include this vertex.

    (c) For every contour of LC_i (potential surface of an object), the projective invariants of its vertices are computed as well as their invariant sensibility with respect to the projection. The invariants, which sensibility is below a certain threshold, are eliminated from the list. The list ($LC_{V_j^E}$) is increased with the associated invariants and their invariant sensibility.

2. **Initial hypothesis**

    (a) The invariants associated to the vertices (V_i^q) of each model M_q are matched with the invariants of the list ($LC_{V_j^E}$) of the potential objects of the scene. As a result of the matching a list of the object vertices and the models to which they match is obtained. This list includes all potential models which can be in the image. However since the number of models can be high to be verified, the list is ordered through a index which indicates the degree of matching between each model to each potential object of the scene.

3. **Verification**

    (a) The initial hypothesis process uses little information to generate the list of candidate models. Information about the model, orientation of the object or the neighbour faces for example, is not used in that process. The verification process use the information of the recognized model to guide the search of additional data in order to confirm the candidate model. The steps of the verification process are:

    i. *Vertex characterization* : For each group of 4 object vertices, V_j^E, of the candidate list which belongs to the same model, M_i, the orientation and position of the 4 vertices is computed. Initially there are not requirements in the selection of the vertices, however there are some configurations of the 4 vertices which are less sensitive to the position errors. The method applied is explained in (Añaños y Sanfeliu, 1988).

ii. *Vertex verification* : Every V_j^E is located in the sphere of vertex-face features of the model in order to identified the neighbour vertices. If a *significant* number of vertices are identified, (by checking their projective invariants, incident planes and orientations and positions) the object is validated with respect to the reference model and a similarity measure is computed. A significant number of vertices means that at least a minimum number of the visible vertices have to be identified. If there are not enough vertices which match with the model, then the model is rejected.

iii. *Final verification* : An object can be recognized by more than one model, then some additional features are checked to eliminate the ambiguity. However, sometimes the ambiguity could not be eliminated due to the lack of information. This situation happens when the object has overlapped a large portion. In this case the object can not be identified.

The time complexity of the method shown is function of the number of vertices to be compared. If there are r scene vertices and s model vertices (total number), the time complexity of the *Initial hypothesis* process is $C_T = O(rs)$. The time complexity of the *Verification* process depends on the three steps. The first step requires to select groups of vertices to obtain their 3D position and orientation. A first approach does not require to verify the best solutions, which implies that the selection is linear with respect to the number of vertices in the list. A deeper approach requires to verify all combinations of groups of four vertices to obtain the best results. The second step requires a linear time complexity with respect to the number of vertices of the model (Chen and Kak, 1989). The last step requires a time complexity linear with the number of identified objects. In conclusion, the time complexity meanly depends on the *Initial hypothesis* process. If the number of models is high compared with the highest number vertices of the models, then the time complexity is $C_T = O(s^2)$.

4   Conclusions

The work presented in this paper describe a method based on projective invariants which permits identify partially occluded objects in a scene from one of its projective views. The identification method is independent of the position and orientation of the objects with respect to the camera, permits to located partially occluded objects and it is very efficient with respect to time complexity. Conversely, the method depends on the sensibility and the extraction of the vertices in a projective view and that at least are available five vertices in every face. The method is now being implemented.

5   References

1. Añaños M. y Sanfeliu A. (1988) *Posicionamiento y verificación de objetos 3D parcialmente ocultos representados por fronteras conocidos 4 puntos de su proyección.* III Simposium Nacional de Reconocimiento de Formas y Análisis de Imágenes, Oviedo 27-30, Sept.

2. Brooks R. (1981) *Model-based three dimensional interpretations of two dimensional images.* Proc. 7th INt. Joint Conf. Artificial Intell., Vancouver, B.C., Canada, Aug., pp.619-624.

3. Chen C.H. and Kak A.C. (1989) *A robot system for recognizing 3-D objects in low-order polynomial time.* IEEE Transactions SMC Vol.19, No.6, Nov./Dic.

4. Grimson W.E.L. and Lozano-Perez T. (1985) *Recognition and location of overlapping parts from sparse data in two and three dimensions.* IEEE Comput. Soc. Int. Conf. Robotics, St. Louis, MO, Mar..

5. Horn B.K.P. (1984) *Extended gaussian image.* Proc. IEEE, Vol.72, No.12, pp.1671-1686.

6. Ikeuchi K. (1987) *Generating and interpreting tree from a CAD model for 3D object recognition in bin-picking tasks.* International Journal of Computer Vision, Vol.1, No.2.

7. Llorens A. (1991) *Proyectividades e invariantes algebraicos en visión por computador.* Doctoral Thesis, Polythecnical University of Catalunya.

8. Lowe D. (1985) *Visual recognition from spatial correspondence and perceptual organization.* Proc. IJCAI-9, pp.952-959.

9. Oshima M. and Shirai Y. (1983) *Object recognition using three dimensional information.* IEEE Trans. on Pattern Analysis and Machine Intelligence, VOL. PAMI-5, NO.4, Jul., pp.353-361.

10. Sanfeliu A. (1987) *Parallel straight segments in the recognition of 3D objects.* Instituto de Cibernética, Technical document IC-DT-1987.04.

11. Sanfeliu A. and Añaños M. (1989) *A CAD based vision system for identifying industrial work pieces.* 6th IFAC/IFIP/IFORS/IMACS Symposium on Information Control Problems in Manufacturing Technology, Sept. 26-29, Madrid (Spain).

12. Sanfeliu A., Añaños M. and Dunjo M.J. (1989) *Integrating driving model and depth for identification of partially occluded 3d models.* NATO Advance Research Workshop on Multisensor Fusion and Computer Vision, Chamrousse, Grenoble, France, June 26-30.

ELASTIC MATCHING USING INTERPOLATION SPLINES

J. Serrat , E. Marti and J. J. Villanueva

Department d'Informàtica, Universitat Autònoma de Barcelona, 08193 Bellaterra, Spain

ABSTRACT

In this article we present a new method to match planar shapes. This method deals with the interpretation of the regions of an image from its edge points and according to a model represented by a series of vertices. The interpolation of these creates a curve, which is quite similar to the one of the model. The matching process aims to find on the image the corresponding points. This is an elastic matching because it allows local distortions with regard to the model. Further more, one of the characteristics of this method is its ability to allow different degrees of tolerance concerning deformations in every part of the model. Finally, some results in the identification and classification of certain bones of the hand from digital radiographs and a few models from an atlas are also presented.

1. Introduction

Matching is an important topic in pattern recognition and computer vision. It is a process which puts in correspondence two existing representations : a model previously stored and a set of imput data acquired by a sensor. The basic matching process can be formulated in the following way[1] : given two sets of data, the model M and the pattern P, use some essential information from the model and the pattern to find a mapping C which, under certain constrains, gives the best possible match in terms of predefined similarity measure S. The mapping C usually consists of registration, which is always global, and matching, which can be local or global, depending on the information used.

A very common situation in image analysis is the existence between model and pattern of a global transformation of scaling, rotation and traslation but also local distortions. This very last point implies that the establishment of the relation between the two representations, that is the matching process, must be elastic in the sense of tolerating relatively small distortions. Whenever the model on which we are working shows exactly the shape that we want, we can use tecniques such as correlation, chamfer matching ,etc. By using these, we only have to obtain the parameters of the global transformation that maximizes the measure of coincidence of the model and the image. If the objects have an arbitrary shape or features, there is no model. The intermediate situation arises when we work neither on an arbitrary shape nor on a fixed one, but when there is a tendency towards an average shape (the model). This implies that there are infinite possibilities around it being an elastic matching method required.

One of the first works on this field goes back to Burr[2]. Given two contours formed by linear segments, he proposes a method that approaches both contours by successive iterations. The changes are based on displacement vectors that are assigned to each end of the segment. They can be understood as forces that "push" and "pull" the points of a contour to the other one. Another method of elastic matching is based on Fourier's elliptic descriptors[3]. Firstly a vector p is formed by the parameters of every ellipse, for all the terms used. Associated to it and bearing the model in mind, a probability measure $P(p)$ is defined. That is how matching becomes a problem of maximization of contour similarity $C(p)$ –correlation to the gradient image– weighted by $P(p)$. Another approach to find the best possible interpretation allowing deviations from the model is the one that uses dynamic programming[4]. This has been used to register satellite images and maps. The similarity to the model and the coincidence with the contours of the image is obtained by searching the minumum cost path in a graph. The nodes are the possible associations between edge points and points on the map, the weight of arches is the compatibility of a couple of nodes to be united.

Finally there is a series of works based on elasticity theory, in which objects are modeled as deformable bodies. Kass et al.[5] gave rise to *snakes*, curves which are attracted by external forces towards outstanding features of the images, such as lines or contours, while internal forces resiting to deformations impose smoothness constraints. Matching is formulated as a problem of energy minimization. The different forces that intervene may be weighted to fit them to the desired behaviour. In [1,6] the application of an elastic matching method to the analysis of X-ray tomographies of the crane according to a brain model is described. After global alignment the brain model is deformed by external forces correcting local disparities. The process stops as soon as a satisfactory coincidence is obtained and an equilibrium between external and internal forces resisting to deformation is reached.

In this article we present a new method to perform elastic matching of planar shapes described by their closed contour. We want to interpret a region of an image according to this kind of model, that is, we want to extract a new shape out of it. This shape will look on the one hand quite enough like the model and on the other hand will correspond to the features detected on the image. The combination of these two measures of similarity will let us evaluate how accurate and good the interpretation is. This focusing is interesting if we have to choose among different interpretations owing to the existence of several possible models for the same set of data, i.e. when we come across the problem of classifying as well as the problem of matching.

According to the foregoing formulation of the matching problem, whenever we face a new method we should specify[1] :

- what to match, that is, which is the representation for each model M and for the pattern P

- which are the constraints to observe to establish the correspondence C

- how to put in relation the two representations of M and P, in order to obtain consitent results.

- how to evaluate the match, that is, how to define the similarity measure between P and $C(M)$

In the following sections we will see each one of these points :

- Representation : We consider P and M two contours of a planar shape represented by a series of points which by interpolating a spline curve create a quite faithful approximation to these contours. The points of interpolation are chosen for being of the most significance in terms of information content, that is, chosen among the local curvature extrema (section 2).

- Constraints : We formulate the hypothesis on the basis that we can esteem the parameters of the global alignment transformation as well as some intervals around them in which the optimal values of each parameter are found. This will allow us to delimit a region R in which P will be located, if it corresponds to the model chosen presently (section 3)

- Matching process : First of all we chose those edge points in R considered to be compatible with the curve according to the position and direction of the gradient. Then we choose a set C_i of candidates to i-th vertex of P for each point m_i of the representation of the model. The matching process will consist of finding the best combination of candidates, one for each set, to maximize the measure S (section 4)

Finally, in section 5 we present some results of the method applied to the identification of certain bones on radiographs of the hand. The problem in question lies in classifying them under seven or eight development stages, in order to diagnose growth disorders in children.

2. Representation

The model contours are represented by a sequence of points which creates a curve quite similar to the model. We have chosen cubic spline curves from the interpolation curves class because they are easy to calculate, C^2 continuous and flexible enough to represent regular shapes.

Given $p_i = (x_i, y_i), i = 0 \ldots m$, we obtain an interpolation curve through cubic splines by finding between each two succesive points p_i, p_{i+1}, the coefficients of each two cubic polynomials $X_i(u), Y_i(u), u \in [0, u_{i+1} - u_i]$, such that :

$$
\begin{aligned}
Y_{i-1}(u_i - u_{i-1}) &= Y_i(0) = y_i \\
Y_{i-1}^{(1)}(u_i - u_{i-1}) &= Y_i^{(1)}(0) \\
Y_{i-1}^{(2)}(u_i - u_{i-1}) &= Y_i^{(2)}(0)
\end{aligned}
\tag{1}
$$

and similar equations for $X_i(u)$ polynomials. Thus, we obtain a (parametric) C^2 curve. In the case of a closed curve, i.e. $p_{m+1} = p_0$, these requirements give rise to a system of linear equations not difficult to solve due to the fact that its matrix is almost tri-diagonal[7]. If not, we come up with $4(m-1) + 2$ linear equations and $4m$ unknowns (the coefficients of the m cubic polynomials). One way to provide the two lacking conditions is fixing the second derivative at zero on the first and the last points (natural cubic splines).

The variable u controls the spacement between vertices. The kind of distance between them may alter the shape of the interpolated curve. In order to avoid unnatural oscilations we have chosen a spacement equal to the euclidean distance instead of an uniform spacement :

$$
u_i - u_{i-1} = ((x_i - x_{i-1})^2 + (y_i - y_{i-1})^2)^{\frac{1}{2}}, \quad i = 1 \ldots m+1
\tag{2}
$$

Owing to the fact that the more points we put in relation, the higher the computational cost of the process is. Therefore, we are interested in a representation with only a few vertices but which, at the same time, can represent faithfully the shape of the model. The data received by human visual system are in many cases redundant, that is to say, a series of dominating points along the contours of an object and their spatial relationships are sufficient to recognize it. In planar shapes they are corners, holes, protruding areas on the contours, etc. Hence, we have chosen dominating points as those on which the curvature shows a local maximum or minimum. From them we will chose the vertices which will represent each model.

Let Q be a parametric curve twice derivable with regard to each component, $Q(t) = (x(t), y(t))$. Then curvature $\kappa(t)$ is defined as the variation of the tangent angle on a curve per unit arc length :

$$
\kappa(t) = \frac{d\alpha}{ds} = \frac{x'(t)y''(t) - x''(t)y'(t)}{(x'^2(t) + y'^2(t))^{3/2}}
\tag{3}
$$

In practice the models are not given as continuous functions $x(t), y(t)$, but as sequences of points $\{(r_i, s_i), i = 1 \ldots n\}$ resulting from sampling spatially some curve. In order to soften the effects of this discretization, which causes false local concavities and convexities in the curve, we have to smooth it before calculating the curvature. On the other hand, this calculation is based on differentiation, an operation that amplifies high frequencies which constitute the noise of discretization. As a consequence, we soften the discretized contour by eliminating high frequencies using a low-pass filter. The procedure is as follows :

- Given the sequence $\{(t_i, u_i), i = 1 \ldots n\}$, we calculate the Fourier descriptors of the sequence of complexes $\{z_i = t_i + ju_i, i = 1 \ldots n\}$. Its power spectrum appears as in figure 1b.

- We apply an ideal low-pass filter and anti-transform its result. This gives a contour $\{(v_i, w_i), i = 1 \ldots n\}$ which is very similar to the original one but lacking the irregularities of the discretization process (figure 1c)

- We calculate a discrete and normalized version of the curvature k_i by approximating the derivative of each component on a particular point by the difference between its value on the preceding and following points (figure 1d).

- We calculate the local extreme points of κ.

Now we have to choose the vertices that will represent the model from these points. There is a great deal of non-representative points because of the small magnitude of their curvature as a result of oscillations in the contour, which are alien to the shape of the model. Then the algorithm of selection is as follows:

- Select directly all the extreme points on which $|\kappa| \geq 1$. The curvature has been normalized with regard to scaling by multiplying it by $2\pi/$perimeter.

- In the interval between each pair of points chosen, if the error between the sampled version (t_i, u_i) and the interpolated curve is higher than a theshold, we have to add an intermediate extreme point. The error is defined as the longest distance between a point of the sequence (t_i, u_i) in the interval and its corresponding point on the spline curve.

- Repeat the previous point until no segment is divided.

3. Constraints

One of the adopted hypotheses is that it will be possible to esteem the parameters of the global transformation of registration between the model and the image as well as some intervals of confidence around these values. In the foregoing intervals we shall also find the ones of the optimal alignment. Secondly, we presume that possible local deformations of P will also be covered by these intervals. That is, we take intervals wide enough to include P in the region R defined in Eq. 6 in spite of deformations.

By using knowledge on the content of the scene as well as on the image formation geometry, we can often formulate initial hypothesis concerning position, size and spatial relationships among different objects that may arise.

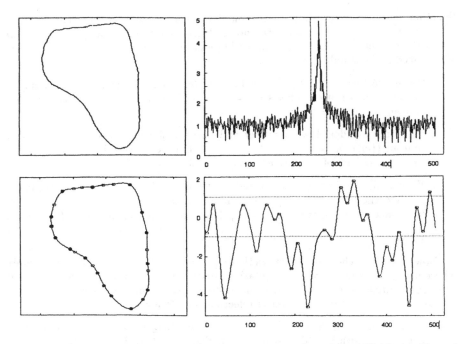

Figure 1: a) discretized contour, b) power spectrum $\log_{10}(1 + |F(z)|)$, c) filtered contour, local extrema of the curvature and selected points (filled) d) normalized curvature.

Let us suppose that there is a transformation $T(S, \Theta, T_x, T_y)$ between the model and the shape of the image, which will give us the best alignment of the model in spite of local deformations. M would be scaled by factor S, rotated by Θ and translated by (T_x, T_y) in this order. The transformation matrix will be therefore

$$T(S, \Theta, T_x, T_y) = \begin{pmatrix} S\cos(\Theta) & S\sin(\Theta) & 0 \\ -S\sin(\Theta) & S\cos(\Theta) & 0 \\ T_x & T_y & 1 \end{pmatrix} \tag{4}$$

The exact value of these parmeters is unknown. However in many occasions we can take advantage of what we know about the scenes we are analysing and about image acquisition to get an estimation $\hat{s}, \hat{\theta}, \hat{t}_x, \hat{t}_y$ and to establish a rank in which the optimal value of each parameter will be contained, $S \in [\hat{s} - L_s, \hat{s} + L_s]$, $\Theta \in [\hat{\theta} - L_\theta, \hat{\theta} + L_\theta]$, etc. Therefore, $\hat{s}, \hat{\theta}, \hat{t}_x, \hat{t}_y, L_s, L_\theta, L_x, L_y$ are such that :

– if (x, y) is a point from the contour of the model, its corresponding point on the image must be located inside the region

$$R(x, y) = \{ \ (x \, s \, cos(\theta) - y \, s \, sin(\theta) + t_x, \ x \, s \, sin(\theta) + y \, s \, cos(\theta) + t_y),$$
$$\mid s - \hat{s} \mid \leq L_s, \ \mid \theta - \hat{\theta} \mid \leq L_\theta, \ \mid t_x - \hat{t}_x \mid \leq L_x, \ \mid t_y - \hat{t}_y \mid \leq L_y \ \} \quad (5)$$

– Consequently

$$P \subset R = \bigcup_{(x,y) \in M} R(x, y) \quad (6)$$

The second constraint consists of taking for impossible the interpretations which exceed a certain initial distortion measure with regard to the model. We will se that the matching process is based on choosing an image edge point for each vertex of the representation of the model. Therefore this constraint imposes that

– the difference between the orientation of the vector v_i, which unites two succesive vertex of the model, m_i, m_{i+1}, rotated $\hat{\theta}$ and the one of vector w_i, that unites the two corresponding points on the image, c_i, c_{i+1}, cannot exceed a certain theshold b_1 (figure 2) :

$$\mid \alpha_i + \hat{\theta} - \beta_i \mid \leq b_1 \quad (7)$$

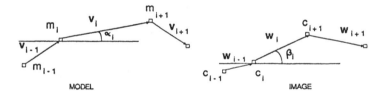

Figure 2:

– it occurs similarly in the relation between their lengths and the scaling factor $\hat{s}$:

$$\text{if } r_i = \hat{s} \, \frac{\mid v_i \mid}{\mid w_i \mid}, \ \text{then } \mid 1 - r_i \mid \leq b_3 \quad (8)$$

b_1 and b_3 are two of the parameters used in the matching process for measuring local distortion between sections of the contour and the model.

4. Matching Process

The aim of matching process is getting from the image a representation of the shape P analogous to the one used by the model –a list of vertices– such that maximizes the measure of similarity S, which is calculated as a combination of the two following factors :

- Similarity to the model in size as well as in shape

- Fitting to the data of the image, that is, the coincidence with the contours that have been previously detected. At fitting we take into account the magnitude as well as the direction of their gradient vector

This process is divided up into three stages :

4.1. Selection of Image Edge Points

We will have previously applied the method of contour detection by zero-crossings of the second directional derivative[8], which give us information on both the module and the direction of the gradient. For each point (x, y) of the interpolated model curve we will choose those edge points p such that

- $p \in R(x, y)$ as it has been defined in Eq. 5
- For some $u \in [0, u_{j+1} - u_j]$, $(x, y) = (X_j(u), Y_j(u))$, the orientation of the gradient at the point p, $\phi(p)$, and the direction of the vector perpendicular to the curve tangent at the point (x, y) differ less than L_θ :

$$\mid \phi(p) - tg^{-1}(\frac{dY_i(u)/du}{dX_j(u)/du}) + \pi/2 \mid \leq L_\theta \qquad (9)$$

- The magnitude of the gradient in p exceeds a certain low theshold t

t is used to reject the points which are likely not to be meaningful contours but resulting from noise and textures. On the other hand owing to the fact that these points usually form short but numerous segments, their elimination allow the number of candidates chosen in the second stage to decrease. Therefore, matching is accelerated. Figure 6a-e shows an example of this phase.

4.2. Selection of Candidates

For each vertex m_i we obtain a set C_i of image edge points which are candiates to become the i-th vertex in the representation of P. Any $c \in C_i$ must accomplish the three preceding conditions but in this case with regard to m_i. This would give an excessive number of candidates, many of which would be adjacent or too close to each other, representing the same shape in this part of P. Hence, for each m_i the points that accomplish the three conditions with regard to m_i are organized in contour segments, from which we consider only the central point as candidate (figure 6e). Note that these sets may be empty or non-disjoint.

4.3. How To Obtain the Best Combination of Candidates

If n is the number of model vertices we have, we have the same number of candidate sets. We want to choose a point for each non-empty set such that S becomes maximized. Therefore the number of possible combinations is

$$\prod_{i=1}^{n} \max(1, \#C_i) \tag{10}$$

The combinatory explosion hinders the study of every combination of candidates. Spline interpolation curves have a certain degree of local control[9], although it is not as great as in B-spline curves. However, they are fitting curves and cannot therefore be used in this method. The influence of a vertex on the shape of the curve decreases and can even disappear the more the number of intermediate vertices increases, especially if we consider that the curves will be discretized in the image. Consequently, we do not consider the combinations of every set of candidates, but k successive adjacent groups of sets. Then, the total number of combinations is noticeably smaller :

$$\sum_{i=1}^{n/k} \prod_{j=1}^{k} \max(1, \#C_{(i-1)k+j}) \tag{11}$$

In order to guarantee coherent transitions between the candidates chosen from successive groups of sets when testing the combination of sets $C_{(i-1)k+1}$ to C_{ik}, we interpolate $e_{(i-1)k}, c_{(i-1)k+1}, \ldots, c_{ik}$ in which e_j stands for the candidate previously chosen of C_j.

Let us consider a combination of a group of candidates which we will denote $c_1, c_2 \ldots c_{k+1}$ for sake of simplicity. S has two components, namely

Correspondence with the Image

We want to check the degree of coincidence of a combination with the contours selected in phase 1. We interpolate a cubic spline curve among the candidates and we add the condition that the second derivative is equal to zero at c_1 and c_{k+1}. The curve is then discretized and the correlation –weighted by distance– to the contours (in magnitude) inside a neighbourhood is calculated. We will call the result S_c.

Correspondence with the Model

Demanding the maximum coincidence with the image is not sufficient. The presence of contours with high gradient may be a result of overlapping objects, of other objects which intersect the region R in question, of their internal structures and finally of pronouced textures and noise. The foregoing contours can cause a maximization in the image correspondence S_c but at the price of a strange shape which is far from the model. In order to avoid this situation we weight S_c by another measure S_d of similarity to the model.

According to the definition of $\mathbf{w_i}, \mathbf{v_i}, \alpha_i, \beta_i$ in section 3, if there were no deformations between $m_1, \ldots, m_{k+1}$ and $c_1, \ldots c_{k+1}$,

$$
\begin{aligned}
\alpha_i &= \beta_i + \delta_i - \theta, \quad \delta_i \in [-L_\theta, L_\theta] \\
r_i &= \hat{s}\, \frac{|\mathbf{v_i}|}{|\mathbf{w_i}|}, \quad r_i \in [1 - f, 1 + f], \quad L_s = f\hat{s}
\end{aligned} \tag{12}
$$

would be constant. But as a result of deformations δ_i and r_i vary from one vector to another. According to our formulation, the combination $c_1 \ldots c_{k+1}$ will be similar in shape to $m_1 \ldots m_{k+1}$ if the two following conditions are accomplished :

- the differences in orientation are small or if they are great it is a difference which remains constant. That is to say, each $\mathbf{w_i}$ has the same orientation that $\mathbf{v_i}$ rotated $\hat{\theta}$ or there is an additional rotation between them which is the same one for each couple of vectors.

- The length of each vector $\hat{s}\mathbf{v_i}$ is approximately equal to the $\mathbf{w_i}$ one or if there are greater differences, these are constant. That is to say, the scaling factor is near to $\hat{s}$ or it is different but constant along the whole combination.

Therefore we should quantify the degree in which the folling facts arise :

- $\delta_i \approx 0 \; \forall i$ or the variation of $\delta_i, i = 1 \ldots k$ is small

- $r_i \approx 1 \; \forall i$ or if it is not, the variation of $r_i, i = 1 \ldots k$ is small

We should use a non-absolute quantificator which can allow us to fix the meaning of "small" and "near to zero". Fuzzy sets have been used to represent terms of this kind, that is, at quantifying subjective concepts. In the theory of fuzzy sets two functions denoted by $S(x; a, b, c)$ and $\Pi(x; b, c)$ which give the probability of an element x to belong to the sets "x is big" and "x is c" respectively (figure 3).

$$
S(x; a, b, c) = \begin{cases}
0, & x \le a \\
2[(x - a)/(x - c)]^2, & a \le x \le b, \quad b = \frac{1}{2}(a + c) \\
1 - 2[(x - a)/(x - c)]^2, & b \le x \le c \\
1, & x \ge c
\end{cases} \tag{13}
$$

$$
\Pi(x; b, c) = \begin{cases}
S(x; c - b, c - (b/2), c), & x \le c \\
1 - S(x; c, c + (b/2), c + b), & x > c
\end{cases} \tag{14}
$$

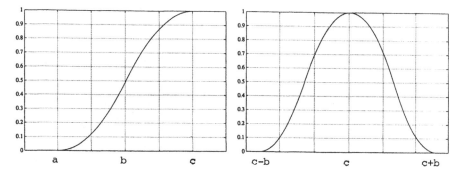

Figure 3: functions S and Π

In order to see if δ_i is close to 0 for every i, we should choose the result of the worst case, $\min_i(\Pi(\delta_i; b, 0))$, but owing to the fact that Π is decreasing for $x > 0$ and symmetric with regard to the y-axis,

$$\min_i(\Pi(\delta_i; b, 0)) = \Pi(\max_i \mid \delta_i \mid; b, 0) \qquad (15)$$

To state if r_i is near to 1 for every i, we apply the function Π to each r_i, being $c = 1$. However according to the same argumentation

$$\min_i(\Pi(r_i; b, 1)) = \Pi(\max_i \mid r_i - 1 \mid; b, 0) \qquad (16)$$

As far as variations are concerned, we quantify the difference between the maximum and minimum value although other measures such as variance could also be used. Therefore, we would calculate

$$\begin{aligned}
p_1 &= \Pi(\max_i \mid \delta_i \mid; b_1, 0) \\
p_2 &= \Pi(\max_i \delta_i - \min_i \delta_i; b_2, 0) \\
p_3 &= \Pi(\max_i \mid 1 - r_i \mid; b_3, 0) \\
p_4 &= \Pi(\max_i r_i - \min_i r_i; b_4, 0)
\end{aligned} \qquad (17)$$

The parameters $b_1 \ldots b_4$ allow us to vary the quantification of each concept. These four factors must be combined to create a single measure S_d. To this purpouse when we have a disjunction between two terms "a or b", we translate it as $\max(p(a), p(b))$, that is, we take the best case. Inversely "a and b" will be expressed as $\min(p(a), p(b))$. Therefore,

$$S_d = \min(\max(p_1, p_2), \max(p_3, p_4)) \qquad (18)$$

In figure 4 we can see the values that this measure takes if the position of a vertex is varied, and in consequence the angle and the length of the adjacent vectors.

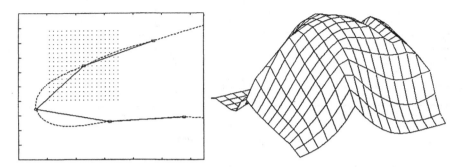

Figure 4: Value of S_d if we shift one vertex of the model

For each group of vertices S is computed as

$$S = S_c \, S_d \tag{19}$$

and we will choose the combination which shows a higher measure. Finally the measure of goodness of the interpretation for a certain model is obtained by adding S of each group. In this way we can decide the best interpretation of data for a given model. And also if there are severals possible models, which is the most suitable.

Next, we will show that the matching process proposed is able to include explicitly knowledge on variation patterns of a single model. As we have already said, during the matching process parameters $b_1 \ldots b_4$ remain constant all along the curve. If the shape we are trying to identify and extract cannot vary at random around the average shape which constitutes the model, that is, if there are certain deformations more likely to occur, then we can assign different values of b_1 and b_3 to each vertex and different values of b_2 and b_4 to each group.

Another possible situation is the need of being more tolerant to deformations in certain directions than in others in a specific vertex, as we shall see in section 5. For example if we do not consider concavity and convexity equally in a region of the contour, then the parameters for calculation of p_1 depend on the sign of δ_i. To cope with it, we define the function $\Lambda(x; \lambda_1, \lambda_2, c)$ starting from the function Π which is able to reflect this duality (figure 5). For every vertex we will calculate $p_1 = \Lambda(\delta_i; b_1, b_1, 0) = \prod(\delta_i; b_1, 0)$ apart from those which need to reinforce a special behaviour, in which λ_1 and λ_2 will receive different values.

$$\Lambda(x; \lambda_1, \lambda_2, c) = \begin{cases} \Pi(x; \lambda_1, c) & \text{if } x \geq c \\ \Pi(x; \lambda_2, c) & \text{if } x < c \end{cases} \tag{20}$$

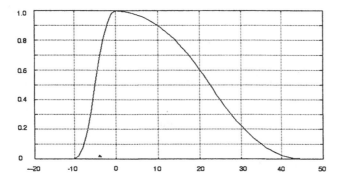

Figure 5: function $\Lambda(x; 10, 45, 0)$

5. Results

We will present some results concerning identification and classification of bones in hand radiographs. The objective is the automation of the TW2 method for the assesment of skeletal maturity or bone age. The evaluation of physiological maturity in children is a widely spread technique in paediatrics practice in order to diagnose hormonal and growth disorders. TW2 method[10] is based on the evolution of hand and wrist bones as they are seen in X-ray films. An atlas contains, for each bone, a growth sequence as a series of 7 or 8 maturity stages. Each stage in turn is described by a typical contour and some written criteria on differentiating features. Once we have classified each bone in the hand radiograph in its closest atlas stage, the method gives us the the bone age, which is compared to the chronological age for diagnosis purposes. Figure 6a shows an example of radial epiphysis and figure 6c three of its stages.

Hence we face a problem dealing with both extraction of a bone from a region in the image and classification of it in its proper stage. Even more, matching must be elastic because, like in many problems of biomedical image analysis, we hardly find in these images exact copies of the models given but version, more or less close to them, which radiologists can interpret. In our case the differences are due to the following causes:

- A wrong position of the hand when taking the radiograph, with regard to the ideal one described in TW2 atlas

- The growth process of each bone is continuous but we only know a few milestones

- Mainly, variability in shape among different people

In figure 6 we can see an example of radial epiphysis (a) and three of the most morphologically similar models (c), from which we will consider the central one. We can lessen the complexity of the problem by esteeming the parameters $\hat{s}, \hat{\theta}, \hat{t}_x, \hat{t}_y$ of the global alignment transform. This can be achieved by using knowledge of size and relative positions of bones in each stage with regard to references in the image which can be automatically extracted. In addition to the rank of variation of each parameter, this estimation allow us to delimit the region R of the image in which the bone will be contained. Provided that this bone is in the stage we are considering (d). The selection of edge points will only maintain the ones in figure 6e, which shows the candidates of each set C_i surrounded by a box. Despite the substantial difference between the model of this stage and the bone in the image, the overlapping of the bone on the two others and the existence of inner structures (the whiter region), a good interpretation is achieved.

In figure 7 we give an example showing how to weight differently distortions with regard to the model by using measure S_d. Both radial epiphysis (figures 7a,b) are in a stage characterized by the white region which appears inside it. It is due to a palmar surface, that is to say, of a protrusion in the plain of the image which causes an increase in the density of this zone. In the upper part of this region, the contour :

- Is quite close to the upper contour of the bone and in great extent parallel to it.

- Has a high gradient because the contrast between the region and the bone is greater that the one between the bone and the background.

- The direction of the gradient in each point is approximately the same as the bone contour one.

Hence, this contour line is chosen during the matching process (figures 7c,d). Further more, owing to its gradient, which is higher than the one of real contour points in this part, S_c will be greater and the resulting curve has a tendency to coincide with this line. We would obtain, therefore, a result like the one shown in figure 7e,f, in which the extracted shape is wrong because of the pronounced concavity in the upper part. This situation can be avoided by penalizing more $\delta_i < 0$ than $\delta_i > 0$ in some vertices of the upper part of the contour. In figures 7g,h the new result is shown, now it does coincide with the external contour of the bone in spite of the low gradient in it (minor S_c but compensated by a major S_d).

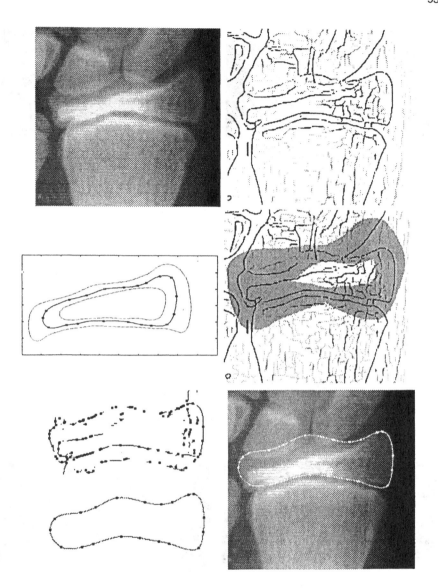

Figure 6: matching process for the radial epiphysis

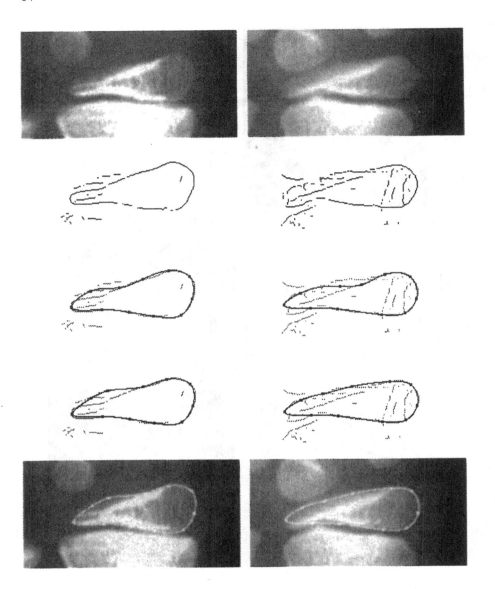

Figure 7: example of different weighting of distorsions

References

1. R. Bajcsy and S. Kovacic, "Multiresolution elastic matching", *Computer Vision, Graphics and Image Processing* **46** (1989) p. 1-21.

2. D. J. Burr, "Elastic matching of line drawings", *IEEE Trans. on Pattern Analysis and Machine Intelligence* **3** (1981), p. 708-713.

3. L. H. Staib and J. S. Duncan, "Parametrically deformable contour models", *Proc. of IEEE Computer Vision and Pattern Recognition* (1989) p. 98-103.

4. H. Maître and Y. Wu, "Elastic matching versus rigid matching by use of dynamic programming", *Proc. 9th Int. Conf. on Pattern Recognition* (1988) p. 79-81.

5. M. Kass, A. Witkin and D. Terzopoulos, "Snakes : active contour models", *Proc. First Int. Conf. on Computer Vision* (1987) p. 259-268.

6. R. Bajcsy, R. Lieberson and M. Reivich, "A computerized system for the elastic matching of deformed radiographyc images to idealized atlas images", *Journal of Computer Assisted Tomography* **5** (1983) p. 618-625.

7. R. H. Bartels, J. C. Beatty and B. A. Barsky, *An introduction to splines for use in computer graphics and geometric modelling* (Morgan Kauffmann, 1987).

8. R. M. Haralick, "Digital step edges from zero crossing of second directional derivatives", *IEEE Trans. on Pattern Analisys and Machine Intelligence* **6** (1984) p. 56-68.

9. T. Pavlidis, *Algorithms for Graphics and Image Processing* (Springer-Verlag, 1982)

10. J. M. Tanner, R. H. Whitehouse, W. W. Marshall et al. *Assessment of skeletal maturity and prediction of adult height (TW2 Method)* (Academic Press, 1983).

AN APPROACH TO NATURAL SCENE SEGMENTATION BY MEANS OF GENETIC ALGORITHMS WITH FUZZY DATA

J. Albert (*), F. Ferri (*), J. Domingo (*) and M. Vicens (**)

(*) Dept. Informática y Electrónica. Univ. de Valencia
(**) Instituto de Robótica. Universidad de Valencia
Av. Dr. Moliner 50, 46100 Burjassot (Valencia), Spain
e-mail (earn) : jesus@image2.eleinf.uv.es

ABSTRACT

This paper introduces a method for low level image segmentation. The pixels of the image are classified according to their chromatic features. A quadratic classifier in the SH-space is constructed in order to produce a fast image classification process. The classifier is obtained using a genetic algorithm which makes use of the information obtained from a fuzzy labelling process made over a training set. Finally, the paper shows the results of applying the method to fruit detection in natural scenes taken in the field.

1. Introduction

Within the area of computer vision, one of the more important and complex problems is that of segmentation. There is an extensive bibliography on the different aspects of image segmentation[1,12] where more or less general methods and numerous applications are described.

In this paper the task we are dealing with is the segmentation of natural scenes in color applied to the location of fruit for its automatic harvesting. With this aim the variability introduced by natural lighting (uncontrolled) adds to the complexity of the underlying problem (chromatic characterization of fruit, possibly in different ripe states) giving special connotations to the problem. Besides this, due to the type of application, it will be necessary for the on-line segmentation procedure to be fast enough to work together with the corresponding robotic system.

As stated above low level approximation has been chosen, so the bigger objects to be dealt with are the image pixels and their associated features. This allows the application of simple and, above all, quick classification methods rather than the high level segmentation methods based on borders or regions.

This work has been partially supported by grant N°ROB89-0285 of Spanish CICYT.

In following sections a method will be introduced for low level segmentation of color images based on a previous phase of unsupervised training, able to manage the imprecision and variability mentioned above by means of a fuzzy clustering process[4], as well as on the later use of a genetic algorithm[13] to infer a simple discriminant function (DF)(quadratic classifier) allowing for separating the zones of interest in the image.

This approximation is going to permit adding the working speed of the DF to the well-known efficiency of fuzzy clustering on segmenting color images[14], as well as its easy hardware implementation.

The following sections will discuss every part of the task at hand. First, in section 2 some of the characteristics and problems associated with color representation are summed up; section 3 shows the scheme used for obtaining a discriminant function in the color space. Sections 4, 5 and 6 deal with each of the subtasks which occur: the automatic labelling of samples by means of a fuzzy clustering process, and obtaining an optimal classifier using a genetic algorithm. Finally, some experimental results will be presented, from a problem dealing with the detection of objects in agricultural environments.

2. Considerations on Color Representation

The experimental laws of color-matching are summed up in the trichromatic generalization[16]. This states that over a wide range of observation conditions many colors can be matched completely by additive mixtures in suitable amounts of three fixed primary colors. The choice of these primary colors, though very extensive, is not entirely arbitrary. Any set in which none of the primaries can be matched by a mixture of the other two may be used. This implies that any color represented by a $\vec{C}$ vector can be expressed as:

$$\vec{C} = r\,\vec{R} + g\,\vec{G} + b\,\vec{B} \tag{1}$$

where $\vec{R}$, $\vec{G}$ and $\vec{B}$ are the vectors representing unitary quantities of the three primary colors. And the r, g and b coefficients are known as the triestimulus values of the $\vec{C}$ color.

However, the triestimulus theory does not correctly reproduce the perceptive phenomena, since the eye has the ability to distinguish colors in terms of other different parameters, chromaticity and lightness.

In the experiments on color discrimination, an observer assesses differences or equalities in his perception of certain perceptual attributes of the color of the test samples. The principal attributes for object colors are Hue, Saturation and Lightness. The scaling of the attributes has to be constructed from the judgement of the observers.

Consider a set of color samples all having a particular fixed lightness; their representative points will generate a surface, and two pairs of samples belonging to this surface that are judged by observers to present the same difference in chromaticity will not generally be represented by pairs of points separated by the same distance. The question is to find a transformation to another space such that these pairs of samples are represented by points that lie at an equal distance.

Most current arrangements for grading chromaticity are organized in terms of loci of constant Hue and Saturation on a surface of constant Lightness; these loci form a polar coordinate system. The central point represents gray, points on a circle represent colors of constant Saturation, and points on a radial line starting at the center represent colors of the same Hue.

To be more specific, we will now consider the system of chromaticity and lightness coordinates employed in this paper which can be obtained from the color signals generated by a TV camera[15].

TV cameras generate three signals R, G, B which are proportional to the red, green and blue measures in the formed image. For transmission and with the object of compatibility with the old B/W devices, a lightness signal is generated,

$$Y = 0.3\,R + 0.59\,G + 0.11\,B \tag{2}$$

so that it fits the human eye patterns.

Since most of the scenes contain little color information and it is desirable that the color signals emitted cancel each other out when the scene is gray, signals are used that correspond to color differences between the R, G, and B and lightness.

These differences are normalized in such a way that the maximum amplitude of the chromatic signals does not exceed 1.33 times the maximum amplitude of the monochrome images. This produces two new variables:

$$U = 0.877\,(R - Y) \text{ and } V = 0.493\,(B - Y) \tag{3}$$

which together with the Y signal permit complete recuperation of the original R, G, B.

These new coordinates are such that if we place ourselves on the line $U = V = 0$, we always obtain achromatic images, and for a certain $Y = const$ the colors situated on the lines passing through the origin all have the same Hue. The color Saturation varies along this line, the most saturated being far from the origin.

Due to the fact that the UV coordinates represent values centered in the origin, and such that the saturation of the colors is approximately represented by lines passing through it, and that those of equal Hue are circles with centers in the origin, we can consider that this space has a euclidean metric, in the sense that the measured distances are proportional to those noticed by a human observer. For this reason, this chromatic subspace will be used in the first part of this work which deals with sample labelling by fuzzy clustering.

We can also, make a transformation to polar coordinates:

$$\begin{aligned} I &= Y \\ S &= \sqrt{U^2 + V^2} \\ H &= arctan\left(\frac{V}{U}\right) \end{aligned} \tag{4}$$

so that in this space the lines of equal Hue correspond to those of $H = const$ and the lines of equal Saturation correspond to $S = const$. In this SH space, small deviations around one color, in Hue as well as in Saturation occur which originate ellipses centered in this color and whose axes are parallel to the S and H axes. This allows us to find a simple discriminant function (quadratic classifier) in the SH color space. This will be the objective of the second part of this paper.

3. Color Image Classification

As has been shown in section 1, the method developed consists of a low level segmentation (pixel classification) in which the color information is used as a main discriminant feature eliminating the lighting component of the image as much as possible. This yields a bidimensional feature space in which a separation border or discriminant function between the zones of interest and the rest of the zones is obtained.

A possible approach to this problem could consist of obtaining a set of samples (pixels) manually labelled in order to later apply a supervised learning process of DF^9. This process irremissibly produces training sets with a considerable amount of badly classified samples which make the results obtained through the usual procedures almost disastrous. This makes it impossible to think of any approximation in this sense without previously undertaking an elimination process for these undesirable samples.

A classical approach to the same problem would consist of performing a clustering process in the feature space, which in general produces very good results, although it is difficult to apply due to the high computational cost of these procedures. This is precisely what leads us to propose an automatic labelling process by means of the use of a clustering algorithm, as a previous step to obtaining a quadratic classifier which in some way reflects the results of this clustering.

The labelling of the samples will be fuzzy which will permit us to represent the information in a more real way. In short, the algorithm used in this paper is the fuzzy c-means (FCM) whose efficacy level has been sufficiently tested[14] and which, moreover, admits a broad range of variants and adaptations[4]. A fuzzy labelled training set (FLTS) will be obtained that will be used as input for a genetic algorithm whose aim will be the search, in a certain subspace of the quadratic classifiers, of the classifier which best separates the selected class from the others, all of this in fuzzy terms. This procedure will be tackled as a minimization process of certain objective function defined in terms of the fuzzy labelling of the samples. The use of a genetic algorithm assures obtaining an optimal solution (or very close) within the self-imposed constraints when defining the search space[8].

This way, what is achieved, in a certain sense, is a concentration of the information about the fuzzy partition we are interested in, which is given by the fuzzy clustering, in a simple classifier (quadratic) with all the computational and implementational advantages that this implies.

Figure 1 shows a diagram of the method introduced.

Figure 1. Diagram of the employed method.

4. Fuzzy Clustering. The Fuzzy c-Means Algorithm

The aim of a clustering algorithm is to make a partition of a data set in a certain number of natural and homogeneous gatherings, so that the elements of each subset are as similar as possible and present considerable differences with respect to the other subsets. In classical clustering techniques it is implicitly assumed that it is possible to find disjoint gatherings of the data set. In practice, there are many cases in which the clusters are not completely disjointed and, therefore, the separation of these clusters is a fuzzy notion. In these cases, it is necessary to describe the data structure in terms of fuzzy subsets.

Definition: Let $X = \{x_1,...,x_n / x_k \in R^p, 1 \leq k \leq n\}$. It is said that u is a fuzzy subset of X if $u:X-- > [0,1]$ assigns to each x_k in X its degree of membership to the fuzzy set u.

A point x_k in X presents a strong association to the subset u if the value of $u(x_k)$ is close to 1. On the contrary, a value $u(x_k)$ close to 0 indicates a weak association to this set.

Definition: Let $X = \{x_1,...,x_n / x_k \in R^p, 1 \leq k \leq n\}$; V_{cn} the set of real cxn matrices, and c an integer, $1 < c < n$. It is said that $U = [u_{ik}] \in V_{cn}$ is a non-degenerated fuzzy c-partition of X if it satisfies:

$$u_{ik} \in [0,1] \;, \; 1 \leq i \leq c, 1 \leq k \leq n \tag{5}$$

$$\sum_{i=1}^{c} u_{ik} = 1 \;, \; 1 \leq k \leq n \tag{6}$$

$$\sum_{k=1}^{n} u_{ik} > 0 \;, \; 1 \leq i \leq c \tag{7}$$

The ith row of the matrix U shows the values of the ith membership function (fuzzy subset) u_i in the fuzzy c-partition U of X,

$$u_i : X --> [0,1] / u_i(x_k) = u_{ik}, 1 \leq i \leq n, 1 \leq k \leq n \tag{8}$$

Since the sum in each column is 1, the total membership of each point x_k to X is 1, although this membership can be arbitrarily distributed among the fuzzy c subsets $\{u_i\}$ of X. Equation (7) tells us that the partition can not have empty subsets.

The available criteria for carrying out a fuzzy description of a data set are multiple. However, among all of them probably the best known algorithm and the most widely used one is the fuzzy c-means algorithm (FCM). This algorithm was initially developed by Dunn[10] and generalized for an infinite family of objective functions by Bezdek[2]; it is based on the iterative minimization of an objective function J_m that generalizes the least-squared error criterion. The J_m function is defined as:

$$J_m : M_{fc} \times R^{cp} \rightarrow R^+ \tag{9}$$

$$J_m(U,v) = \sum_{k=1}^{n} \sum_{i=1}^{c} (u_{ik})^m (d_{ik})^2 \tag{10}$$

where M_{fc} is the fuzzy c-partitions space of the X set, and U is a fuzzy c-partition of X; $v = (v_1,...,v_c) \in R^{cp}$, $v_i \in R^p$ being the center (prototype) of the cluster u_i, $1 \leq i \leq c$, and $d_{ik}^2 = ||x_k - v_i||^2$, where $||.||$ is any norm induced by an inner product on R^p.

The weight exponent m, $1 \leq m \leq \infty$, determines the nature of the clustering, so that the imprecision of the partitions increases with m. If m --> 1 the algorithm converges to the classical "hard" (not fuzzy) version, i.e., $u_{ik} \in \{0,1\}$ $\forall i,k$. On the contrary, if m --> ∞, we have the most imprecise solution possible, since u_{ik} --> $1/c$ $\forall i,k$ (all the points belong equally to all the clusters) and the cluster centers tend to converge to the centroid of the data set. Therefore, the bigger the m, the more imprecise the membership assignment will be.

For m > 1, Bezdek obtained the necessary conditions to iteratively minimize $J_m(U,v)^2$:

$$v_i = \frac{\sum_{k=1}^{n} (u_{ik})^m x_k}{\sum_{k=1}^{n} (u_{ik})^m} \tag{11}$$

$$u_{ik} = \frac{1}{\sum_{j=1}^{c} \left(\frac{d_{ik}}{d_{jk}}\right)^{\frac{2}{m-1}}} \quad , \text{ if } d_{ik} > 0 \tag{12}$$

If x_k exists such that $d_{ik} = 0$ for some i, then

$$u_{ik} = \frac{1}{|I_k|} \quad \text{if } d_{ik} = 0, \text{ being } I_k = \{j / 1 \leq j \leq c, d_{jk} = 0\} \tag{13}$$

$$u_{ik} = 0 \quad \text{if } d_{ik} \neq 0 \tag{14}$$

In Figure 2 the c-means algorithm is more formally shown.

A fuller description of this algorithm, as well as the proof of its convergence properties can be found in 3,4.

It becomes evident that the shape of the clusters obtained in this way will strongly depend on the metric used. When the data set presents heterogeneous gatherings, the described algorithm can produce unsuitable solutions, due to the fact that the topology induced by the metric used does not fit the characteristics of the set. Along these lines

Fuzzy c-Means (FCM) Algorithm

Input:

Fix c (number of clusters), $1 < c < n$;

Choose an inner product norm metric for R^p, $||.||$,

and a convenient norm to compare partitions;

Fix the parameter m, $1 < m < \infty$;

Initialize the partition $U^{(0)}$;

Fix a threshold T as stop condition;

Then in the iteration l, l = 0,1,2,...:

i) Calculate the c centers of the fuzzy clusters:

$$v_i = \frac{\sum_{k=1}^{n} (u_{ik})^m x_k}{\sum_{k=1}^{n} (u_{ik})^m}$$

ii) Update c-partition $U^{(l)}$:

$$u_{ik} = \frac{1}{\sum_{j=1}^{c} \left(\frac{d_{ik}}{d_{jk}}\right)^{\frac{2}{m-1}}}$$

if any cluster i such that $d_{ik} = 0$ does not exist, otherwise:

$u_{ik} = \frac{1}{|I_k|}$, $I_k = \{ j / d_{jk} = 0, 1 \le j \le c, 1 \le k \le n \}$, if $d_{ik} = 0$;

$u_{ik} = 0$, if $d_{ik} \ne 0$.

iii) Compare U(l) to U(l+1) in a convenient matrix norm,

if this comparison is less than T then stop

else $l = l + 1$ and go to (i).

Figure 2. Fuzzy c-Means Algorithm.

an interesting improvement in the algorithm is the one realized by Gustafson and Kessel[11], in which assuming a different metric for each cluster, the matrix that induces the norm in each one is calculated from its fuzzy covariance matrix, getting gatherings that better fit the natural structure of the data.

However, in the case at hand, the color space, as was pointed out in section 2, offers the practical possibility of using the euclidean metric in the UV space. In this way, the chromatic gatherings present in a data set will be detected making use of the FCM algorithm with the norm induced by the identity matrix.

5. Genetic Algorithms

The topic of genetic algorithms (GA's) was started by Holland13 in 1975. His works introduced two aspects of fundamental importance in this field: (i) the possibility of codifying complex structures through simple representations (bit chains), and (ii) the power of some easy transformations for improving these structures. Holland proved that by following a suitable control scheme, the structures codified as bit chains can be quickly improved when making transformations upon them. This can be done in such a way that a set of bit chains can be made to evolve as if it were an animal species.

A GA is nothing more than a control structure that allows for managing representations of possible solutions for a problem, which have been suitably codified, and fro managing the operations upon them so that these solutions evolve to those that best fit the problem requirements.

An important conclusion of Holland's works was that even in complex search spaces, and under certain conditions, the GA's tend to converge to globally optimal solutions or close to them.

The efficient balance GA's keep between the exploration of those more promising regions of the search space and the assimilation of information about the problem in each new generation (iteration) must be emphasized. In each of the generations, the GA keeps a "population" made up of a subset of possible solutions obtained from the information incorporated in the former generation. All the solutions are evaluated according to their adaptation to the problem. The idealized genetic operators are applied to the solutions which permit obtaining a new generation of solutions. The genetic operators act on the population basing themselves on the evaluation measures, so that the solutions that show a better performance have a greater probability of generating new solutions.

Now let's briefly look at the main elements applicable in a GA:

1) Representation of solutions in terms of "chromosomes". The bit chains are the most common representation, because of their ability to represent a great variety of information. Their properties have been the most widely studied[7].

2) A method to create the initial population. If no previous knowledge about the optimal solution is possessed it is common to generate this population randomly. Random election is also, a good proof of the efficacy of the method, whose final solution does not depend on a good initialization.

3) An evaluation function,

F: S (solutions space) --- > R or Z

This function must measure the performance of each solution in the problem resolution. The process of normalization employed in evaluating the solutions is of great importance. It is advisable to show the differences among the solutions with a higher score, which will permit the algorithm to evolve to the truly better solutions and not be held back at a certain performance level. The result of the GA will be highly sensitive to the normalization technique employed.

4) Some genetic operators that change the composition of the offspring of each generation. The two most common operators are crossover and mutation. Many different operators can be built starting from the basic idea of these two operators. Let's now see a brief description of them:

- Crossover: Crossover is the key to the power of the GA's. This operator selects two solutions from the current population and interchanges some of its parts. If the probability of selecting a solution to perform a crossover increases with its associated score, it is possible to assure that the probability of obtaining a generation with better solutions is increased. The crossover operator also preserves the internal characteristics of the solutions (bit schemes). In terms of search strategy it can be said that this operator has the ability to concentrate the search in regions of greater interest, according to the information given by the evaluation function. For instance:

Solution 1: 1 2 3 4 5 6

Solution 2: a b c d e f

If the points chosen for the crossover are 2 and 4, the resulting structure will be:

Result: 1 b c d 5 6

The crossover points are usually chosen at random.

- Mutation: This operator introduces an accidental change in one or more bits of the solution, in such a way that variability in the search process is introduced, and it is possible to investigate in new regions of the space. It has to be taken into account that the former genetic operator (crossover) only takes the information present in the current population into account and therefore, does not generate completely new prototypes but keeps already existing schemes. The mutation operator supplies a way to introduce non-existent information to the population. For example, if the scheme of a solution is:

1 1 0 1 0 0 1

The mutation applied to the first and third bit could provide some of the following schemes:

$\underline{0}$ 1 $\underline{0}$ 1 0 0 1
$\underline{0}$ 1 $\underline{1}$ 1 0 0 1
$\underline{1}$ 1 $\underline{0}$ 1 0 0 1
$\underline{1}$ 1 $\underline{1}$ 1 0 0 1

5) Values of the parameters of the GA, such as: size of the population, probabilities of application of the genetic operators, etc.

The general scheme of a GA is shown in Figure 3.

The genetic algorithms have their classical areas of application in the following areas: communication network design, layout circuit design, game theory, classifier systems, etc. The characteristics of a GA applied to the search of an optimal classifier will be described in the next section.

<u>Genetic Algorithm</u>

Input:

Fix the size of population;

Choose an evaluation function, F;

Fix the probability of mutation, p_m;

Fix the score needed for succes, P;

Fix maximal number of generations, M;

Generate initial population;

In each generation (iteration) do:

i) For each solution, S_i, in the current population compute $F(S_i)$;

Assign to each S_i a number of descendants, d_i, proportional to its score.

ii) For each S_i choose randomly d_i members from the current population and generate the new descendents by croosover with S_i;

iii) If random_number(0,1) $< p_m$ then choose a bit in the population randomly and change it;

iv) If $(\max(F(S_i)) < P)$ or (generation $< M$) then repeat from (i) else return S_i which gives the maximal value for $F(S_i)$.

Figure 3. Genetic Algorithm.

6. A Genetic Algorithm For Color Classification

In this section the discussion will be centered on the problem of the search of a classifier in the color space. As has been shown in former sections, it will be necessary to find the quadratic function (ellipse) that best classifies the points of the fuzzy labelled training set (FLTS) belonging to the searched class (chromatic tonality). The classification function can be more easily characterized on the representation space SH (Saturation-Hue). In this space it can be assumed, without loss of generality, that the possible solutions to the problem will be ellipses with parallel axes to the coordinates axes, since when realizing the transformation to polar coordinates, what in the UV space was a chromatic distribution around the origin will become a distribution along the H axis in the new space. Also, as the variation in a color hue over the variation in saturation is of greater importance this allows us to assume that the major axis will be parallel to the S axis. Finally, it is possible to describe the searched classification function using the following equation:

$$\frac{(x - cx)^2}{a^2} + \frac{(y - cy)^2}{b^2} = 1 \tag{15}$$

where a and b are the semiaxes of the ellipse with its center at the point (cx,cy).

Once the restrictions of the problem are established, it can be concluded that the search for possible classifiers will take place in a 4-dimensional space (a,b,cx,cy); concretely in a subspace of R^4. However, for practical reasons and in order to accelerate the searching process, the problem has been restricted to search the centers in a "grid" of 512x512 points (sampled SH space) and semiaxes with values in [0,255]. It has been verified that this resolution is sufficient for the objectives of the task[8]. In summary, with the former restrictions there is a space with exactly 2^{34} points, so that:

a, b ∈ [0,255]

cx, cy ∈ [0,511]

In the rest of this section the implementation of an GA for this specific problem will be described. The elements of the problem to be considered are the following:

- The structures which are candidates for solutions to the problem are codified as chains of 36 bits, using 9 bits for each one of the center coordinates (cx,cy) and 8 bits for each semiaxis (a,b), in that order.

- The size of the populations has been selected equal to 100 structures, so that the most promising schemes are guaranteed to have a reasonable transmission probability and reduce the sampling error made when assigning an integer number of descendants to each solution instead of a real number strictly proportional to its score.

- Random election of the initial population must be performed, so that no information about the possible optimal solution is introduced.

- The evaluation function of the GA takes into account the membership information associated to each point of the training set by means of the fuzzy clustering process formerly applied to it. In this way, for each solution of the population, the error committed when classifying the FLTS with that solution is evaluated. The error made by a solution will be given by the following expression:

$$e = \sum_{x \in W^c} u_A(x) + \sum_{x \in W} u_A^c(x) = \sum_{x \in W^c} u_A(x) + \sum_{x \in W} (1 - u_A(x)) \tag{16}$$

Where:

u_A is the membership function associated to the fuzzy A subset (searched class).

u_A^c is the membership function complementary to u_A.

W is the subset formed by the FLTS points in the SH plane enclosed by the considered solution.

The evaluation function F, F: S ---> R, where S is the space of possible solutions, is defined as:

$$F(s) = C - \log(e), s \in S \tag{17}$$

The non-linear definition of F permits increasing the differences between those solutions for which the value of e is small, i.e, for the best solutions. By being able to better distinguish between the solutions close to the maximum of F, an attempt is made to keep the algorithm from converging to a local maximum.

The value of the constant C is determined experimentally so that it is possible to limit F properly according to the problem data.

- The idealized genetic operators, crossover and mutation, are made to act on the 36 bit chains as was described in section 5. Although, in the case of crossover, in addition to considering two breaking points, the "chromosomes" have been treated as if they were circular. This modification which was proposed by Booker[5] slightly improves the search speed.

7. Experimental Results

As stated in the introduction, the problem on which the segmentation scheme presented in this paper was applied, is the detection of objects in natural scenes that can be characterized by a chromatic tonality. This imposes two conditions on the problem: (i) all the objects belonging to the searched class have the same tonality, and (ii) another class with the same tonality does not exist.

As an actual case, this scheme has been applied to the detection of fruit (oranges) on the tree, as a previous step for their automatized harvesting. In this process the fruit can appear under different levels of lightning and in different states of ripeness, so that it is not possible to establish a selection criterion based on only one color. It turns out advisable to eliminate the influence of the lightness component of color.

With this aim, and as an example, the results obtained from a training set formed exclusively by the points of a representative image of the problem (Figure 4a) will be presented next. In this figure well-lighted zones together with zones shaded by the leaves of the tree apart from objects, both fruit and leaves, in which the conditions of the incident solar lighting provokes the appearance of highlights can be observed. The process of labelling the samples through the application of the fuzzy clustering algorithm FCM was performed on this data set without any filtering treatment.

One of the main objections that it is usually raised against the application of this algorithm is its high computational cost for big point sets. For this reason, in order to increase the efficiency of the labelling process an approximated implementation of the FCM (AFCM) based on the one described in [6] has been used, at a practical level. This has achieved an increase in efficacy of about six times that achieved with the FCM algorithm literally transcribed.

With the help of the AFCM algorithm we proceed to assign a membership values to the training set points to each one of the four classes appearing in the image: fruit, leaves, sky, and gray or very dark zones (low saturation).

To measure the deviation of the results from the information perceived by an observer, the difference in distance between the centers of the four classes provided by the AFCM algorithm and the average values of the chromatic features measured manually in selected zones of the image belonging to the different classes has been measured. This data are represented in Table 1, with the results of the AFCM being obtained for a value of the parameter m equal to 2.0.

The result of the clustering was the one shown on Figure 4b. The values of the membership function of the orange class for all the points of the image are represented in this figure using different grey levels, the value 0 being equal to the black level, and the value 1 being equal to the white level.

Therefore, having proven that the results of the fuzzy labelling process approximate fairly well to what seems to be perceived from the image, the values of the membership function of the fuzzy subset corresponding to the searched tonality serve as input for a genetic algorithm whose characteristics were described in sections 5 and 6.

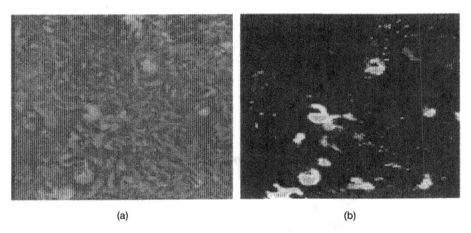

(a)   (b)

Figure 4. Result of the fuzzy labelling process: (a) Original image, and (b) Orange class.

The GA was applied to the representation space SH, as has been mentioned, and after 50 generations, provided the solution shown in Figure 5. In this figure, and in order to check what region of the SH space is enclosed by the solution, points belonging to the image in Figure 4a and labelled manually by an observer into two classes ahve been plotted, those points belonging to orange zones (x) and those belonging to other regions (+). The solution found by the GA enclosed the greater part of the points labelled as orange, the ones outside of the solution being the result of errors in the manual labelling process.

To test the efficacy of the obtained classifier, this classifier was applied to a new image different from the training one. The second image used is shown in Figure 6a. Figure 6b shows the result of the classification of this image. The fact that the results obtained are good enough for the search objetive can be verified.

Table 1. Distances between the prototypes of four classes calculated by AFCM (vi) and average UV values measured in four selected regions of the image (Mf = fruits, Ml = leaves, Ms = sky, and Mg = gray)

$\|\|M_i - v_j\|\|$	Mf (-32.90,18.13)	Ml (-13.27,2.17)	Ms (15.96,-27.30)	Mg (-0.18,-0.29)
v1 (-28.98,17.52)	**3.97**	21.96	63.47	33.86
v2 (-11.96,0.94)	27.09	**1.80**	39.71	11.84
v3 (13.35,-24.84)	63.13	37.92	**3.59**	28.03
v4 (-1.92,-2.74)	37.35	12.37	30.38	**3.01**

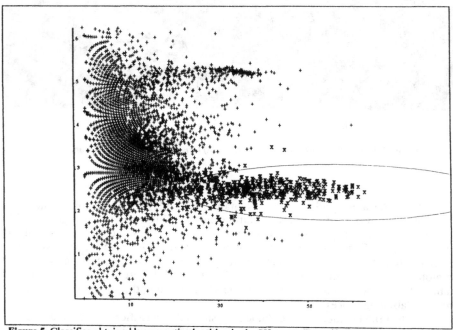

Figure 5. Classifier obtained by a genetic algorithm in the SH space. To verify the results points belonging to training image and classified by an observer in two classes have been plotted: (x) orange points, (+) other.

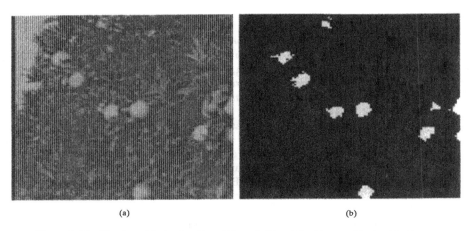

(a)   (b)

Figure 6. Classification with the classifier of figure 5: (a) Original image, (b) Classified image.

8. Concluding Remarks

In this paper we introduce a method for rapidly classifying the the pixels of natural scenes according to their chromatic features, making use of a discriminant function which reduces the high computational cost of a clustering process for all the images. The solution obtained can be considered optimal because, by using a genetic algorithm, a classifier with minimal error in the SH color space has been found. The genetic algorithm improves the classical methods in cases in which there is an intrinsic non-separability (noisy samples). Moreover, it gives a good convergence rate for reasonable classifier complexity and for a moderate number of classes.

The performance of every solution in terms of the fuzzy labels associated with the points of the training set has been measured in the genetic algorithm. These labels have been assigned to the points in an automatic way, performing a fuzzy clustering process on the training set as a previous task. It is important to point out that this process reduced the errors committed when labelling samples manually.

The labelling process could be improved introducing partial supervision in the clustering algorithm. With this aim experiments with new objectives functions including supervision are now being made.

There are also some other possible extensions to the method, for instance using other color features or a more general classifier than the quadratic one, as well as applying the method to other kinds of scenes and to other search spaces.

9. References

1. D.N. Ballard and C.M. Brown, *Computer Vision*, (Prentice Hall, 1982).
2. J.C. Bezdek, *Fuzzy Mathematics in Pattern Classification*, Ph.D. dissertation, (Appl.Math., Cornell Univ. Ithaca, NY, 1973).
3. J.C. Bezdek, *A Convergence Theorem for the Fuzzy ISODATA Clustering Algorithms, IEEE Trans. on Pattern Analysis and Machine Intelligence,* **IEEE PAMI-2, No.1** (1980).
4. J.C. Bezdek, *Pattern Recognition with Fuzzy Objective Function Algorithm*, (Plenum Press, NY, 1981).
5. L.B. Booker, *Improving Search in Genetic Algorithms*, in *Genetic Algorithms and Simulated Annealing*, (Morgan Kauffman Publ.Inc., 1987).
6. R.L. Cannon, J.V. Dave and J.C. Bezdek, *Efficient Implementation of the Fuzzy c-Means Clustering Algorithms,IEEE Trans. on Pattern Analysis and Machine Intelligence,* **IEEE PAMI-8, No.2** (1986).
7. L. Davis and M. Steenstrup, *Genetic Algorithms and Simulated Annealing: An Overview,* in *Genetic Algorithms and Simulated Annealing*, (Morgan Kauffman Publ.Inc., 1987).
8. J. Domingo, J. Albert, F. Ferri, V. Cerverón, *A Learning Method Based on Genetic Algorithms Applied to Colour Image Segmentation, Proc. of Fourth International Symposium on Knowledge Engineering*, (Barcelona, 1990).
9. R. Duda and P.E. Hart, *Pattern Classification and Scene Analisys*, (Wiley, New York, 1973).
10. J.C. Dunn, *A Fuzzy Relative of Isodata Process and Its Use in Detecting Compact Well-Separated Clusters, J. Cybernet.* **Vol.3, No.3** (1974).
11. D.E. Gustafson and W. Kessel, *Fuzzy Clustering With a Fuzzy Covariance Matrix, Proc. IEEE-CDC,* **Vol. 2** (K.S. Fu, ed.), (IEEE Press, 1979).
12. R.M. Haralick and L.G. Shapiro, *Image Segmentation Techniques, Computer Vision, Graphics and Image Processing,* **29** (1985).
13. J. Holland, *Adaptation in Natural and Artificial Systems*, (Ann Arbor, University of Michigan Press, 1975).
14. T.L. Huntsberger, C. Jacobs and R.L. Cannon, *Iterative Fuzzy Image Segmentation, Pattern Recognition* **Vol. 18, No.2** (1985).
15. W.K. Pratt, *Digital Image Processing*, (John Wiley and Sons, Inc., 1978).
16. G. Wyszecki and W.S. Stiles, *Color Science*, (John Wiley and Sons, Inc., 2nd. edition, 1982).

REAL TIME PATTERN RECOGNITION USING AN OPTICAL CORRELATOR

I. Juvells, S. Villmitjana, S. Boch, J. Campos
A. Carnicer and J. R. de F. Moneo

Laboratori d'Optica de Física Aplicada i Electrònica
Universitat de Barcelona, Diagonal 647, 08028 Barcelona, Spain

ABSTRACT

The general procedures for optical implementation of cross-correlation between two-dimensional functions are revised. An optical set-up for real time pattern recognition is described. It is designed as a joint transform optical correlator (JTC) where the output of the first stage is detected by means of a CCD camera and simultaneously introduced as an input object for the second stage, using a low cost commercial liquid crystal television (LCTV) screen. A tele-diffractometer system for the adjustment between the physical dimensions of optical transforms and spatial light modulators is used.

The experimental results for a character recognition process are presented. Intermediate results indicate two main difficulties to be solved for a widespread practical usefulness of the method: the non-availability of high resolution, high contrast linear LCTV displays at present and the development of a procedure to eliminate the phase distortions which these screens originate in transmitted light. Within these practical limitations, the final detection is successfully achieved, making this technique a promising one.

1. Introduction.

In the field of pattern recognition methods, optical techniques are usually based on the analysis of the cross-correlation between the two dimensional functions representing the scene and the target. This correlation is normally carried out in Fourier space, as a simple multiplication of functions[1]. Target identification and localization is established upon determination of peak values inside the two-dimensional cross-correlation intensity.

Optical pattern recognition methods have an inherent capability for parallel processing, which results in a much higher operating speed than digital pattern recognition techniques. In practice, the ability of optical coherent systems to perform two-dimensional Fourier transforms of light distributions at the same time as light propagation occurs may allow real time processing. Moreover, the number of grey levels in images is very high and the computation method is intrinsically analogic. Many optical processing methods are founded on the matched filter technique, which may be manufactured following a holographic procedure[2]. This type of filter acts as a multiplicative function in the Fourier plane. This procedure is spatially invariant, i.e., it may detect the target in any position within the scene; but it is not rotationally or scale invariant: the target cannot be rotated or scaled inside the scene. There are also experimental difficulties in manufacturing the holographic filters and placing them in the optical set up, thus preventing any possibility of real time realisation of the whole method.

An alternative approach to overcome these difficulties is formulated on the basis of the joint transform correlator (JTC). This optical set up does not need to work with an optical filter in the Fourier space, conversely the reference is in the same space of the scene[3].

Nowadays, the practical utility of the JTC is being revised because of the great advances in technology of spatial light modulators[4], which may allow practical real time pattern recognition methods based on its use[5].

In this work, first we study the methods to realize the two-dimensional cross-correlation by optical means. One of the problems encountered in experimental work is to adjust the size of the optical transforms to the physical dimensions of light detectors and modulators. To solve this type of difficulty, a scale-tunable diffractometer is analyzed. Finally, as the aim of this work is to use optical correlation techniques for real time pattern recognition, a particular study for the joint transform correlator is carried out and some experimental results are presented. The input scene and target are photographic registers, the optical systems are scale tunable tele-diffractometers, the light detector used is a CCD camera and the light modulator for the second optical transformer is a commercially available low cost LCTV system [6, 7]. In spite of the limited performances of these LCTV units (poor resolution, low contrast, few grey levels,...) the practical results in our experimental conditions are satisfactory.

2. Optical correlation.

Two-dimensional cross-correlation by optical methods is usually accomplished by Fourier transforming the product of the Fourier transforms of the two initial functions (one of these complex conjugate)[8]. There are two main practical operating procedures: the Vander Lugt architecture and the JTC.

2.1. Vander Lugt type set-up.

The basic configuration for this optical correlator is shown in figure 1. It consists of two converging lenses (or lens systems), placed in such a way that the back focal plane of the first one coincides with the front focal plane of the second. Let us name the two complex two-dimensional functions $h(x_1,y_1)$ and $g(x_1,y_1)$. In a pattern recognition process $h(x_1,y_1)$ would be the scene analyzed and $g(x_1,y_1)$ the pattern to be detected. When the complex distribution in the front focal plane of the first lens (L1) is $h(x_1,y_1)$, the corresponding distribution in the back focal plane of L1 due to light propagation and diffraction is given by its Fourier transform $H(u,v)$[9]

$$H(u,v) = \int\int h(x_1, y_1) \exp\{i2\pi(x_1u + y_1v)\} \, dx_1 \, dy_1 \qquad (1)$$

where $u = x_2/\lambda f$ and $v = y_2/\lambda f$ are the spatial frequencies, λ the wavelength and f the focal length of lens L1.

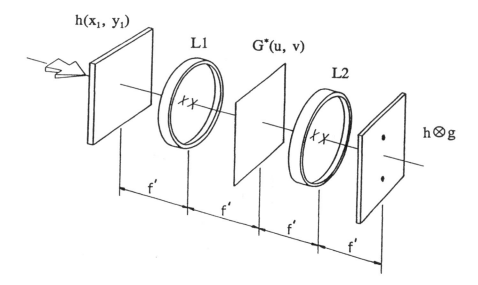

Figure 1.- Diagram of the optical correlator.

116

If a complex multiplicative filter $G^*(u,v)$ modifies the light distribution on this plane (where G^* is the complex conjugate of the Fourier transform of $g(x_1,y_1)$), the resulting complex amplitude will be $H(u,v)\ G^*(u,v)$, which upon a similar transformation in the second lens (L2) will give rise to the correlation $h(x_3,y_3) \otimes g(x_3,y_3)$ in the last plane[8].

The main drawback to the practical realization of this process is the difficulty in making the filter $G^*(x,y)$, because it corresponds to a complex function. The usual methods for this codification entail optical or digital holography[2, 10].

2.2. Joint-transform correlator.

The joint transform correlator is an experimental set up which may perform the correlation between two functions optically, without the need of any complex filter codification. The optical design of this correlator is given in figure 2.

The object plane includes both the pattern to be detected $g(x_1,y_1)$ and the scene $h(x_1,y_1)$, which includes additional objects. We take the scene centred with respect to the optical axis, while the pattern is placed at a distance y_0 from it. Thus, the light distribution in the object plane is: $\qquad g(x_1,y_1-y_0)\ +\ h(x_1,y_1)$

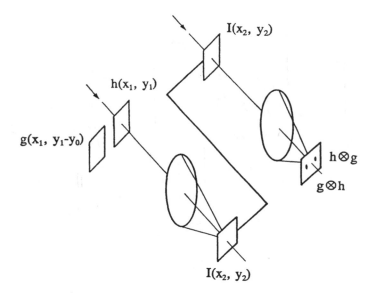

Figure 2. Joint transform optical correlator.

Lens L1 performs a first Fourier transform: in the back focal plane we have

$$A(x_2,y_2) = G(x_2/\lambda f, y_2/\lambda f) \exp(-i\frac{2\pi}{\lambda f}y_0y_2) + H(x_2/\lambda f, y_2/\lambda f) \qquad (2)$$

where (x_2,y_2) are the spatial coordinates and G and H are the Fourier transforms of g and h. The constant f is the focal length of lens L1 and λ the wavelength of the coherent illuminating light.

Any physical (square-law) light detector placed in this plane will give the corresponding intensity of the previous amplitude distribution. Namely,

$$I(x_2,y_2) = |A(x_2,y_2)|^2 = G^2 + H^2 + G\,H^* \exp(-i\frac{2\pi}{\lambda f}y_0y_2) + G^*H \exp(i\frac{2\pi}{\lambda f}y_0y_2) \quad (3)$$

This intensity may be the input of a second optical correlator which performs the same transformations. The complex amplitude on the back focal plane of lens L2 will be:

$$U(x_3,y_3) = g\otimes g + h\otimes h + (g\otimes h)*\delta(x_3,y_3-y_0) + (h\otimes g)*\delta(x_3,y_3+y_0) \qquad (4)$$

where $\otimes$ stands for the cross-correlation and $*$ for the convolution between two-dimensional functions.

The first and second terms correspond to the auto-correlations of g and h respectively, centred at the origin of the axis. The other two terms are the cross-correlations between g and h symmetrically displaced from the origin by a distance y_0. Any of these correlation terms may be studied to perform the pattern recognition analysis, usually by identification of intensity peak values which allow us to find the target inside the scene. Note that no filter has been used.

3. Adjustment of transform size. Tele-diffractometer.

In any optical correlation set-up, it is necessary to match the sizes between the light transforms and the filters or optoelectronic spatial modulators included. The easiest way is to alter the size of the Fourier transforms given by the optical systems. The usual optical diffraction set-up, working with common converging lenses, is not particularly suitable as they usually give too small light distributions and the range of size variation is too low[9].

Taking into account the mathematical expressions given in the previous paragraph, it is apparent that for fixed initial objects the scale of the Fourier transforms is defined by the constant value λf (which divides the spatial coordinates). Thus, to enlarge the transforms it is necessary to increase the value of λf. A noticeable increase in λ would lead to non-visible wavelength. To increase f would make optical combinations on the bench very long. With slightly modified optical arrangements it is possible to have a variable scale transformer, but only within a limited range[11].

A practical approach to increasing f without increasing the overall length is to use a tele-objective type diffraction lens. This is accomplished by inserting a diverging lens behind the usual converging one (figure 3).

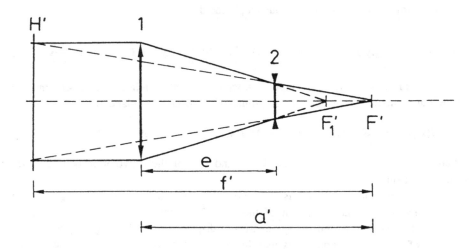

Figure 3.- Drawing of a tele-diffractometer.

The resulting focal length f' is a function of the two focal lengths f'_1, f'_2 of the two lenses and the distance between them e. The explicit expressions are the following (notation corresponds to figure 3):

$$f' = - \frac{f'_1 f'_2}{e - f'_1 - f'_2} \qquad\qquad a' = \frac{e^2 - e f'_1 - f'_1 f'_2}{e - f'_1 - f'_2} \qquad (5)$$

These expressions were obtained by coupling two-lens optical systems[12].

Let us define the gain attained as the relation between the resulting focal length and the length of the diffractometer $g = f'/a'$. Then,

$$g = \frac{f'_1 f'_2}{e^2 - f'_1 e + f'_1 f'_2} \qquad (6)$$

These formulae allow the analysis of the capabilities and limitations of a tele-diffractometer in order to change the size of the transforms.

Using normalized (dimensionless) distances $f = f'/f'_1$, $f_2 = f'_2/f'_1$, $a = a'/f'_1$, figure 4 shows the variation of the resulting focal length f as a function of f_2 and a. It can be seen that long focal length (i.e., large size transforms) with short overall length requires a short f_2 value. With commonly available lenses one may have $f_2 \approx 0.1$. For example, the combinations used by other authors[13, 14] give $f_2 = 0.05$ and $f_2 = 0.066$ respectively.

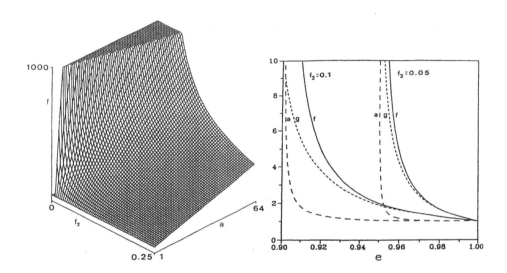

Figure 4.- Variation of resulting focal length.

Figure 5.- Focal, length and gain as a function of relative distance e.

For a fixed pair of lenses, the performances of the tele-diffractometer depend on the relative distance e between them. For $f_2 = 0.1$ and $f_2 = 0.05$, figure 5 sketches the resulting normalized focal f, the normalized length a, and the gain g as a function of e. In the graph the meaningful e zone is bounded by $1-f_2$ and 1.

Changing the distance between these limits, any gain is theoretically attainable.

The variation range for e is small, decreasing with the value f_2. This implies a critical adjustment, which is noticeable in the graphics where small position variations yield large focal length changes (or gain changes), mainly for long focal lengths.

There is an almost plane zone in the curve of the diffractometer length a versus the mutual distance e. Here it is possible to considerably increase the gain with only a small length increment. Moreover, looking at fig. 5, it is apparent that the smaller f_2 then the higher the slope and the thinner the zone where the length remains constant. Therefore the position of every element becomes more critical.

Table I shows some relevant numerical values. It can be seen that long focal lengths (about 10 m) are attainable with moderate size diffractometers (approximately 1 m or 0.5 m), obtaining gain values of 10 or 15. Similarly, we can have medium focal lengths (about 1 m) with short length (18 o 15 cm). Gain increases with decreasing f_2 , the cost being a critical lens positioning, as we have already shown.

TABLE I. Numerical values of focal length (f'), overall length (a') and gain (g) for different values of normalized distance (e), taking $f_2 = 0.1$ and $f_2 = 0.05$.

e	f' (cm)	a' (cm)	g
.901	100	10.80	9.26
.905	20	2.80	7.13
.910	10	1.81	5.52
.920	5	1.32	3.79
.950	2	1.05	1.90
1.000	1	1.00	1.00

$f_2 = 0.1$

e	f' (cm)	a' (cm)	g
.9505	100	5.90	16.95
.9525	20	1.90	10.50
.9550	10	1.41	7.12
.9600	5	1.16	4.31
.9750	2	1.02	2.05
1.0000	1	1.00	1.00

$f_2 = 0.05$

An important point to take into account when using a tele-diffractometer is the quadratic phase factor which multiplies the Fourier transform at the output plane. This implies that the amplitude itself is not the exact Fourier transform of the input. Of course, this is not prominent when only the intensity is to be detected, but becomes important when analytic Fourier transforms are required. Clearly, this exactness in phase would be obtained when the input is in the front focal plane of the tele-diffractometer, making the overall length as long as any normal diffractometer. Regarding only the length of the set up, the optimum position for the input is the converging (first) lens plane. Under these circumstances, the amplitude at the output plane is the Fourier transform multiplied by

$$\exp\ [-i\pi\ (e'-f_2')(x_2{}^2+y_2{}^2)/(\lambda\ f'\ f_2')].$$

Notice that this is not relevant for the JTC, because of the intensity detection in the exit planes of the correlators.

4. Experimental set up.

The drawing of our experimental set up is shown in figure 6. It is based on a joint transform correlator.

The experimental results are obtained using both photographic target $g(x_1,y_1)$ and scene $h(x_1,y_1)$. Live scenes at video rate could be handled using a TV camera and a spatial light modulator (as the LCTV) for the input of the coherent system.

The intensity at the exit of the first optical system (joint power spectrum) is detected by means of a CCD camera and simultaneously inserted in the second optical Fourier transformer using the LCTV modulator.

Our spatial modulator was a liquid crystal screen taken from a commercial black and white TV set CASIO-200. It was removed from the original unit and adapted to be used for transmitted light. The main characteristics are:

- Size: 30 x 38 mm.
- Number of pixels: 110 x 140
- Pixel size: 280 x 277 μm.
- Grey levels: 8 nominal. Under our working conditions, we have only measured
  4 grey levels.
- Contrast ratio: 14/1

At the final stage, another CCD camera detects the intensity of the correlation and displays it on a TV monitor. It may be also introduced into a computer by means of an analogic/digital converter, allowing direct digital analysis.

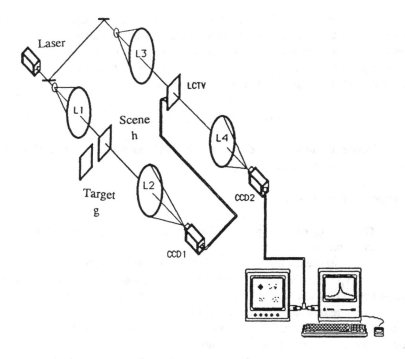

Figure 6.- Sketch of the experimental joint transform correlator.

5. Results.

The scene used in the experiment is shown in figure 7. The target to be detected is the letter K.

In figure 8-a we show the output (intensity) of the first optical processor and 8-b is the distribution as it appears on the LCTV, i.e., the input for the second optical processor.

Figure 9 is the intensity at the correlation plane, following expression (4). An axial zone is apparent where auto-correlations are superimposed together with two symmetrical lateral zones including the cross-correlations between the scene and the target.

The lack of central symmetry in the intensity distribution of fig 8 is worth noting. This may only be explained by the non-real character of the photographic images corresponding to scene and target: although we used a liquid gate[9] for the film substrate, the resulting complex amplitude transmittance is not constant in phase, leading to a non-real input function. This is even enhanced on the LCTV screen due to non-linear transformations in the CCD camera and the screen itself[15].

The LCTV screen is also a non constant phase object (non-real function) and a liquid gate arrangement is also necessary. Even now, final figure 9 is not perfectly symmetrical, giving two cross-correlation distributions which are not perfectly equivalent. Nevertheless, the change in the intensity peaks is not very important and gives similar final detection results.

Finally, figure 10 shows the cross-correlation between the scene (figure 7) and the target (letter K). The experimental results with the explained method are good. With our binary objects (constant intensity in dark background), the discrimination is good even between two characters as similar as K and H.

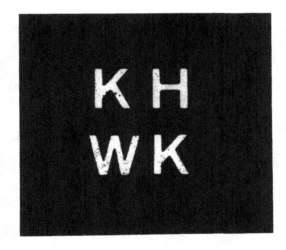

Figure 7. Scene

124

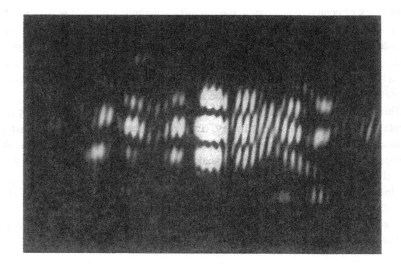

Figure 8.   a) Output from the first processor.

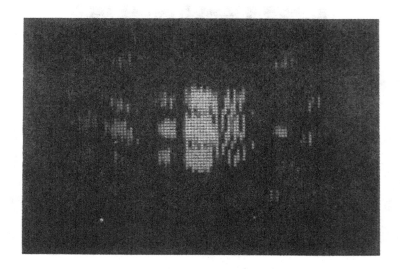

Figure 8.   b) Input to the second processor.

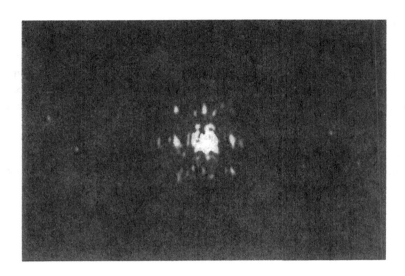

Figure 9. Output intensity at the correlation plane.

Figure 10. Optical cross-correlation.

6. Conclusions.

A set up for optical correlation by joint transform method (JTC) is presented. The intensity at the output of the first processor is detected by means of a CCD camera and simultaneously introduced in the second transformator using a LCTV screen. This obviates the need for a photographic process, allowing a real time pattern recognition process.

Experimental results using simple binary objects are reported, showing good discrimination capability. The application of the method to more difficult situations would demand a development of more sophisticated optoelectronic devices to increase the resolution and optical quality of our LCTV screen.

7. Acknowledgements.

This work has been supported in part by DGICYT, project number PB87-0177.

8. Bibliography.

1. H. Bartlet, in *Optical Signal Processing*, ed. H.J. Horner (Acad. Press, San Diego, 1987) p.97.
2. A.B. Vander Lugt, *IEEE Trans. Info. Theory*, **IT-10**, (1964) 139.
3. C.S. Weaver and J.W. Goodman, *Appl. Opt.*, **5**, (1966) 1248.
4. U. Efron, *Proc. SPIE*, **960**, (1988) 180.
5. F.T.S. Yu and X.J. Lu, *Opt. Commun.*, **52**, (1984) 10.
6. H.K.Liu and T.H. Chao, *Appl. Opt.*, **28**, (1989) 4772.
7. F.T.S. Yu, S. Jutamulia, T.W. Lin and D.A.Gregory, *Appl. Opt.*, **26**, (1987) 1370.
8. A. Papoulis, *The Fourier integral and its applications* (Mc Graw-Hill, New York, 1962).
9. J.W. Goodman, *Introduction to Fourier Optics* (McGraw-Hill, New York, 1968).
10. G. Tricoles, *Appl. Opt.* **26**, (1987) 4351.
11. B.J. Thompson, in *Optical Data Processing*, ed. D. Casasent (Springer-Verlag, Berlin 1978) p. 15.

12. M. Born and E. Wolf, *Principles of Optics*, (Pergamon Press, Oxford, 1975) p. 155.

13. D.L. Flannery, J.S. Loomis, M.E. Milkovich and P.E. Keller, *Opt. Eng.*, **27**, (1988) 309.

14. J.A. Davis, M.A. Waring, G.W. Bach, R.A. Lilly and D.M. Cottrell, *Appl. Opt.*, **28**, (1989) 10.

15. B. Javidi, *Appl. Opt.*, **28**, (1989) 2358.

COMPARISON OF SEVERAL EDITING AND CONDENSING TECHNIQUES FOR COLOUR IMAGE SEGMENTATION AND OBJECT LOCATION

F. Ferri[†]

Departamento de Informática y Electrónica
Universidad de Valencia, Av. Dr. Moliner 50
46100 Burjassot, Valencia, Spain

and

E. Vidal[‡]

Departamento de Sistemas Informáticos y Computación
Universidad Politécnica de Valencia
Camino de Vera s/n, 46020 Valencia, Spain

ABSTRACT

Several Editing and Condensing techniques are considered for implementing a Nearest Neighbour classifier which is applied to an Image Segmentation and Object Location problem. This problem arises in the development of the Vision System of a robotic citric harvesting device and essentially consists of the detection of the different image zones of interest on the basis of their colour and certain contextual and morphological aspects; all this strongly conditioned by the extremely variable lighting conditions in which the system is intended to work. The proposed solution to this problem through Nearest Neighbour pointwise classification is presented and the need for Editing and Condensing to design the required classifier is discussed. Different Editing and Condensing algorithms are presented along with comparison experiments to evaluate their relative merits for the proposed task. The results suggest the Multiedit algorithm of Devijver and Kittler along with the MNV-ordered Condensing of Gowda and Krishna as the most adequate choices for this task.

1. Introduction

Recently a new approach has been proposed for supervised colour image segmentation and object location with particular application to the vision subsystem of a robotic citric harvesting device [8]. This approach relies basically on a Nearest Neighbour (NN) classifier [7] which classifies each image point into either of the two classes of interest: fruit, non-fruit. By choosing an appropriate representation of image points and using a sufficiently large reference set of points with known classification, this rather straightforward approach has been shown capable of accounting for the regularities of colour and shape of fruit versus the random-like

(†) Work partially supported by grant N° ROB89-0285 of the Spanish CICYT.
(‡) Work partially supported by grant N° TIC-0448/89 of the Spanish CICYT.

appearance of leaf-regions and other uninteresting parts of the images. However, given the extremely variable lighting conditions in which the system is intended to work and the very different pigmentation that is exhibited by fruit depending on its actual variety and/or ripeness, the design of the above indicated classifier is not trivial at all.

In fact, although appropriate (quasi-optimal) asymptotical behavior has been shown for the error-rate of the NN classification rule [7], in practice, only finite sets of prototypes are available, generally leading to error-rates which are usually far from being appropriate. In particular, it can easily be seen that the presence of mislabelled prototypes and/or "outlyers" can strongly degrade classification accuracy. Furthermore, the probability of collecting such noisy or erroneous data grows proportionally with the number of references; but theory dictates large (and fair) reference-sets in order to approach optimal accuracy!. It should be recognized that, for the application to our pixel classification problem, this is just half of the trouble, since we have to achieve both accuracy and speed: if large sets of prototypes are used, the NN rule is, in principle, computationally prohibitive.

In order to give a solution to both the above problems we have adopted two interesting related families of techniques known as Editing and Condensing. Given a large finite set of samples or prototypes, the combined technique of Editing and Condensing aims at obtaining a consistent and reduced subset of these prototypes, whose corresponding Nearest-Neighbour decision frontiers closely approximate the Bayes classification frontiers for the minimum error in the underlying classification task. The Editing techniques aim at selecting, from the original reference set, only those prototypes that would belong to the Bayes acceptance region of each class. The Condensing techniques, on the other hand, attempt to drastically reduce the size of an Edited reference set by retaining only a small subset of prototypes whose associated NN decision frontiers closely approximate the NN frontiers of the Edited set.

Several specific techniques belonging to these two families have been proposed in the literature. Among the earliest, the Editing approach of Wilson [19] is worth noting . Also, Devijver and Kittler have proposed their own techniques for editing as well as the Multiedit algorithm [5]. Similarly, the earliest approach to Condensing is that proposed by Hart [11] which led to many other related techniques. Gates [9] suggested a procedure for further reducing the resulting condensed set. Gowda and Krishna [10] introduced the idea of ordering the references for posterior application of Hart's procedure, and Yalabik et al. [20] proposed an independent application of the Condensing procedure to pairs of "neighbour" classes of references. Other approaches have been proposed for the Condensing problem such as those of Tomek [15], Chang [4], and Wang [18].

While all the works on Editing are often accompanied by the appropriate mathematical analysis to establish the corresponding (asymptotic) behavior, this is not the case of Condensing techniques which are rather heuristic and whose corresponding behavior is often only established through (simulation) experiments.

The application of these techniques to real problems, on the other hand, has been carried out for printed character recognition [17], and speech recognition [2,20]. All these works, however, have practically been restricted to the use of Devijver and Kittler's Multiedit and Hart's Condensing.

Apart from the above mentioned works, we have recently applied the same techniques to Colour Image Segmentation and Object Location [8]. While the results obtained with these particular techniques were satisfactory, other Editing and Condensing approaches were seen as possibly more appropriate for the considered task, thus requiring the corresponding comparison experiments. This paper is devoted to reporting on these experiments. It should be pointed out that while it is both theoretically established and generally accepted that Multiedit is the best editing technique currently available, this superiority strongly relies upon the availability of large sets of references. In practice, however no such large sets can be afforded, either because of computational limitations or because of the large human-time required to collect these sets. Correspondingly other, perhaps more primitive, editing techniques can be seen as possible or perhaps better alternatives. In particular, in this work we have considered the original Editing of Wilson [19] and that of Devijver and Kittler, as well as the more popular Multiedit [5] which had already been adopted in our previous works. On the other hand, the Condensing variant of Gowda and Krishna [10] has been used and compared with the original one of Hart [11] which was adopted in our previous work.

The rest of this paper is organized as follows. The algorithms implementing the different Editing techniques are discussed in Section 2, and those of Condensing in Section 3. Section 4 presents the preprocessing procedures applied to our specific (image) data and Section 5 outlines the whole process of designing and using a (Multi)Edit-Condensing-NN classifier in our Colour Image Segmentation and Object Location task. The experiments comparing the different techniques are presented in Section 6, and Section 7, summarizes the work and draws some conclusions.

2. Editing Algorithms

Although at the present time, the (k-)NN rule is a simple and well-known classification procedure of wide-range applicability, there are quite a few tasks in Pattern Recognition in which reference selection difficulties tend to produce noisy training sets with uncontrolled prototypes (or "outlyers") which usually lead to excessive error-rates. A solution to this drawback consists of selecting a subset of the original set whose classification performance would be better than those of the complete set. The Editing idea, first proposed by Wilson [19], helps us to achieve this goal. This approach is based on selecting a representative subset of the Reference Set (RS) that allows NN classification to achieve a performance which is close to or better than the theoretical performance of NN classification with the original RS.

Most common Editing algorithms are based on the idea of discarding certain prototypes of the RS which are responsible for misclassification of (some of) the

132

remaining ones (for which correct classification is possible). Under the large-sample assumption, this procedure tends to eliminate prototypes that lay in the neighbourhood of the boundaries of the Bayes classifier for the underlying classification task.

The Editing algorithm of Wilson develops this idea by performing a closed classification test in a leaving-one-out fashion using the k-NN rule.

Wilson Editing Algorithm

Input:
    R :   Initial Reference Set.
    $k \in N$:   Number of Neighbours for the Classification Rule.

Output:
    R :   Edited Reference Set.

Method:
    1.   For each p in R,
                classify p with the k-NN rule using R-{p} as RS.

    2.   Discard those references that were misclassified in
                step 1 and with the remaining ones form a new set R.

Some of the theoretical results reported by Wilson were disproved by Penrod and Wagner [12]. The controversy was settled by Devijver and Kittler who stated that the difficulty with Wilson Editing is due to its leaving-one-out type of closed classification. Devijver and Kittler proposed a modification of Wilson's technique, based on the "holdout" or partitioning technique, which is as follows:

Holdout Editing Algorithm
// holdout version of Wilson Editing [5]//

Input:
    R :   Initial Reference Set.
    $k \in N$:   Number of Neighbours for the Classification Rule.
    $m \in N$:   Number of blocks in each partition, $m \geq 3$

Output:
    R :   Edited Reference Set.

Method:
    1.   Randomly divide R into m subsets R(i), i=1..m

    2.   For i=1..m, classify the references in R(i) with the
                k-NN rule using R((i+1)mod m) as Reference Set.

    3.   Discard those references that were misclassified in
                step 2 and with the remaining ones form a new set R.

Intuitively speaking, the effect of this holdout Editing is the same as that of Wilson Editing: it aims to eliminate the references that do not belong to the Bayes acceptance regions of each class; but this procedure has theoretical evidence of an improvement of the asymptotic performance over the k-NN rule. More concretely, it has been shown that the asymptotic conditional probability of error $\varepsilon_k(x)$ of the edited NN rule defined above is given for the two-class case by:

$$\varepsilon_k(x) = \frac{e_1(x)}{2\left[1-e_k(x)\right]} \le e^*(x)\frac{1-e^*(x)}{1-e_k(x)} \le e_k(x) \qquad (1)$$

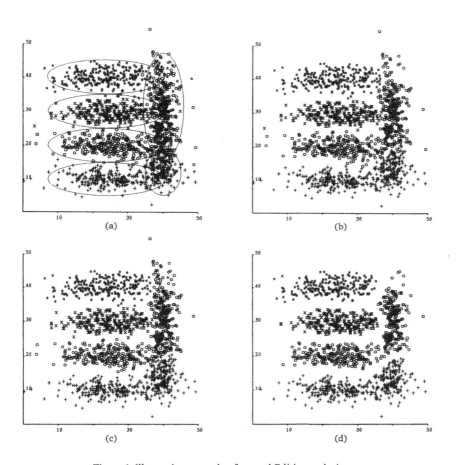

Figure 1. Illustrative example of several Editing techniques

Set of references generated from different gaussian distributions for each of four classes (+ , o , x , *). (a) Original set with constant probability density contours superimposed, (b) Result of Wilson Editing procedure, (c) Result of Holdout Editing, and (d) Result of Multiedit .

where $e_k(x)$ is the asymptotic conditional probability of error of the k-NN rule without editing, and $e^*(x)$ is the corresponding Bayes error [5].

By further pursuing the Holdout Editing framework, Devijver and Kittler proposed their Multiedit algorithm which somewhat reduces the number of references selected and further improves classification performance. Multiedit makes repeated use of holdout Editing according to the following algorithm:

Multiedit Algorithm

Input:
- R : Initial Reference Set.
- I ∈ N : Stopping Criterion
- m ∈ N : Number of blocks in each partition, m≥3

Output:
- R : Edited Reference Set.

Method:
1. Perform Holdout Editing with R, m and k=1.

2. If the last I iterations elapsed with no editing, then STOP else go to step 1.

Devijver and Kittler provided both theoretical and experimental evidence that this procedure converges asymptotically -in the number of iterations- to the Bayes decision rule. They proved also that the proportion of samples discarded by the Multiedit algorithm is bounded from above by two times the error-rate of the 1-NN rule [6].

Illustrative examples of the behavior of different editing algorithms with synthetic reference sets in two dimensional Euclidean space are shown in Figure 1.

It should be noted that, in practical situations, Multiedit requires a substantially large number of references to be effective. This number, on the other hand, is related to the dimensionality and statistical complexity of the reference set. This is not the case with the previous editing algorithms for which this number is not, in principle, as critical as for Multiedit.

3. Condensing Algorithms

Even in the case of performing NN classification with a "clean" set of references (perhaps obtained by means of some editing procedure), the strong conditions this rule imposes in terms of storage and computational requirements make its use quite inadvisable in many situations. For circumventing this problem, several approaches have been proposed in the literature. One of these approaches, which will not be pursued in this paper consists of the development and use of nearest neighbour searching algorithms (see e.g. [16]); The other main approach is that of Condensing.

The Condensing approach, adopted here, consists of searching for a <u>minimal</u> <u>consistent</u> subset of the original (possibly edited) set. A subset of a set of labelled references is said to be <u>consistent</u> with the entire set if it correctly classifies all the references in the set with the NN rule.

It should be noted that a consistent subset by no means needs to provide the same NN classification frontiers as those of the original set. While the problem of finding a smallest subset of references which exactly provides the same original NN classification frontiers can in fact be properly formulated, no general solution is currently known for such a problem and therefore the above weaker consistency criterion needs to be adopted.

The Condensing technique was originally suggested by Hart [11] who proposed the algorithm:

Condensing Algorithm

<u>Input:</u>
  R :   Edited Reference Set.

<u>Output:</u>
  S :   Condensed Reference Set. Initialized to the empty set.

<u>Method:</u>
  1.   Select some reference from R and join it to S

  2.   For each p in R,
           classify p with the current contents of S as Reference Set.
           if p is incorrectly classified, transfer it from R to S.

  3.   If no transfers occurred during the execution of step 2
           or R is exhausted, then STOP else go to step 2.

It is easily seen that this algorithm obtains as a result a <u>consistent</u> subset with respect to the input set, but there is no theoretical knowledge of how well the resulting set represents the original statistical distributions of the different classes or how close the resulting NN frontiers are from the original ones. In this sense, it is said that this algorithm is not optimal.

An important modification of Hart's Condensing algorithm was proposed by Gowda et al. [10]. Due to the strong dependence of Hart's Condensing on the order in which the prototypes are taken into account, it is possible to constrain the behavior of Condensing using a prior ordering phase according to certain criterion. In this sense, the Mutual Nearest Value (MNV) is defined for each prototype as a measure of its closeness to the nearest neighbour of a different class [10]. Therefore, prototypes with small MNV are those which are located close to the boundaries of different class clusters and, by selecting first these prototypes in the Condensing algorithm, smallest condensed sets are expected. It should be noted, however, that although this procedure decreases in fact the number of retained prototypes, it does not necessarily improve the classification performance of the original condensing technique.

136

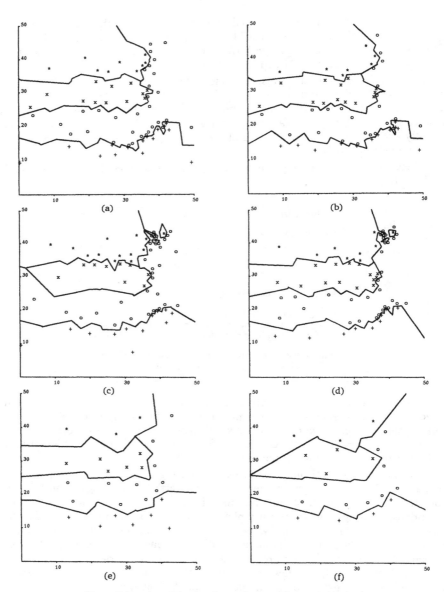

Figure 2. Results of Condensing techniques for synthetic data.

Condensed sets with corresponding Voronoi diagrams obtained from the edited sets of Figure 1.
(a) and (b) Result of Condensing and MNV-ordered Condensing from Figure 1b (Wilson Editing),
(c) and (d) idem of Figure 1c (Holdout Editing), (e) and (f) idem of Figure 1d (Multiedit).

Other approaches proposed in the literature for the Condensing problem are not considered for the purposes of this work.

Figure 2 shows the results of applying both Hart's Condensing algorithm and the MNV-ordered variation to the edited sets of Figure 1.

4. Pointwise Representation of Colour and Shape

In order to apply the above outlined techniques and to perform NN classification, an appropriate representation and metric is required for the samples or references. In our case, sam,)les are image points that have to be classified into two major classes: fruit/non-fruit.

Although colour may in fact constitute one of the main discriminating features between fruit and leaves, sky or other artifacts, the large, disturbing pigmentation and lighting variabilities that were discussed in section 1 make it strongly advisable to adopt an extended representation that would incorporate some appropriate information about shape and/or surface also. A variety of more or less robust techniques have been proposed in the literature that aim at extracting such information (see e. g. [3]). However, in order to keep the computational requirements within practical acceptable limits, a quite pragmatic approach has been adopted here. In this approach, each discrete image point is represented by a vector that includes not only the colour components of the corresponding pixel itself, but also the components of four of its neighbours. By collecting a sufficiently large number of references, this crude, straightforward representation can in fact capture both the shining and shading regularities that come from the spherically-shaped surfaces of fruit, and the (also important) randomly textured appearance of leaf regions.

The resulting vector representation of each image point would thus encompass five times the number of components of a single pixel colour representation. The colour space used in this work is based on the well-known YUV coordinates which are defined in terms of RGB values by [13]:

$$\begin{pmatrix} Y \\ U \\ V \end{pmatrix} = \begin{pmatrix} 0.229 & 0.587 & 0.114 \\ -0.147 & -0.289 & 0.437 \\ 0.615 & -0.515 & -0.100 \end{pmatrix} \cdot \begin{pmatrix} R \\ G \\ B \end{pmatrix} \tag{2}$$

Since coordinate Y only contains information about intensity, it is not considered to represent the colour components of an image point. This amounts to the following 10-dimensional representation, x, of a point at image coordinates (i,j):

$$x(i,j) = (U(i,j), V(i,j), U(i+h,j), V(i+h,j), U(i-h,j), V(i-h,j), U(i,j+h), V(i,j+h), U(i,j-h), V(i,j-h))$$

Where $U(i,j)$ and $V(i,j)$ are, respectively, the colour components of the pixel located at (i,j) and h is a neighbourhood parameter that is to be chosen in accordance with the expected size of image fruit pieces, given the (known) optics and camera-to-scene distance.

5. NN Pixel Classification from Edited and Condensed References and Object Location

Once we have seen how reduced and consistent sets of references or prototypes can be derived and how to obtain an adequate pointwise representation of the information that is expectedly useful for our task, we will briefly outline the whole set of procedures that designing and using our harvesting vision system entails. This comprises a <u>preprocessing</u> phase of prototype selection through Edit-Condensing and a <u>testing</u> or <u>working</u> phase involving NN point classification and <u>object location</u>.

In order to select an adequate set of references, a series of images are required in which all the expected lighting and pigmentation variabilities are sufficiently well-represented. With these images, the classes of interest (fruit, leaves and, possibly, sky) are manually separated by means of a rather inexpensive interactive procedure which simply consists of hand marking the image regions that are spanned by these classes. All the points (pixels) in each class are then collected together and vector-represented as described in Section 4. Since the overall number of points collected in this way is usually huge, a pseudo-random pre-selection step is carried out prior to any further processing. This step is aimed at both reducing the set of references to a manageable size and smoothing the usually large differences between the number of references in each class (Note that the regions of interest -fruit- tend to span only very small areas of the whole image). Let R be the set of n references that are obtained through this procedure.

The next step consists of <u>Editing</u> R. Depending on the specific technique that is used, this may require choosing an appropriate number of neighbours, k, a partition size, m, and an equally adequate threshold for the number of no-change iterations, I (stopping criterion). In the case of Multiedit, taking into account the number of iterations, the computational cost can roughly be estimated as $\Omega(nI/m)$. The quality of results, on the other hand, also tends to increase with I and to decrease with m, since more iterations tend to improve the results and large numbers of blocks in the partition cause the classes to be poorly represented in each block. Consequently, the trading of accuracy for speed in the preprocessing phase dictates choosing small values of m in conjunction with rather large values of I.

The next preprocessing step is to <u>condense</u> the results of multiediting. The Hart's condensing procedure has no parameters to be chosen, but its results may significantly depend on the order in which references are taken into account. The relatively low computational cost of this procedure makes it advisable to run it several times with different random orderings so as to avoid obtaining a particularly bad condensed result. The MNV-ordered condensing, on the other hand, gives deterministic results and only one execution of the algorithm makes sense.

Once a small set of consistent references has been obtained, the system is ready for the <u>testing</u> or <u>working</u> phase. Now, a new, fresh (test) image is given and all its points (pixels) are then linearly scanned while simultaneously obtaining their corresponding vector representations and NN classifications with respect to the reference prototypes. In passing, the sets of connected-component points with equal (fruit) classification can be assembled using the appropriate Merge-Find-Set procedure [1,14]. As soon as one of these sets gets closed, it is submitted to trivial size and shape verifications and, if finally assessed as a possible piece of fruit, the corresponding coordinates of its center can be readily sent to the robot's arm subsystem, thus effectively finishing the <u>object location</u> step. Control can then be concurrently granted to the arm subsystem to launch the appropriate fruit picking action, while the linear image scan continues its search for further pieces of fruit.

6. Experiments and Results

The whole process explained in previous sections has been followed in several experiments. In order to compare the relative merits of the different Editing and Condensing techniques, in this section <u>quantitative</u> results concerning <u>pixel classification</u> will be presented that are independent of the final object location phase. Final fruit location is also reported as a <u>qualitative</u> result in Figure 3e.

Seven representative RGB images are considered in the forthcoming experiment. In order to reduce computation, the images are captured into arrays of 128x128 pixels. All seven images are hand-segmented as explained in Section 5; three of them are taken as training images and the other four as test images.

In order to reduce the effects of misclassification in the manual segmentation, pixels in the frontiers of two different classes are discarded (in fact, a morphological erosion of small size is performed for each class in the segmented images). Finally, by applying the random reduction process mentioned in Section 4 to the three training images, we obtain a training set (R) which encompasses 4008 image points. Each of these points is converted into a 10-dimensional prototype as indicated in Section 4.

All the Editing procedures described in Section 2 were applied, with appropriate parameters, to the set R. To be more specific, different numbers of neighbours were considered for Wilson's Editing and Holdout Editing (k=5 and k=7) and, for the latter, a partition size (parameter m) of 5 was selected. On the other hand, the Multiedit algorithm was applied with two different values of the stopping criterion (I=5 and I=10) and a larger partition size (m=7) in each iteration was used in order to reduce the computation time which was significantly greater in this case. The Condensing method was applied in the two versions discussed in section 3 to each of the six edited reference sets: with random ordering, and taking into account the references depending on their MNV. Various random-condensed sets were generated and only one was selected on the basis of a rather inexpensive closed classification test. The results corresponding to the whole experiment are shown in Table I.

It should be pointed out that, from the point of view of our Image Segmentation and Object Location problem, these results should only be taken as merely illustrative, in the sense that the NN error rate of a given image does not provide

Table I

Results of size and classification performance for
different editing and condensing procedures

		Original Set	Editing (Wilson) k=7			Editing (Wilson) k=9			Holdout Editing m=5 k=5			Holdout Editing m=5 k=7			Multiedit m=7 l=5			Multiedit m=7 l=10		
			edit	cnd	MNV	edit	cnd	MNV	edit	cnd	MNV	edit	cnd	MNV	edit	cnd	MNV	edit	cnd	MNV
size	total	4008	3875	136	97	3876	106	87	3823	93	81	3811	87	72	3579	26	16	3573	23	15
	fruit	1500	1455	70	41	1450	54	38	1426	40	35	1424	31	25	1266	12	6	1246	9	7
	leaves	2100	2020	55	44	2023	46	39	1996	43	39	1988	43	37	1923	11	8	1936	11	6
	sky	408	400	11	12	403	6	10	401	10	7	399	13	10	390	3	2	391	3	2
Iterations		-	-	5	3	-	4	3	-	3	3	-	3	3	52	3	2	111	3	2
% NN errors		15.63	14.33	18.40	20.31	14.12	17.15	19.37	13.18	16.26	16.80	13.20	17.67	15.47	10.63	13.15	11.00	10.29	12.58	12.93
		18.19	16.30	16.18	21.67	16.35	16.08	24.65	12.75	14.44	15.59	13.99	16.18	16.76	10.70	12.24	11.16	10.62	17.91	8.87
		30.64	28.29	36.53	41.06	28.12	36.39	42.68	26.69	33.38	34.26	26.58	34.38	31.80	26.69	37.25	25.79	27.13	33.12	34.16
		28.73	28.75	33.14	35.56	28.78	31.17	33.26	28.53	30.82	30.28	28.45	30.00	29.71	28.25	31.90	28.03	28.16	29.11	30.92
% average errors		23.30	21.92	26.06	29.65	21.84	25.20	30.00	20.28	23.73	24.23	20.55	24.56	23.44	19.06	23.64	19.00	19.05	23.18	21.72

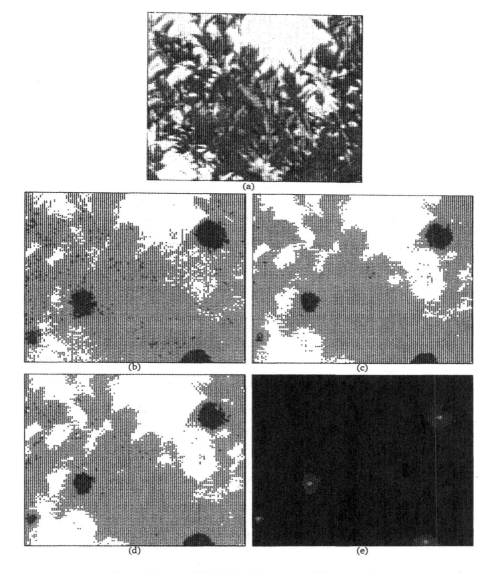

Figure 3. Results of Pixel Classification and Object Location.

(a) Gray level representation of the scene, (b) Classification using Original set,
(c) Multiedited set, and (d) Condensed set with MNV-ordering. (e) Located objects and Centroids.

very reliable information as to how well fruit is to be detected. In fact, only the amount of object location error is what will characterize the final system performance. However, the results are interesting in the sense that the classification errors with the edited and condensed sets tend to follow the predicted behavior with respect to the error with the original R. The edited sets significantly improve the NN classification accuracy with respect to that observed with the original set and, the more sophisticated the Editing procedure, the better the improvement is. On the other hand, the condensed-set results tend to worsen, but remain better (on the average) than those of the original set, at least for the MNV-ordered Condensing. Furthermore, the relative performance of the MNV-ordered Condensing with respect to the non-ordered one tends to improve for progressively good edited sets. This could be interpreted as a tendency of the MNV-ordering scheme to improve the performance of Condensing only if a truly good edited input set (sufficiently "clean" and representative of the probability distributions) is given.

It is important to note the large difference in size between the original and edited sets versus the condensed ones. This dramatic size reduction is in fact what definitively makes possible the application of these techniques to our harvesting vision task.

Figure 3 shows the results of pixel classification for one of the test images used in the experiments with three different sets of references: original, multiedited and MNV-condensed. With the good results obtained from pixel classification it is relatively easy to currently obtain the correct location of the searched objects. For this final phase we have implemented a connected component labelling algorithm which is based on the well-known disjoint union-find algorithm [1]. Area, perimeter and centroid of each object are calculated, on the fly, through the single image scan that is carried out by the algorithm. The final results, using area and perimeter as assessing parameters, are also shown in Figure 3.

7. Conclusion

This paper has dealt with a comparative study of different (Multi)Editing and Condensing procedures as applied to a difficult (pixel) classification task which arises in the development of the vision subsystem of a robotic harvesting device. This study complements previous works of ours in which only the Multiedit-Condensing technique was used. As far as Editing is concerned, the results of the present work clearly confirm the theoretically expected superiority of our initial choice for Multiedit. The Condensing variant here tested, on the other hand, has shown a consistent improvement over the performance of the traditional Condensing technique, at least for the good edited results obtained through Multiediting. Although computationally more expensive than traditional Condensing, this variant is still significantly cheaper than Multiedit and, therefore, the results obtained in this work clearly suggest the use of MNV-ordered Condensing in the design of a pixel classifier for our Image Segmentation and Object Location task.

The final results obtained are judged as sufficiently fast and accurate to enable an adequate implementation of the vision system of a robotic harvesting device which is capable of working in quite variable environments and/or lighting conditions.

8. References

1. A. V. Aho, J. E. Hopcroft, J. D. Ullman. *The Design and Analysis of Computer Algorithms* Addison-Wesley.(1974)

2. P. Aibar, M.J. Castro, F. Casacuberta, E. Vidal. *"Multiple Template Modelling of Sublexical Units" in Speech Recognition and Understanding: Recent Advances, Trends and Applications,* P. Laface (ed). Springer-Verlag (1990)

3. W.E. Blanz, J.L.C. Sanz, D. Petkovic. *"Control-Free Low-Level Image Segmentation: Theory, Architecture, and Experimentation." Advances in Machine Vision,* J.L.C. Sanz(ed) Springer-Verlag(1989).

4. C. Chang *"Finding Prototypes for Nearest Neighbor Classifiers"* *IEEE Trans. on Computers,* Vol **C-23**, N⁰ 11, pp. 1179-1184 (1979)

5. P. A. Devijver, J. Kittler. *Pattern Recognition, A Statistical Approach* Prentice Hall, (1982)

6. P. A. Devijver. *"On the editing rate of the multiedit algorithm."* *Pattern Recognition Letters* 4, pp. 9-12 (1986)

7. R. Duda, P.E. Hart. *Pattern Classification and Scene Analysis* Wiley. (1973)

8. F. Ferri, E. Vidal *"Colour Image Segmentation and Labelling through Multiedit-Condensing".* Submitted.

9. G. W. Gates *"The Reduced Nearest Neighbor Decision Rule"* *IEEE Trans. on Inform. Theory,* Vol **IT-18**, pp. 431-433 (1972)

10. K. C. Gowda, G. Krishna. *"The Condensed Nearest Neighbor Rule using the Concept of Mutual Nearest Neighborhood"* *IEEE Trans. Info. and Theory,* Vol **IT-125**, pp. 488-490. (1979)

11. P. E. Hart. *"The Condensed Nearest Neighbor Rule."* *IEEE Trans. Info. Theory,* Vol. **IT-14**, pp. 515-516 (1968)

12. C. S. Penrod, T. J. Wagner *"Another look at the Edited Nearest Neighbor Rule"* *IEEE Trans. on Systems, Man and Cybernetics,* Vol **SMC-7**, pp. 92-94 (1977)

13. W. K. Pratt *Digital Image Processing* John Wiley and Sons, Inc. (1978)

14. H. Sammet, M. Tamminen *"An Improved Approach to Connected Component Labelling of Images" Proceedings of Computer Vision and Pattern Recognition* (**CVPR'86**).(1986)

15. I. Tomek *"Two Modification of CNN" IEEE Trans. on Systems, Man and Cybernetics,* Vol **SMC-6**, pp. 769-772 (1976)

16. E. Vidal *"An Algorithm for Finding Nearest Neighbors in (aproximately) Constant Average Time" Pattern Recognition Letters,* Vol. **4**, pp. 145-157 (1986)

17. J. Voisin, P. A. Devijver. *"An Application of the Multiedit-Condensing Technique to the Reference Selection Problem in a Print Recognition System." Pattern Recognition,* Vol. **20**, N⁰ 5, pp. 465-474 (1987)

18. Q. R. Wang *"Boundary Patching CNN and Edit-partition Tree Classifiers"* *Intl. Conf. on Pattern Recognition,* **ICPR'86**, pp. 1127-1129, Paris (1986)

19. D. L. Wilson *"Asymptotic Properties of Nearest Neighbor Rules using Edited Data"* *IEEE Trans. on Systems, Man and Cybernetics,* Vol **SMC-2**, pp. 408-420 (1972)

20. N. Yalabik, F. Yarman-Vural, A. Mansur. *"Modified Condensed Nearest Neighbor Rule as Applied to Speaker Independent Word Recognition." Speech Comm.* 7, pp. 411-415 (1988)

NON-SUPERVISED CHARACTERIZATION OF GALAXIES USING DIFFERENT APPROACHES

J. A. Garcia, R. Molina and N. Pérez de la Blanca

Departamento de Ciencias de la Computación e I.A.
Universidad de Granada. 18071 Granada. Spain.

ABSTRACT

In this paper we present some results for automatic characterization of galaxies from digital images. In a first approach we try to characterize spirals and elliptical galaxies as realizations of MRF with different interaction parameters. In a second approach we attempt the characterization using some points on the galaxy contour that represent the shape of the galaxy, more precisely those with highest local curvature. Then we reduce the dimensionality of the problem using the boundary to characterize a galaxy shape.

1   Introduction

The first time the problem of galaxy classification appeared in literature was in 1786, when William Herschel[7] published the first volume of his catalog of nebulae and star clusters, classifying them into five types of nebulae -bright, faint, very faint, planetary and very large- and three types of clusters. Since then many authors have proposed systems to classify galaxies but the most important classification system of galaxies was created by Hubble[8].

Hubble's work published in 1926[9] proposed a new classification system of extragalactic nebulae which extended his previous work[8]. The scheme is the following:

> *Type: A: Regular*
> > *1. Elliptical: E_η ($\eta = 0, 1, \cdots, 7$. The numeral*
> > *η indicates the elipticity multiplied by 10)*
> > *2. Spiral:*
> > > *a) Normal spirals: Sa (early), SBb (intermediate)*
> > > *and Sc (late)*
> > > *b) Barred spirals: SBa (early), SBb (intermediate)*
> > > *and SBc (late)*
> > *B: Irregular*

In his book *The Realm of the Nebulae* published in 1936, Hubble[10] presented the so called tuning fork diagram, introducing at the junction of the fork the SO type. The reason for that introduction was the smooth transition between E7 and Sa by the discontinuity between E7 and Sa.

Toward 1950, Hubble modified his tuning fork diagram into the form which is described in *The Hubble Atlas of Galaxies* published by Sandage[13] in 1961.

Although some authors have extended the Hubble's tuning fork[10], his classification scheme still remains as the bons of any classification system of galaxies based on morphological features.

In this work we will concentrate on the extraction of the morphological features determining a galaxy: general shape, the appearance of spiral arms and bars, the relative proportion of the spheroidal component in size and luminosity and so on. Many authors believe that any galaxy classification system conduted in this way is esentially qualitative and inevitably subjective to some degree and they propose what they call a quantitative classification. We want to see how much automatization can be achieved on the extraction and classification of morphological features.

2 Parameter estimation on the contour of a galaxy

Taking into account that the two building blocks of galaxies are spirals and ellipses, in this section we will try to characterize these two objects as realizations of Markov Random Fields (MRF) (see below) with different interaction parameters.

We will consider here binary images with just an spiral or ellipse, the spiral being defined by the expression $r = \alpha exp(b\theta)$ proposed by Danver[3] to model the arms of galaxies, where α determines the distance to the center of the galaxy and b determines the size of the angular increment.

These images are considered realization of the following MRF:
We focus our attention on discrete 2D random fields defined over a finite $N_1 \times N_2$ rectangular *lattice* of points defined as $L = \{(i,j) : 1 \leq i \leq N_1, 1 \leq j \leq N_2\}$. We assume that the random field X consists of discrete random variables $\{X_{ij}\}$ taking values in $\{0,1\}$. The distribution is specified in terms of second order neighborhood system η^2 and cliques are those associated with η^2. For convenience, we simplify the labeling of x_{ij} to x_t with $t = j + N_2(i-1)$. The set of first order spatial neighbors is denoted by $\{x_{t:r}; r = +1, -1, +2, -2\}$ and the set of second order spatial neighbors by $\{x_{t:r}; r = +3, -3, +4, -4\}$ (see Geman[6]). The joint distribution is of the form

$$P(X = x) = \frac{1}{Z} \exp^{-U(x)}$$

where

$$Z = \sum_x \exp^{-U(x)}.$$

Only cliques of size 2 are involved in a pairwise interaction model. The energy function for a pairwise interaction model can be written in the form Besag[1] :

$$U(x) = \sum_{t=1}^{M} F(x_t) + \sum_{t=1}^{M} \sum_{r=1}^{K} H(x_t, x_{t:+r})$$

where $H(a,b) = H(b,a)$, $H(a,a) = 0$ and K depends on the size of the neighborhood around each site. Funtion F(.) is the potential funtion for single-pixel cliques and H(.,.) is the potential function for all cliques of size 2. For example, K is 4 for neighborhoods of order 2.

We use the Derin-Elliott[4] model in which

$$F(x_t) = \alpha x_t \ and \ H(x_t, x_{t:+r}) = \beta_r I(x_t, x_{t:+r})$$

where $I(.,.)$ is the indicator function

$$I(a,b) = -1 \ if \ a = b \ and \ 1 \ if \ a \neq b$$

and the parameters β_r, $r = 1, 2, 3, 4$, influences spatial dependence in the horizontal, vertical, diagonal and opposite-diagonal directions respectively.

Since the information to discriminate between the spirals and ellipses is contained in the contour of such objects we will perform the estimation of the $\{\beta\}$ only on those points. Taking into account that the ellipses have isotropic properties the spirals lack we expected the second order parameters $\{\beta_r; \ r = 1, 2, 3, 4\}$ to be different for both objects.

$\beta = \{\beta_r; \ r = 1, 2, 3, 4\}$ were choosen to maximize

$$PL = \prod_{\text{pixels}} P[X_{ij}/X_{kl} \ with \ (k,l) \neq (i,j), \beta] \qquad (1)$$

see Besag[2]. Optimization of (1) was performed using a quadratic search routine Press et al[12].

The results are shown in table 1 and table 2.

b	β_1	β_2	β_3	β_4
0.12	6.195440	5.022793	2.568366	2.733341
0.13	6.195440	5.022793	2.733341	2.568366
0.15	2.135317	1.923415	1.397863	1.359995
0.17	2.135317	1.923415	1.397863	1.359995
0.19	2.135317	1.923415	1.397863	1.359995
0.20	2.683971	2.302599	1.552279	1.510072
0.25	2.135317	1.923414	1.359995	1.397863

Table 1

e	β_1	β_2	β_3	β_4
0	3.966667	3.966666	2.083679	2.083679
5	7.596351	6.412594	3.180444	3.180444
11	3.093205	2.404890	1.626428	1.626428
15	3.128371	2.340688	1.596411	1.596411
30	3.216230	1.701586	1.404316	1.404316
50	9.215978	2.288349	2.115880	2.115880
80	6.630832	1.428520	1.405486	1.405486

Table 2

It can be observed that the estimated parameters β_3 and β_4 are different values on a contour of a spiral arm (table 1), hence the associated model is second order non-isotropic. While the estimation on an ellipse (table 2) produces equals values of parameters in both diagonal directions, obtaining the associated model as a second order isotropic.

It is obvious from the above tables that although the elliptical objects posses isotropy which the spirals lack, the difference between the parameters for both images is not significant even for binary an perfect images. A different approach to the problem is necessary. It will be discused in the next section.

3 Characterization using landmarks

We now try to reduce the dimensionality of the problem using the curvature curve associated to the boundary of a galaxy shape to characterize the galaxy. More precisely, we suppose that all the information necessary to characterize a 2D galaxy shape it is on its boundary, and the characterization is possible using the information provided by their curvature curve and particularily their landmark points.

Then the first step is to get a boundary estimation. To do this we need to divide the astronomical image into galaxy and background.

A possible model includes an unknown greylevel η_b outside and a greylevel η_g inside the galaxy ($\eta_b < \eta_g$). The pixel values have Gaussian distributions $N(\eta_g, \sigma_g)$ inside the galaxy and $N(\eta_b, \sigma_b)$ on the background. If the parameters η_b and η_g can be estimate, then a non-contextual rule could be used to classify a pixel. This model produces an unsatisfactory solution (see -B- in figure 1).

Instead we use a model proposed in Geman[6] (see -C- in figure 1). The idea is to construct a MRF consisting of two coupled processes, one accounting for the labels and the other for the edges. The edge process is an auxiliary process. Let $S^P = \{ (i,j) : 1 \leq i, j \leq N \}$ and let S^E be the dual lattice consisting of all nearest-neighbor pairs $< s, t >$ from S^P. The elements of S^E are referred to as edge sites and correspond to the location of a edge between the corresponding pixels.

The label process is now denoted $X^P = \{X_s^P, s \in S^P\}$ and the edge process by $X^E = \{X_r^E, r \in S^E\}$. As usual, $X_s^P \in \Lambda = \{0, 1, \cdots, L\}$ whereas $X_r^E \in \{0, 1\}$, with $X_r^E = 1(resp.0)$ indicating the presence (resp. absence) of an edge at r.

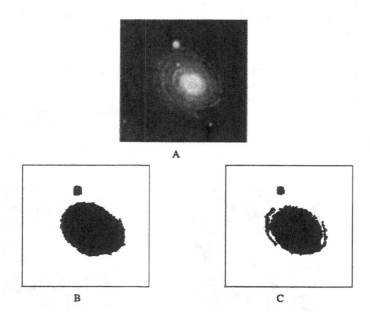

Figure 1: (A) Original Image. (B) Non-MRF model. (C) MRF model.

We now consider the process $X = \{X^P, X^E\}$ with index set $S = S^P \cup S^E$ and configuration space $\Omega = \Lambda^{S^P} \times \{0, 1\}^{S^E}$. The neighborhood system is $\eta = \{\eta_s, s \in S\}$, the neighborhood η_s of each pixel $s \in S^P$ consists of the eight adjacent pixels and the edge sites associated with s, and the dual neighborhood η_s of each edge site $s \in S^E$.

The energy $H(x) = H(x^P, x^E)$ has two terms, reflecting expectations about interactions between intensities and edges and about boundary organization. Specifically,

$$H(x) = H^1(x^P, x^E) + H^2(x^E).$$

We select

$$H^1(x^P, x^E) = \theta_1 \sum_{(r,t)} \phi(x_r^P - x_t^P)(1 - x_{(r,t)}^E)$$

where $\phi(u) = -1$ if $u = 0$ and 1 if $u \neq 0$, and $\theta_1 > 0$.

150

The organization of x^E is controlled by

$$H^2(x^E) = -\theta_2 \sum_D W_D(x^E) \ , \ \theta_2 > 0$$

where the sum extends over all cliques D in S^E (see Geman[6]).

The segmentation is based on simulated annealing with the logarithmic temperature schedule

$$t_k = \frac{c}{\log(1 + k)}$$

where t_k is temperature during the k'th sweep, $c = 3.5$, $1 \le k \le 100$.

Our experimental results indicate that it's necessary to segment using four classes (L=4) instead of two classes (L=2). The reason is that inside the galaxy three different regions appear: center, high greylevel pixels and medium greylevel pixels (see figure 2). The competition between the four regions increases the quality of the segmentation, recovering the basic geometric structure of the regions, while the use of only two classes produces an excessive smoothing and interpolation.

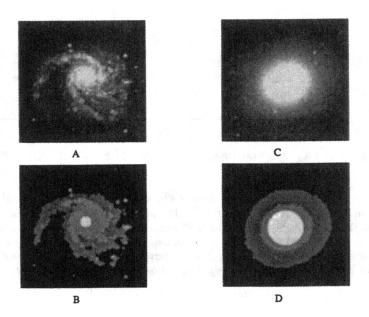

Figure 2

We now use the curvature curve associated to the estimated boundary (frontier between galaxy and background) to characterize the galaxy shape, following the methodology given in Fdez-Valdivia et al[5].

The points on the curve -boundary- representing the shape of the galaxy choosen to determine its shape are those with the highest local curvature. In particular we have to estimate the curvature values in each point of the curve and the minimum number of landmarks necessary to characterize the shape of the curve.

The main problem when we are estimating curvatures on a discrete curve is the noise from the discretization process. To avoid this effect we have estimated the gaussian curvature at each point using the method proposed in Knoerr[11].

Once we have estimated one adequate smooth curvature curve, we estimate the landmark points following the method given in Knoerr[11].

Some results are showed in Figure 3 and Figure 4. The presence of more than one landmark can be observed by each arm in the contour of a spiral galaxy. In contrast the curvature values in each point on the boundary of an elliptical galaxy are almost equal values and there are no landmarks in the shape. In all experiments we fix the maximum number of landmark points that can be obtained.

4 Conclusions

We have presented two different approaches to characterize galaxies. In the first we obtain that the elliptical objects possess isotropy which the spirals lack, although the difference between the parameters for both images is not significant. In the second we show that it is very promising to try to characterize a galaxy shape using a landmark point set of the estimated contour, which reduces the dimensionality of the characterization problem.

Acknowledgement: The authors want to acknowledge the programming assistance given by Dr. Fdez-Valdivia.

References

[1] Besag,J. *Spatial interaction and the statistical analysis of lattice systems.* Journal of Royal Statistical Society, Ser. B, 6, (1974).

[2] Besag,J. *On the statistical analysis of dirty pictures.* J. Royal Statist. Soc., Ser. B, 48, (1986).

[3] Danver, C.G. Ann. Obs. Lund, No. 10, (1942).

[4] Derin, H., Elliott, H. *Modelling and segmentation of noisy and textured images using Gibbs random fields.* IEEE Transactions on Pattern Analysis and Machine Intelligence, PAMI 9, (1987).

[5] Fdez-Valdivia, J., Pérez de la Blanca, N. *Characterization of shapes in microscopical digital images,* 7th SCIA, Alboorg, (1991).

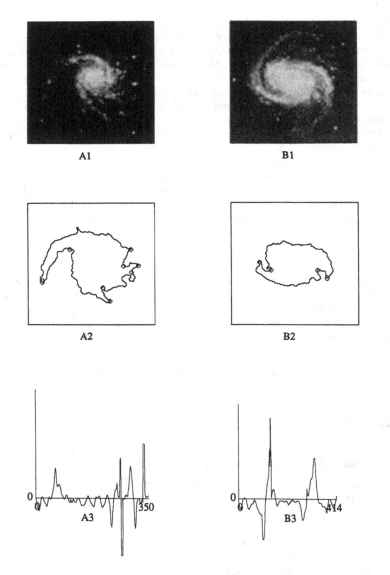

Figure 3: (A1),(B1) Spiral galaxies. (A2),(B2) The landmark point sets in the estimated contours A1,B1. (A3),(B3) The associated curvature curves to the contours A2,B2.

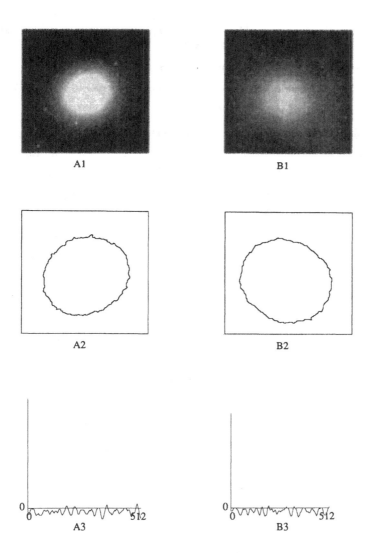

Figure 4: (A1),(B1) Elliptical galaxies. (A2),(B2) No landmark points in the estimated contours A1,B1. (A3),(B3) The associated curvature curves to the contours A2,B2.

154

[6] Geman, D. *Random Fields and Inverse Problems in Imaging.* Personal comuni-cation, University of Massachusetts.

[7] Herschel, W., Philosoph. Trans., 76, (1786).

[8] Hubble, E., Memorandum to the Commission on nebulae of the IUA, (1923).

[9] Hubble, E, Astrophys J., 64, (1926).

[10] Hubble, E, *The Realm of the nebulae*, (Yale University Press, 1936).

[11] Knoerr, A. *Globals Models of Natural Boundaries: Theory and Applications.* Report in Pattern Theory 148. Brown University, (1988).

[12] Press, W. et al, *Numerical recipes in C*, (Cambridge University Press, 1988).

[13] Sandage, A, *The Hubble Atlas of Galaxies*, (Carnegie Institution of Washington, Washington, D.C., 1961) .

ANALYSIS AND OPTIMIZATION OF THE K-MEANS ALGORITHM FOR REMOTE SENSING APPLICATIONS

P. Montolio, A. Gasull, E. Monte, L. Torres and F. Marqués

Department. Teoría Señal y Comunicaciones
Univ. Politécnica de Catalunya, Barcelona, Spain

ABSTRACT

This paper deals with the k-means algorithm. A formal interpretation of the method is presented, and it is shown that it is possible to spread the k-means algorithm by means of other kinds of distance measurements that are well known in classification techniques. Moreover, an optimized implementation of the algorithm is presented. This implementation can save up to 30 % of the number of operations in the case of Landsat V images for remote sensing purposes.

1. INTRODUCTION

Nowadays there are several satellites that scan the Earth sending images of its surface. This observation is a source of enormous information about it. The remote sensing techniques are envisioned to interpret this information very fast, with the least computational cost possible and with as little intervention of specialists as possible.

A remote sensing system is usually divided in several modules[2] : the extraction of characteristics, learning, classification, presentation, etc. Some of the most used algorithms are based on methods of minimum distance and on unsupervised learning algorithms, due to the fact that in these algorithms the intervention of the operator is minimum. These methods are widely used in remote sensing and other areas of pattern recognition.

One of the most popular algorithms for non-supervised learning is the k-means method. In this paper a formalization of the algorithm is

This work was supported by the PRONTIC grant nº 105/88.

presented. This formalization is used as a basis in order to make extensions to any other distance measures, like distances derivated of probabilistic concepts (Bayes). At the end of the paper, a simple implementation of the k-means algorithm is presented, that allows substantial savings in the processing time.

These and other methods are applicated to Landsat satellite images. These satellites yield a digitalized image (with a resolution up to 30x30 m^2/pixel) which has multiband information (bands of the visible spectrum, (R, G, and B) and infrared and thermic bands).

2. EUCLIDEAN MINIMUM-DISTANCE CLASSIFICATION

In the wide range of classification algorithms, we have a family of algorithms that make the classification by means of minimum distance. These algorithms assign a point or pixel of an image, (which is characterized by a vector of brightness x_i), to the nearest class W_j, of all the classes that have been found during the learning stage. That is

$$x_i \in W_j \quad \text{if} \quad d\left(x_i, W_j\right) < d\left(x_i, W_k\right) \quad \forall \, k \neq j \tag{2.1}$$

The classifier by minimal euclidean distance is the most simple of the classifiers of minimal distance. It is also the algorithm which requires the least computational burden. This algorithm characterizes each class by means of a class center vector C_j, which indicates the mean brightness of the pixels of that class. Afterwards, a measure of the euclidean distance is used in order to evaluate the distance between the pixel and the class center

$$d\left(x_i, W_j\right) = \left\| x_i - C_j \right\|^2 \tag{2.2}$$

This gives the decision rule for the classifier

$$x_i \in W_j \quad \text{if} \quad \left\| x_i - C_j \right\|^2 < \left\| x_i - C_k \right\|^2 \quad \forall \, k \neq j \tag{2.3}$$

In this case the classification process is composed of two parts

1) Find the classes which are suitable and the class (cluster) center of these classes.
2) Classify all the pixels of the image by means of the decision rule mentioned in (2.3).

In order to find a set of valid classes, one can begin with data that is alien to the image to be classified, data normally supplied by the user, and thus obtain the classes and their associated centers (supervised learning). One can also use automatic algorithms that with only the information of the input image, search for a set of possible classes, without the need of supplying any additional information (non-supervised learning). The iterative k means algorithm belongs to this last group.

3. THE K-MEANS ALGORITHM

Normally the non-supervised techniques search for a set of classes that optimize a cost function, for instance, to minimize the distance between the classes and the points, or other similar cost functions.

The non-supervised learning algorithm known as k-means[1], is designed in order to minimize the total error or cost in the classification, taking as a measure of this error the squared euclidean distance between a pixel and the center of the class to which it belongs.

Thus, the error when the point x_i is assigned to the class W_j is the following

$$\varepsilon\left(x_i, W_j\right) = \left\| x_i - C_j \right\|^2 \tag{3.1}$$

where C_j is the center of the class W_j.

If the decision rule of the classifier that uses the minimal euclidean distance is used, we will assign the point x_i to the nearest class. So, the cost in the classification of the point x_i is

$$\varepsilon\left(x_i\right) = \underset{C_j}{\text{MIN}} \ \left\| x_i - C_j \right\|^2 \tag{3.2}$$

for $C_j=0,...,F-1$, with F being the number of classes to be determined.

If the total cost of all the pixels of the image, $x_0...x_{m-1}$, is added, we have

$$\varepsilon(I) = \sum_{x_i} \underset{C_j}{MIN} \left\| x_i - C_j \right\|^2 \tag{3.3}$$

The best situation of the class center will be the one that minimizes the cost $\varepsilon(I)$. Therefore, the gradient of this cost with respect to the components of the class center C_j is computed and set equal to zero

$$\nabla_j \varepsilon(I) = \begin{pmatrix} \dfrac{\partial \varepsilon}{\partial c_j^0} \\ . \\ . \\ . \\ \dfrac{\partial \varepsilon}{\partial c_j^{n-1}} \end{pmatrix} = 0 \tag{3.4}$$

Taking into account that

$$MIN(a,b,c) = MIN(a, MIN(b,c)) \tag{3.5}$$

and that

$$\nabla_x \ MIN(x,a) = 1 - u(x - a) \tag{3.6}$$

where u(x) is the Heaviside function defined as

$$u(x) = \begin{cases} = 1 & \text{if } x > 0 \\ = 0 & \text{if } x < 0 \end{cases}$$

(3.7)

the gradient can be calculated. Then, in order to obtain the best set of class centers, the following equations have to be solved

$$\nabla_j \varepsilon(I) = \sum_{x_i} \left[1 - u\left(\|x_i - C_j\|^2 - \underset{k \neq j}{MIN}\left(\|x_i - C_k\|^2 \right) \right) \right] (x_i - C_j) = 0$$

(3.8)

with j=0...F-1 .

This system of equations has several problems. It is not a linear system of equations, so iterative numerical methods have to be used to solve it. In order to compute C_j from (3.8) we have the following iterative rule

$$C_j = \frac{\sum_{x_i} \left[1 - u\left(\|x_i - C_j\|^2 - \underset{k \neq j}{MIN}\left(\|x_i - C_k\|^2 \right) \right) \right] x_i}{\sum_{x_i} \left[1 - u\left(\|x_i - C_j\|^2 - \underset{k \neq j}{MIN}\left(\|x_i - C_k\|^2 \right) \right) \right]}$$

(3.9)

This expression allows us to compute a new set of clusters $C_j{'}$ from the set C_j. This iterative process has to be repeated until the remaining error is below a fixed threshold or until the new set of centers do not present significative changes with respect to the preceding positions. It leads to the same solution as the k means algorithm. A diagram of this algorithm is shown in figure 1.

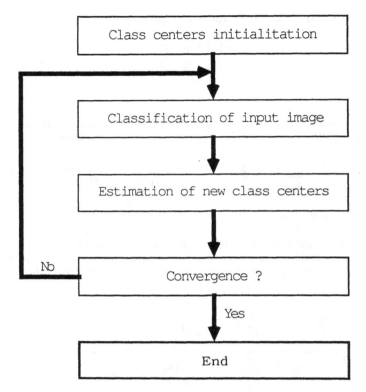

Figure. 1: Implementation of k-means algorithm

When initializing the iterations one should start from a set of centers initialized in an arbitrary point. Due to the fact that the initialitation has a great influence on the computational time needed in order to reach convergence, it is necessary to find methods of initialitation adequate for the image. There are also local minimums for the cost $\varepsilon(I)$, and the method converges to one or another minimum depending on the initial centers, which is another reason for using a good initial estimation of the centers.

4. BAYES CLASSIFIFERS AND AN APPROACH TO OPTIMUM LEARNING

There are several possible classifiers in the literature[1,4] based on the rule of minimal distance, depending on the metric that are convenient for each case of detection. As the previous classifier based on the euclidean minimum distance, there are other distances based on criteria of probabilistic decision.

These distances are based on assigning the pixel to the class to which it is more probable that it belongs, thus the decision rule is the following

$$x_i \in W_j \quad \text{if} \quad p\left(W_j / x_i\right) > p\left(W_k / x_i\right) \quad \forall k \neq j \tag{4.1}$$

if we suppose that the statistics of the classes is Gaussian, we get the following decision rule

$$x_i \in W_j \quad \text{if} \quad -\left(x_i - C_j\right)^t \sigma_j^{-2}\left(x_i - C_j\right) - \ln\left(\left|\sigma_j^2\right|\right) + \ln\left(p\left(w_j\right)\right) >$$

$$> -\left(x_i - C_k\right)^t \sigma_k^{-2}\left(x_i - C_k\right) - \ln\left(\left|\sigma_k^2\right|\right) + \ln\left(p\left(W_k\right)\right) \quad \forall k \neq j \tag{4.2}$$

One can think if there might be another algorithm, similar to the k-means algorithm, that were adequate for classifiers of this kind. In order to find this algorithm the same procedure as in the case of the k-means will be followed.

The probability that a pixel of the class W_j takes a value x_0, if Gaussian statistics is supposed, is

$$p\left(x_0 / W_j\right) = \frac{1}{\sqrt{2\pi\left|\sigma_j^2\right|}} e^{-\left(x_0 - C_j\right)^t \sigma_j^{-2}\left(x_0 - C_j\right)} \tag{4.3}$$

162

If the classes are supposed equally likely a priori, the probability that a pixel of an image takes the value x_0 will be the mean of the probabilities of each of the classes, that is

$$P(x_0) = \sum_j p(x_0/W_j)p(W_j) \propto \sum_j \frac{1}{\sqrt{2\pi|\sigma_j^2|}} e^{-(x_0-C_j)^t \sigma_j^{-2}(x_0-C_j)}$$

(4.4)

The same will be valid for a pixel x_1 in the neighbourhood of the previous one, with the additional hypothesis of the stationarity of the image. The probability of finding in an image I a set of N pixels of values $x_0 \dots x_{N-1}$, knowing that there are pixels that belong to the set of classes $W_0 \dots W_{F-1}$, will be denoted $p(I/W_0 \dots W_{F-1})$. If the statistics of $W_0 \dots W_{F-1}$ is Gaussian and the classes are a priori equiprobables, this probability takes the value

$$p(I/W_0 \dots W_{F-1}) = \prod_{x_i} p(x_i/W_0 \dots W_{F-1}) \alpha$$

$$\propto \prod_{x_i} \sum_j \frac{1}{\sqrt{2\pi|\sigma_j^2|}} e^{-(x_i-C_j)^t \sigma_j^{-2}(x_i-C_j)}$$

(4.5)

When the Bayes rule is used, the opposite concept can be calculated, i.e. the probability that a set of classes exists in an image where the pixels take the values $x_0 \dots x_{N-1}$

$$P(W_0 \dots W_{F-1}/I) = \frac{p(I/W_0 \dots W_{F-1})p(W_0) \dots p(W_{F-1})}{p(I)} =$$

$$= \frac{p(I/W_0 \dots W_{F-1})p_c^F}{p(I)}$$

(4.6)

which, from (4.5) is

$$p(W_0 \cdots W_{F-1} \mid I) \propto \prod_{x_i} \sum_j \frac{1}{\sqrt{2\pi \left| \sigma_j^2 \right|}} e^{-\left(x_i - C_j\right)^t \sigma_j^{-2} \left(x_i - C_j\right)}$$

(4.7)

The last expression gives a way of computing how good is the set of classes that has been found. An optimal system for a Bayes classifier, with the above hypothesis, will be the one that finds the classes and their centers such that the probability $p(W_0 \cdots W_{F-1} /I)$ is maximized.

In order to find the maximum of that probability, the gradient of that probability with relation to the components of each one of the centers should be computed, and set equal to 0. The following system of equations is obtained

$$\sum_{x_i} \frac{\dfrac{1}{\sqrt{2\pi \sigma_j^2}} e^{-\left(x_i - C_j\right)^t \sigma_j^{-2} \left(x_i - C_j\right)}}{\sum_{C_k} \dfrac{1}{\sqrt{2\pi \sigma_j^2}} e^{-\left(x_i - C_k\right)^t \sigma_j^{-2} \left(x_i - C_k\right)}} \left(x_i - C_j\right) = 0$$

with j = 0...F − 1

(4.8)

that can be written as:

$$\sum_{x_i} \frac{p(x_i; W_j)}{\sum_{W_k} p(x_i; W_k)} \left(x_i - C_j\right) = 0$$

(4.9)

where:

$$p(x_i; W_j) = \frac{1}{\sqrt{2\pi\sigma_j^2}} e^{-(x_i - c_j)^t \sigma_j^{-2}(x_i - c_j)}$$

(4.10)

To solve these equations, an iterative algorithm is used, based on the recurrent rule

$$c'_j = \frac{\sum_{x_i} \dfrac{p(x_i; W_j)}{\sum_{c_k} p(x_i; W_k)} x_i}{\sum_{x_i} \dfrac{p(x_i; W_j)}{\sum_{c_k} p(x_i; W_k)}} \quad \text{with} \quad j = 0 \dots F - 1$$

(4.11)

5. WEIGHTING FUNCTIONS

If the recurrent rules for the k-means algorithm and for the Bayes algorithm are compared, see (3.9) and (4.9), it can be noticed that in both cases the new center is computed as a weighted mean of the pixels of the image, xi, with weighting functions that tend to 1 when the pixel is very near the class j and to 0 when it is far from it. The meaning of near and far is related to the distance from the pixel to the class center and the distance to the rest of the class centers.

The selection of a good weighting functions or even the adequate approximations for the numerical computation, will have influence on the speed of convergence, because it has an influence on the cost of the computation of one iteration and on the number total of necessary iterations to the convergence. Also, this selection have influence in the quality of the final set of centers, because the weighting functions with big steps (as is the case of the Heaviside functions) have a greater tendency to fall on local minima than smooth functions (as the Gaussian).

6. OPTIMIZATION OF THE COMPUTING TIME OF THE K-MEANS ALGORITHM

As it can be seen from figure 1, the k-means algorithm is implemented by doing a serie of classifications of the image, which are based on the minimum euclidean distance. From these classifications, a new set of optimal class centers is computed. This set is more optimal in the sense that the classification cost is lower than with the initial set.

If the classifications are done using the decision rule of equation (2.3), then for each pixel the distance to each of the centers should be computed, as well as the class that gives the lower distance. This represents a hard cost in computing time.

In order to save some of this calculations, a rule derivated of equation 2.3 can be used

Before the classification, and for all class W_j, the class W_l that has the center nearest to the center of the class W_j is found

$$W_l \quad \text{such that} \quad \left\| C_l - C_j \right\| \leq \left\| C_j - C_k \right\| \quad \forall \; k \neq j, k \neq l \tag{6.1}$$

So, it is known (see figure 2) that if the pixel x_i is nearer to C_j than $\| C_l - C_j \| / 2$, then it will be assigned to the class W_j because, for definition of W_l, there will not be another center nearest to the pixel

$$x_i \in W_j \quad \text{if} \quad \left\| x_i - C_j \right\| \leq \frac{\left\| C_j - C_l \right\|}{2} \tag{6.2}$$

(sufficient condition but not necessary).

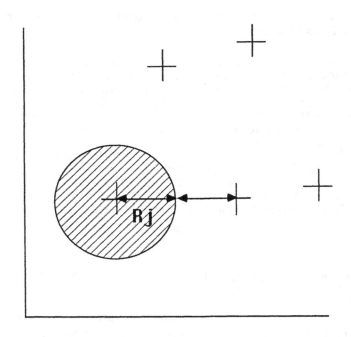

Secure decision zone

Figure 2: Distance threshold of a class

In this way with only the computation of one distance pixel-center, one can be sure that the pixel belongs to the class.

In order to implement the modification of the algorithm **3** one should do

1)For all the classes W_j compute which is the other class W_1 with the nearest center and save the threshold distance $R_j = | | C_1 - C_j | | /2$.

2)For all the pixels, do an hypothesis of the class to which it belongs. Then, compute the distance between this class and the pixel. If this distance is lower that the threshold, the point belongs to the class. If the distance is higher than the threshold, the usual decision rule should be used in order to find the class.

This implementation can be seen in figure 3.

167

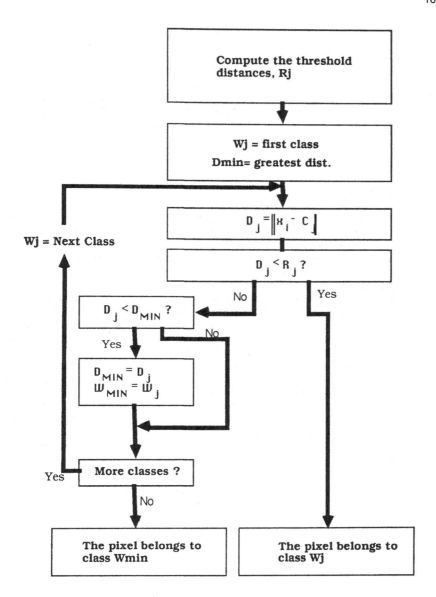

Figure 3: Optimizated implementation of the k-means algorithm.

An issue that appears is which is a priori the most probable class of a point. This depends on the additional information that is available. In a single classification, if the image is supposed to be more or less uniform, the most probable class is the class of the previous pixel in the image, and this class should be the first one used in the classification of pixel. In case of the successive classifications in an iterative algorithm, one can take as the most probable class for each pixel the class to which the pixel was assigned in the previous classification. It is supposed in this case that if the classification is done on the same image and with two sets of similar class centers, the majority of pixels will not change of class from one iteration to the following one.

7. RESULTS

The algorithms that we have described have been used on remote sensing applications of Landsat images, without supervision, which allows us to distinguish between the classes that due to the lack of continuity (rivers or other abrupt zones) would be difficult to mark by means of a supervised learning.

The optimization that we have described for the classifier of minimal distance gives a saving on the number of computations of distances necessary for the classification of images. This saving is greater on uniform images (as colour photographs) and in classifications that have been done during the learning stage, because the number of times that the correct class is guessed is higher.

The results which have been obtained for different experiments are shown in table 1. The type of images were different as well as the number of classes used in the classification, in the learning system or as a simple classifier. The ratio of improvement N.O. shows the number of computations (distance between pixel and class center) that have been necessary for the classification, compared always with the number of computations necessary for the same classification without the optimization of the algorithm. That is

$$\text{N.O} = \frac{\text{number of realized calculations}}{\text{number of calculations without optimization}} \qquad (7.1)$$

IMAGE TYPE	OPERATION	Centers	N.O.
LANDSAT	Classification	20	85%
LANDSAT	Classification	5	90%

TRANSFORMED LANDSAT	Classification	5	55%
PHOTOGRAPHY	Classification	5	40%
LANDSAT	Learning	20	75%
LANDSAT	Learning	5	45%
TRANSFORMED LANDSAT	Learning	5	50%
PHOTOGRAPHY	Learning	5	35%

Table 1 Optimization results.

It can be observed that the number of operations (with respect to the total number without optimization) decreases when the image is smoother (colour photograph or transformed image) or when o an iterative learning is done.

It has also been seen that the use of learning and classification with probabilistic measures of distance, compared with the use of euclidean distance, gives a substantial improvement in the results, so that the work previous to the extraction of characteristics and prepossessing can be reduced.

8. CONCLUSIONS

A formal deduction of k-means algorithm has been provided. It is shown, in preliminary results, that the extension of this algorithm to distances based on probabilistic concepts increase the quality of the obtained results.

On the other hand, an implementation of the k-means algorithm that saves a great amount of computational cost has been presented. This optimization saves a 30% of computations in Landsat images classification. Moreover, this optimized implementation can be easily modified in order to be used with other distance measurements.

9. REFERENCES

1. J.T. TOU and R. GONZALEZ, in *Pattern Recognition Principles*, Addison-Wesley.

2. J.A. RICHARDS, in *Remote Sensing Digital Image Analysis*, ed. Springer-Verlag.

3. E. VIDAL RUIZ, *An algorithm for finding nearest neighbours in (approximately) constant average time*, in Pattern Recognition Letters 4 (1986), p. 145-157.

4. K.S. FU, *Pattern recognition and machine learning*, ed. Plenum.

SPEECH RECOGNITION

FEATURE SELECTION IN SPEECH RECOGNITION

E. Lleida, C. Nadeu and J. B. Mariño

Department Signal Theory and Communications, U.P.C.
Apdo 30002, 08080 Barcelona, Spain

ABSTRACT

In this paper we investigate the use of a feature selection step in a isolated word recognition system. The feature selection step tries to model the correlation among adjacent feature vectors and the variability of the speech. Thus, the feature selection is performed in two steps. The first step takes into account the temporal correlation and redundancy among feature vectors in order to obtain a new set with a minimum number of feature vectors. The second step takes into account the frequency discrimination features which discriminate each word of the vocabulary from the others or a set of them. Thus, the new feature vectors are uncorrelated in time and discriminant in frequency. The result obtained in the recognition of the digit data base are reported.

1. Introduction

Most of the speech recognition systems make use of the pattern-matching approach for the classification of the recognition units, words, syllables, demisyllables, etc. The first step of this systems is the feature extraction procedure. LPC analysis has been successfully applied in speech recognition. Speech is known to be composed of stationary parts and transitions, and much of the perceptual information of the speech signal is concentrated around the transitions parts. Thus, it is interesting to introduce a feature selection step after the feature extraction to select the relevant information for the recognition process. In addition, the speech recognition systems based on pattern matching use dynamic programming

---

This work was supported by the PRONTIC grant number 105/88

174

methods for time alignment between two utterances. However, the computational expenditure grows proportionally to the square of the pattern length. Thus, it is interesting to introduce a compression step before the classification process,

The data compression and selection can be undertaken in the same process from two points of view; the temporal selection and the frequencial selection, related with the time dimension and the frequency dimension of the patterns [1]. Figure 1 shows a diagram of the selection process.

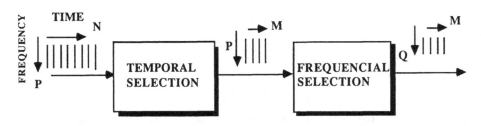

Figure 1. Two step feature selection procedure (M<N; Q<P)

A classical approach to data compression and selection is to remove those feature vectors which are similar. This techniques are based on the fact that the stationary segments of the speech signal are the most affected by variations on the speaking rate. Thus, a spectral (LPC vectors) sequence redistribution can be carried out exploiting the similarity among spectra belonging to stationary segments [2,3,4,5].

Another approach is to assume that there is an underlying set of "real" uncorrelated features, and the features we are working on are "impure" in the sense that they are a linear combination of those "real" features. Then, the objective is to find a transformation which recovers the "real" features [6].

These two approaches select the feature in the time dimension, that is, it is a temporal selection. Thus, the temporal selection obtains a new template where the feature vectors are uncorrelated or without temporal redundancy.

However, the temporal selection does not take into account the variability and separability among words. Thus, a frequencial selection step which reduces the within-class variability and increases the separability among words is needed [7,1]. In this case, taking the new feature vectors of the temporal selection, a transformation matrix associated with each vector of a word is sought. This is the second step proposed in our feature selection procedure which can be seen as a method for finding a specific distance for each feature vector.

To test the feature selection procedure, the recognition experiments were made using a data base consisting of ten repetitions of the Catalan digits {1 /u/,2 /dos/,3 /tres/,4 /kwatrə/,5 /siŋ/,6 /sis/,7 /sɛt/,8 /buit/,9 /nou/,0 /zɛru/ } uttered by six male and three female speakers (900 words) and recorded in a quiet room.

The organization of this paper is as follows. Section II describes the temporal selection procedure from two points of view, similarity and representation. Section III introduces the frequencial selection. Section IV describes the recognition experiments. Finally, section V contains the conclusions.

2. Feature selection in the time domain

The feature selection in the time domain (temporal selection) takes as starting point the study of the temporal evolution of the speech spectra. From this point of view, two criteria can be defined; the similarity criterion where the feature vectors are selected and compressed by means of a similarity measure and the representation criterion where the new set of feature vectors is obtained by means of a transformation matrix which removes the correlation among feature vectors.

2.1. Similarity Criterion

The temporal selection by means of the similarity criterion is based on the search of those feature vectors which keeping some constraints given by a cost function can represent a portion of the speech signal. Thus, in the feature extraction process, the speech signal is represented by means of a set of vectors corresponding to an uniform sampling of the temporal evolution of the spectrum. This evolution shows portions where there are a great similarity between spectra and portions where there are spectral changes. The former have redundant information and the later are transitory portions with a lot of information. Thus, it can be made a new sampling process, in the feature vector space, which selects a reduced set of feature vectors. This new sampling process is uniform in the similarity dimension which gives a non-uniform sampling in the time dimension depending on the similarity measure.

The non-uniform sampling will mark those feature vectors which exceed a threshold of dissimilitude. The new set of feature vectors could be built by those feature vectors which exceed the threshold or by a linear interpolation of the closest vectors to the sampling point or by an average of the feature vectors between two sampling point.

These selection methods can be classified in two groups: variable length methods and fixed length methods [4]. If we want the same number of feature vectors for all the words, a fixed length method must be select. However, if the length is not a constraint, a variable length method can be selected.

2.1.1. Cost Function

The cost function tells us the additional cost or information increase provided by a feature vector with regard to others. The distance measure between vectors could be a measure of similarity. Thus, a cumulative distance D_n is defined among the n-th spectral vector and the "S" previous ones [8]

$$D_n = \frac{\sum_{i=1}^{S} w(i) d^r(n, n-i)}{\sum_{i=1}^{S} w(i)} \tag{1}$$

where D_n is interpreted as the innovation of the n-th vector with regard to the "S" previous ones weighted the temporal difference between vectors by a window $(w(i) = \beta^{i-1})$. $d^r(n, n-i)$ is the distance measure between the n-th vector and the n-i th vector, and its definition depends of the features (Euclidean distance, Itakura distance, etc.). The exponent r controls the non-uniform degree of the sampling process. For r equal to 0 the sampling process is uniform, as r is greater than 0 the gradient get steeper in the transitions between sounds. In this way, the cost function or sampling function is defined as the sum of the cumulative distances of each vector, defining a trace

$$J(N) = \sum_{n=1}^{N} D_n \tag{2}$$

The cost function is a increase monotony function. Its gradient is depending of the spectral changes or information increase. Great gradients point out a great information change, soft gradients point out redundancy.

2.1.2. Variable Length Selection

This methodology makes a sampling of the feature vectors keeping fixed the threshold of dissimilitude (ϕ_0) for all words. Thus, the number of new feature vectors depends on the select threshold and the spectral changes of the utterances. If the utterance has N feature vectors, the sampling points are obtained as follow:

```
j=1;øj = ø0;
For i=1 to N
        Compute J(i);
        if J(i) > øj then
                sampling point = i; j=j+1; øj= ø0 * j
        Endif
EndFor
```

This methodology can be applied in real time at the same time that the extraction procedure gives a feature vector.

2.1.3. Fixed Length Selection

This methodology keeps fixed the number of feature vectors for all utterances. From the sampling point of view, this means that the number of sampling points is the same for all utterances. In this way, the dissimilitude threshold is variable with the utterance. Once, the final cost or trace is found, the sampling space is divided in M-1 portions of equal similitude, being M the number of new feature vectors. Thus, if N is the number of feature vectors obtained in the feature extraction process, the sampling period is given by

$$\theta = \frac{\text{final cost}}{M\text{-}1} = \frac{J(N)}{M\text{-}1} \qquad (3)$$

This methodology needs to have all the feature vectors before starting the process.

In our experiments, the new set of feature vectors is obtained by means of a linear interpolation of the two closest vectors to the sampling point, independently of the method, fixed or variable length. Figure 2 shows an example of the feature selection by the fixed length method of an utterance of the word /zeru/.

2.2. Representation Criterion

The similarity criterion obtains a new set of feature vectors based on the idea of removing redundancy. However, the purpose of the representation criterion is to obtain a time compression by removing the

178

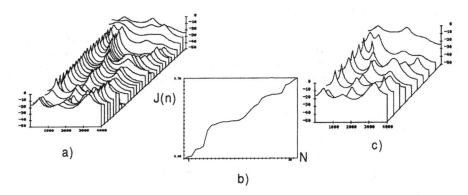

Figure 2. a) spectral sequence of an utterance of the word /zɛru/. b) cost function for this utterance. c) new spectral sequence selected by the fixed length method with M=10.

correlation of the temporal evolution of the spectrum. Basically, the problem is to represent the sequence of spectra by a linear combination of the members of an orthogonal family of functions so the template is represented with less coefficients.

Given a NxP matrix Y of spectral parameters $\{y_i(n)\}$ representing N frames of P "impure" features, the transformation obeys the following formulation

$$y_i(n) = \sum_{m=1}^{N} \alpha_m(i)\phi_m(n) \qquad 1 \leq i \leq P \; ; \; 1 \leq n \leq N \qquad (4)$$

where $\alpha_m(i)$ is the mth "real" feature vector and $\phi_m(n)$ is the mth transformation function of the transformation matrix $\{T\}$.

There are two classes of transformation functions:

1- Data independent transformation functions. The transformation functions are members of a deterministic family of orthogonal functions as the Discrete Cosine Transform (DCT).

2- Data dependent transformation functions. The transformation functions are found from the data using a criteria of minimum square error. The error of representing $y_i(n)$ with M "real" feature vectors is defining as follows

$$\varepsilon = E\{(\underline{y}_i - \underline{\hat{y}}_i)(\underline{y}_i - \underline{\hat{y}}_i)^t\} \tag{5}$$

where $\underline{\hat{y}}_i = \sum_{m=1}^{M} \alpha_m(i)\phi_m(n)$ is the estimation of the"impure" feature vectors with M "real"

feature vectors. As the transformation functions have the constraint of orthogonality, the transformation functions are found solving the eigensystem

$$C_{yy}\phi_m = \lambda_m\phi_m \tag{6}$$

where C_{yy} is the covariance matrix defined as

$$C_{yy} = \frac{1}{P-1}\sum_{i=1}^{P} (\underline{y}_i - \underline{\bar{y}})(\underline{y}_i - \underline{\bar{y}})^t \tag{7}$$

with

$$\underline{\bar{y}} = \frac{1}{P} \sum_{i=1}^{P} \underline{y}_i \tag{8}$$

and $\underline{y}_i = \{y_i(1), y_i(2), \ldots\ldots, y_i(N)\}$ is the temporal vector of the i-th spectral component.

From this eigensystem, N eigenvalues and their corresponding eigenvectors are obtained. However, only the M eigenvectors with the largest eigenvalues are retained. Thus, the transformation matrix {T} is composed by the M eigenvectors with the M largest eigenvalues, ranking them from the largest to the smallest one. Because of the orthogonal property of the transformation functions, the new "real" feature vectors are computed as a linear combination of the "impure" feature vectors as follows [9]

$$\alpha_m(i) = \sum_{n=1}^{N} y_i(n)\phi_m(n) \qquad 1 \le i \le P \; ; \; 1 \le m \le M \tag{9}$$

which is known as the Karhunen-Loève transform (KLT). Then, the new coefficients α_m have information about the interdependency among the feature vectors. The first eigenvector represents the temporal trajectory of the spectrum with the largest variance, the second one represents the best temporal trajectory which can be obtained if the first eigenvector information is removed from the covariance matrix. As the eigenvalue decreases, the associated eigenvector carries information of the small variation of the temporal trajectory of the spectrum.

The main properties of the new representation are:

-Coefficients with largest variances are the "real" features.

-The new "real" features are uncorrelated.

-Feature vectors are arranged in variance order, thus, no time-alignment is needed in the comparison step.

The transformation matrix is computed in the training process. We distinguish two cases:

1- General matrix. A transformation matrix T_g for all the words of the vocabulary. In this case, the covariance matrix C_{yy} is obtained averaging the covariance matrix of each training word.

2- Specific matrix. A transformation matrix T_w for each word of the vocabulary. Then, a covariance matrix C_{yy} is obtained for each word using several repetitions. In the recognition process, the test template is transformed by every specific matrix.

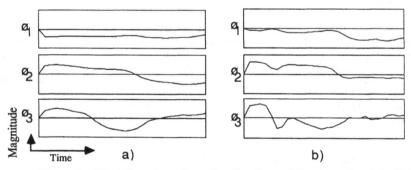

Figure 3. a)First three transformation functions of the general matrix (T_g). b)First three transformation functions of the specific matrix of the word /sɛt/ ($T_{/sɛt/}$).

Figure 3 shows the evolution of the first three transformation functions for the general matrix of the digit data base (a) and for the

181

specific matrix (b) of the word /dos/. The speech signal was analyzed by an LPC processor and 8 Log-Area ratios were extracted in each frame. First of all, note that the functions of the general matrix have a temporal evolution similar to the DCT which is due to the average process done to obtain the covariance matrix. With regard to the specific matrix, the transformation functions describe the temporal trajectory of the Log-Area ratios. Note for example that for the word /dos/, which is composed by two voiced sounds followed by an unvoiced sound, the first eigenvector of the specific matrix carries information of the unvoiced sound /s/, the second one about the voiced sounds /d//o/ and the third one about the transitions in the sound /do/. Thus, the first new feature vector will be a linear combination of the features of the /s/ sound, the second of the /d//o/ sound and the third of the transitions in /do/. This separation in the transformation functions between voice and unvoice sounds shows the high uncorrelation between both sounds.

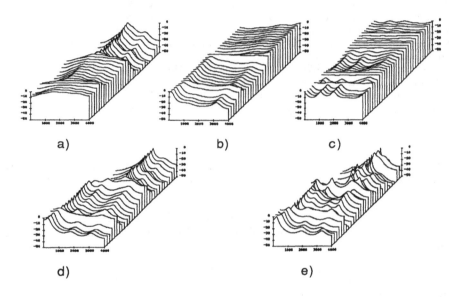

Figure 4. Spectral sequences for the word /dos/. a) Spectral sequence of the first eigenvector. b) idem of the second eigenvector. c) idem of the third eigenvector. d) idem with the first three eigenvectors. e) Original spectral sequence.

Figure 4 shows these effects in the spectral sequence (impure features) estimated with the first three eigenvectors of /dos/ and their corresponding "real" features. When a word has only voiced sounds, the first eigenvector is an average of the temporal evolution of the first Log-Area coefficient. Thus, its associated feature vector is a weighted average of all the word sounds. The second eigenvector which represents the best temporal trajectory that can be obtained if the first eigenvector information is removed, begins to capture the dynamic aspect of the temporal evolution of the features vectors. Thus, the transformation matrix of the digit data base carries more than 95 % of the variance information with only three eigenvectors.

3. Feature selection in the frequency domain

The second step of the feature selection process is to compute a transformation matrix for each new feature vector obtained in the temporal selection in order to discriminate between words. The temporal selection step does not take into account the discriminant properties of the feature vectors. Thus, after the temporal selection, a frequencial selection step is proposed to obtain a set of discriminant features. This step can be seen as a method for finding a specific distance measure for each reference vector. This frequencial selection takes into account the discriminant properties of the feature vectors which reduces the within-class variability and increases the separability among feature vectors. Thus, the frequencial selection step is related with the comparison step. Defining the weighted Euclidean distance between the test vector α_i and the reference vector α_j as

$$d(i,j) = \| F_j (\alpha_i - \alpha_j) \|^2 \qquad (10)$$

a transformation matrix or specific distance matrix $F_j = \{fd_1, fd_2, ..., fd_Q\}$ of Q weighting vectors for each reference vector of each word has to be computed.

In order to find the discriminant matrix F_j, two classes of vectors are defined. For a word 'w', the mth feature vector of any utterance of it forms the correct class (α_{ce}) and the mth feature vector of the other words forms the incorrect class (α_i). Thus, defining the mean interclass distance as the mean distance between the incorrect class vectors and the mean correct class (α_c) feature vector

$$E(D_{inter}) = E(\| F_c (\alpha_i - \alpha_c) \|^2) \qquad (11)$$

where α_c is mean vector of the correct class, and taking into account the matrix relation

$$\|a\|^2 = tr(a\ a^t) \qquad (12)$$

we can rewrite Eq.11 as

$$E(D_{inter}) = tr(F_c \ E((\alpha_i-\alpha_c)(\alpha_i-\alpha_c)^t)F_c^t)) \qquad (13)$$

defining the between-class mean distance matrix as

$$B = E((\alpha_i-\alpha_c)(\alpha_i-\alpha_c)^t) \qquad (14)$$

the mean interclass distance is as follow

$$E(D_{inter}) = tr \ (F_c \ B \ F_c^t) \qquad (15)$$

In order to take into account the within-class variability a mean intraclass distance is defined as

$$E(D_{intra}) = tr \ (F_c \ W \ F_c^t) \qquad (16)$$

where

$$W = E((\alpha_{ce} - \alpha_c)(\alpha_{ce} - \alpha_c)^t) \qquad (17)$$

In this way, the criterion function to be maximized is [1,10]

$$J = tr(fd_k \ B \ fd_k^t) - \lambda(tr(fd_k \ W \ fd_k^t) -1) \qquad (18)$$

The solution of this optimization problem is the eigensystem

$$(W^{-1}B)fd_k = \lambda_k fd_k \qquad (19)$$

Therefore, the specific distance matrix is formed by the Q eigenvectors with the Q largest eigenvalues of $W^{-1}B$, whenever

$$E(D_{inter}) = \sum_{k=1}^{Q} \lambda_k \ >> \ Q = E(D_{intra}) \qquad (20)$$

The discriminant properties can be found in the matrix $W^{-1}B$ because

$$tr(W^{-1}B) = \sum_{k=1}^{P} \lambda_k \qquad (21)$$

This process is made for each reference vector of each word of the vocabulary. In the training process, a mean vector (α_c) for each feature vector is computed and used as reference to compute the within-class and between-class mean distance matrices as well as reference vector for the recognition process. In order to take the best discriminant functions, the number Q of eigenvectors can be adapted to each word or can be fixed and equal to each word. A high eigenvalue indicates a good discrimination property for this feature. Table 1 shows the eigenvalues when M is equal to 3 for the word /dos/. It can be seen how the first three eigenvectors have good discrimination properties. Therefore the word /dos/ can be represented by three vectors of three features.

Q \ M	1	2	3
1	18.63	115.11	18.62
2	9.7	8.01	11.41
3	7.23	7.1	3.45
4	4.81	3.9	2.86
5	2.38	2.5	1.37
6	1.97	1.63	1.02
7	0.7	0.8	0.87
8	0.6	0.5	0.55

Table 1. Eigenvalues of the matrix $W^{-1}B$ for the first three uncorrelated vectors of the word /dos/.

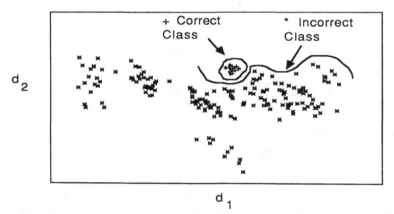

Figure 5. Projection of the first feature vector of several words using the first two discriminant eigenvectors of the word /dos/ (correct class).

Figure 5 shows the projection of the first feature vector of the digits using the first two discriminant eigenvectors of the word /dos/. Note that the variance of the correct class (templates of the word /dos/) is very small with regard to the variance of the incorrect class. Thus, using the mean vectors of the correct class as reference in the recognition process, the probability of confusion among classes and them the recognition error would decrease.

4. Results

For feature extraction, the speech signal was sampled at 8 KHz, preemphasized ($H(z)=1-0.95z^{-1}$) and 8 Log-Area ratios were computed each 15 ms using the LPC analysis of 30 ms. A typical Hamming smoothing window was applied to the data.

The first set of experiments shows the performance of the temporal selection by the similarity and representation criterion. The experiments were made in a dependent speaker approach. Figure 6 shows the results using the similarity criterion with the fixed length method for different values of length and different degrees of non-uniform sampling (r). The experiments were made using a dynamic programming algorithm for time alignment. We want to point up that the same experiments with a variable length method gives worst results [1].

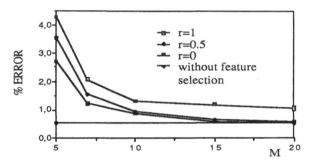

Figure 6. Results for the fixed length method (similarity criterion)

Figure 7 shows the results obtained using the representation criterion with a general matrix. In this case, after the LPC analysis, the templates were normalized to a fixed number N of frames, with N equal to 30. The experiments were made without time alignment, and the minimum error were obtained for M equal to 3, that is, each word is represented by only 3 feature vectors of 8 parameters. The same experiments with a specific matrix gives similar results with an increase of the computational cost. Figure 8 shows the evidence distribution for M equal to 3 defined as Ev=(D2-D1)100/D1, where D2 is the distance to the second candidate and D1 is the distance to the first candidate. The mean value of the evidence distribution is around 80 % which is a higher value than the values obtained with the similarity criterion that are around 40 %.

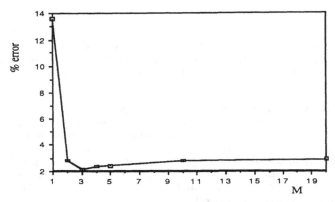

Figure 7. Results for representation criterion with general matrix

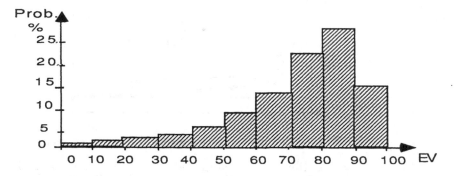

Figure 8. Distribution evidence for M equal to 3 and general matrix

The next set of experiments were made by using the two step feature selection process by means of a representation criterion for temporal selection and the frequencial selection step. A classical pattern recognition system which compares an input template with a set of reference templates by means of a linear frame to frame comparison was used. The references were constituted by a mean feature template obtained in the training process and two sets of transformation matrices. One set is used for temporal selection and the other set is for frequencial selection.

We present two experiments. The first one is a multispeaker experiment. Six repetitions of the nine speakers digit data base are used as training. Figure 9 shows the recognition results obtained for different values of M and Q using both temporal transformation matrices T_g (general matrix) and T_w (specific matrix). For the best result, 0.22% of error rate with M=3, Q=2 (only 6 features per word) and T_g, the mean evidence is 85,4 % showing the good discrimination properties of this feature selection process. Note that the specific matrix, which is the best representation of each word, does not improve the recognition performance of the general matrix. The improvement in the representation is compensated by a degradation in the comparison step.

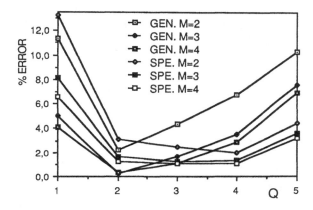

Figure 9. Error rate for several values of M and Q.

In order to have significant results, ten recognition experiments were made taking in each recognition experiment a training set with six different repetitions (multispeaker experiment). In this way, all the data base was used as test. In this experiment M and Q were fixed and equal to 3 and 2 respectively and the T_g matrix was used for temporal selection. Table 2 shows the confusion matrix of this experiment. The worst results are obtained by the word /trɛs/,/u/ and /siŋ/. Nevertheless, the error rate is small, 1.19 % for utterances out of the training set and 0.26 % for utterances inside the training set. An experiment with only the temporal selection step shows a deterioration of the recognition rate to 7 % showing the need of improving this step.

Recognized Word

	0	1	2	3	4	5	6	7	8	9
0	893					4				3
1		888						2		10
2			900							
3		10		885			5			
4					900					
5	8					884		8		
6							900			
7						3	3	894		
8			1						889	
9										900

Total error: 57 (14 (0.22%) within and 43 (1.19%) out of the training set)
mean evidence: 85.4 %

Table 2. Confusion matrix for the multispeaker experiment.

The second experiment is a speaker independent experiment. In this case, the training set is made up by ten repetitions of six speakers of the digit data base, using three speakers for testing. Table 3 shows the results for three different versions: a) classical independent system with a clustering process, DTW and 240 features per reference (N=30, P=8), b) only temporal selection step with 24 features per reference (M=3, P=8) and c) temporal and frequencial selection steps with 9 features per reference (M=3, Q=3). This figure also shows the computational load in number of multiplications per recognized word. It may be noted that the best result is obtained using the two step feature selection process which both increases the recognition rate and decreases the number of features and the computational load.

5. Conclusions

A study of different criteria for feature selection in speech recognition has been presented. This feature selection procedure transform an input template to a new representation in which either the redundancy

		% error	evidence	# references per word	# features per word	computational load
a)	Classical system	2.00	45 %	2	480	48000
b)	Temporal selection	3.00	54 %	1	24	1000
c)	Two steps selection	1.66	77 %	1	9	1500

Table 3. Results for the speaker independent experiments

is removed by means of a similarity criterion or the correlation among vectors is removed by means of the idea of the Karhunen-Loève transform, and the variability and separability among words is taken into account using the idea of discriminant analysis in a frequencial selection step. The best results with a great data compression rate and small computational load is obtained using a representation criterion with a general matrix and the frequencial selection step. As a result, the new template has the feature vectors arranged in variance order; therefore, no time-alignment is needed in the comparison step and each reference vector has associated a specific distance measure which selects the discriminant features.

6. References

1. E.Lleida, *Compresión y Selección de Información en Reconocimiento Automático del Habla*, Ph.D. thesis (in Spanish), Dpto. Teoría de la Señal y Comunicaciones, U.P.C. (1990) 292.
2. R.Pieraccini,R.Billi, *Experimental comparison among data compression techniques in IWR*, Proc. ICASSP-83, 22.2, (Boston 1983).
3. M.H.Kuhn,H.Tomaschewski, *Improvements in IWR*, IEEE. Trans. on ASSP vol-31, pp 157-167, (1983).
4. J.L. Gauvain, J. Mariani, J.S. Lienard, *On the use of time compression for word-based recognition*, Proc. ICASSP-83, pp. 1029-1032, (1983).
5. E.Lleida,C.Nadeu,E.Monte,J.B.Mariño, *Statistical feature selection for isolated word recognition*, Proc. ICASSP-90, (Albuquerque 1990).
6. E. Lleida, C. Nadeu, J.B. Mariño, *Feature selection through orthogonal expansion in isolated word recognition*, MELECON-89, pp. 253-256, (Lisbon 1989).

190

7. E.L.Bocchieri,G.R.Doddington, *Frame-specific statistical feature for speaker independent speech recognition*, IEEE trans. on ASSP, vol 34, (1986).

8. E. Lleida,C. Nadeu, J.B. Mariño, *Speech parametrization and recognition using block and recursive linear prediction with data compression*, European Conference on Speech Technology, pp. 300-303, (Edinburgh 1987).

9. J.J. Gerbrands, *On the relationships between SVD,KLT and PCA*, Pattern Recognition, vol 14, pp. 375-381, (1981)

10. K. Fukunaga, *Introduction to Statistical Pattern Recognition*, Academic Press, (1972).

ISOLATED WORD RECOGNITION BASED ON MULTILAYER PERCEPTRONS*

F. Casacuberta   M. J. Castro[†]
Departamento Sistemas Informáticos y Computación
Universidad Politécnica de Valencia, Valencia, Spain

and

C. Puchol
The University of Texas at Austin, USA

ABSTRACT

Multilayer Perceptrons are a class of artificial neural networks that have been used with success in automatic speech recognition tasks. However, these networks do not adequately represent the temporal variability of the speech signal. In order to overcome this drawback, conventional solutions require high amounts of computational resources. To reduce these requirements, an adequate modelization of time is necessary. Alternatively for some specific tasks, the use of Trace Segmentation can allow for design of a pattern compression interface between the speech signal and the Multilayer Perceptron. This type of interface can transform variable length utterances to fixed length ones.

In order to study this technique, several experiments were carried out with easy and difficult isolated word recognition tasks. Experimental results are reported, achieving a reduction of the computational costs with an increase in the recognition performance in front of the conventional application of Multilayer Perceptron even when Hidden Markov Models are used for the same task.

1. Introduction

Artificial neural networks constitute a promising approach to many problems that appear in automatic speech recognition. Different architectures have been applied with success, but for specific tasks such as Isolated Word Recognition (IWR), Multilayer Perceptrons (MLPs) have been the most widely used during the last few years[1,2,3]. The success of these particular networks comes from the existence of powerful training algorithms from speech utterances, the most important one being the Back-Error Propagation algorithm[4].

* This work has been partially supported by CICYT, under contract TIC-0048/89 and by ESPRIT (BRA) under contract 3279 (ACCOR).
† Supported by a postgraduate grant from Conselleria Cultura, Educació i Ciència of Valencia.

The main problem of the application of MLPs to IWR is that the temporal nature of the speech signal is not adequately represented. While the utterances are of variable length, the number of input units of a conventional MLP is fixed a priori. The first straightforward solution to this problem is to fix the size of the input layer to a value large enough to accept the longest utterance. In this approach, when the utterance is shorter than the input layer, the utterance is filled up with silences. The problem with this solution is the high amount of computational resources that are required. Other solutions consist of fixing the size of the input layer to a given value, and the utterances are expanded or compressed by using linear interpolation[5,6] or dynamic warping[7]. In the proposal that appears in previous works[5,6] the computational costs can be further reduced by using a particular architecture of MLP that is called Scaly Networks. Another interesting technique is Trace Segmentation (TS) that is based on pattern compression using only acoustic properties of the speech signal. TS was originally introduced for the application of Dynamic Time Warping to speaker-dependent IWR[8,9,10,11]. In the last one[11] this technique was used together with MLP for a speaker-independent Italian digit task with limited success.

In this paper exhaustive experiments are presented to explore the capability of the TS to adequately modelize temporal and acoustic features of the speech signal to be used with MLPs and the reduction of the computational costs produced by these techniques is also studied. The corpora used in these experiments correspond to a speaker-independent IWR from easy and difficult vocabularies. Important reductions of computational requirements are achieved in these experiments without degradation in the recognition performance.

2. Trace Segmentation

TS is essentially accomplished by uniformly sampling the trajectory of an utterance in the parametric space of representation (i.e. Cepstral coefficients). This technique allows for the compression or the expansion of an utterance to a fixed number of frames. At the same time it allows for the representation of non-stationary portions of the speech signal with more frames than in the original representation and permits the representation of the stationary ones with less frames. In the rest of this section, a detailed description of TS is presented.

An utterance can be represented by a sequence of N vectors (trace) in the C-dimensional feature space

$$(x_1, x_2, \ldots\ldots, x_N), \quad x_i \in \mathfrak{R}^C, \ 1 \leq i \leq N$$

where C is the number of features used for every frame, and N depends on each utterance.

The main idea is to represent each utterance by M vectors belonging to its trace, in the C-dimensional feature space.

$$(y_1, y_2, \ldots\ldots, y_M), \quad y_i \in \Re^C, \; 1 \le i \le M$$

The TS algorithm performs a subdivision of the trace into $(M$-$1)$ segments of equal length uniformly spaced along the trace itself. Then, the boundaries of such segments are used as the representative pattern vectors of the utterance. For this purpose, the total length $\mathcal{D}$ of the trace in the sequence x is computed as follows:

$$\mathcal{D} = \sum_{i=1}^{N-1} d(x_i, x_{i+1})$$

where d is the Euclidean distance between each pair of consecutive points of the trace. Then, the trace can be divided into $(M$-$1)$ segments of length $L = \mathcal{D} \, / \, (M$-$1)$ using linear interpolation between time consecutive points such as $y_1 = x_1$, $y_M = x_N$, and every intermediate point y_k is chosen such that the distance in the trace from y_i to y_{i+1} is L.

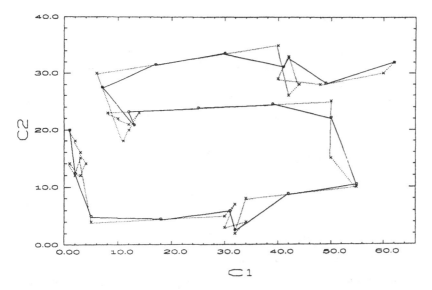

Figure I. An artificial example of the use of the TS technique. The dotted line indicates the trace of an imaginary utterance in the feature space C1-C2. The grouped points correspond to stationary segments, and the rest of the points correspond to transitional segments. The solid line denotes the result of the TS technique.

As an effect of the TS, a better allocation of the points along the trace itself is obtained and, if M<N, a reduction of frame number is obtained (see Figure I for an artificial example). In general, stationary parts of the signal, where the information is redundant, are compressed because the distance between two consecutive frames along the trace is small, while transitional portions of speech, which are represented as long segments over the trace, are maintained or even additional points can be added.

3. Application of the Multilayer Perceptron to Isolated Word Recognition tasks

A MLP is a directed multistage graph $G=(V,E)$, where V is the set of nodes or units that is partitioned into $K \geq 2$ disjoint sets V_i, $1 \leq i \leq K$, and E is the set of edges such that, if $(u,v) \in E$, then $u \in V_i$ and $v \in V_{i+1}$, $1 \leq i < K$. There is also a weight function over the set of edges, $\omega: E \to \Re$ (synaptic connection strengths). The set V_1 is known as input layer, the set V_K as output layer, and the rest of sets V_i, $2 \leq i \leq K-1$, are called hidden layers.

To each unit $v \in V_i$, $i \neq 1$, a procedure is associated to compute an output value S_v

$$S_v = f\left(\sum_{u \in V_{i-1}} \omega(u,v) S_u \right)$$

where f is the activation function that is typically a sigmoid function[4], and $S_u = x_u$ for $u \in V_1$, where x_u is the value of the input unit u. The threshold of each unit is modelized as a weight with an input set to a constant value 1.

A MLP defines a function $F_{MLP}: \Re^{|V_1|} \to [0,1]^{|V_K|}$, and the most important problem of this technique can be established as follows. Given a set of M supervised samples

$$A = \left\{ (x,t) \mid x \in \Re^{|V_1|} \text{ and } t \in [0,1]^{|V_K|} \right\}$$

search a weighted function $\omega: E \to \Re$ that minimizes some criterion function of F_{MLP} and A. Typically, this criterion function is the mean squared error at the output layer:

$$E = \frac{1}{2M} \sum_{(x,t) \in A} \sum_{v \in V_K} (t_v - S_v(x))^2$$

where $S_v(x)$ is the value of the v output node for a stimulus input x.

The Back-error Propagation algorithm[4] is a step-descendant algorithm that allows us to find a local minima of E. In this algorithm a set of input samples are feed-forward propagated through a MLP. For each input pattern, the resulting output value is compared with the corresponding target, and the error is calculated. The weights are then adjusted proportionally to the back propagation of the error. For practical considerations see[4].

The application of MLPs to IWR tasks consists of defining an output layer with a number of units equal to the size of the vocabulary. Let $W(u)$ be the word associated to

$u \in V_K$, the classification of an utterance x is performed according to the following rule:
x is $W(\underset{u \in V_K}{\mathrm{argmax}} S_u(x))$.

Since the length of an uttered word is variable, in the simplest implementation the size of the input layer must be enough to process the largest utterance. For shorter words this layer must be filled up with silences. Under this condition, too many weights from the input layer to the first hidden layer must be processed, and this fact can be an important inconvenience from a computational complexity point of view. A strategy to reduce the amount of these weights is to let the number of input nodes be constant, and the input pattern is time-normalized either by linear expansion or by linear compression to fit the input layer. However, some preliminary experiments showed the inadequacy of this approach[12]. A second approach consists of applying the TS technique that was presented in section 2. In this case the MLP is conventional, but the input pattern is non-linearly expanded or compressed to a fixed number of input nodes.

4. Experiments and Results

In this section we present exhaustive experiments demonstrating the use of the TS with MLP in two IWR tasks. The topology of the MLP used for our experiments is simple, the network has a different number of units in the input and hidden layer, depending on the experiment, and for the output layer one unit for each class that must be discriminated.

4.1. Corpora

Two corpora were used for the experiments that are reported in section 4.2. The first one corresponds to an easy IWR task, the Spanish Digits (DIG) composed by the following ten words: /θero/, /uno/, /dos/, /tres/, /kuatro/, /θinko/, /seis/, /siete/, /oʧo/, /nueβe/. The speech data consisted of 10 repetitions of the ten Spanish digits, which were uttered by ten speakers (five male and five female) in a laboratory environment. This makes a total of 1000 utterances. Each speaker uttered this data in two or more sessions which spread over a period ranging from one day to one month. The acquisition and end-point detection procedures were rather standard and the signal was sampled at 8533 Hz. The acquired speech data were transformed into sequences of 10-dimensional parameter vectors of Cepstrum coefficients which were obtained from a 10 channel Mel frequency scale filter bank plus the energy at a rate of 66.66 vectors per second. This representation was used for the experiments with MLP. This speech data was converted into a string of codeword symbols by using a vector quantization procedure with a codebook of 15 entries. For comparative purposes, this representation was used for experiments with discrete Hidden Markov Models (HMM). The utterances range in duration from 22 to 50 frames.

The second corpora is not an easy task: the Spanish E-Set (SES). This dictionary corresponds to the most confusable subset from the Spanish alphabet, and was composed by the following nine words: /efe/, /ele/, /eλe/, /eme/, /ene/, /eɲe/, /ere/, /ere/, /ese/. The speech data consisted of 10 repetitions of these nine Spanish E-Set which were uttered by ten different speakers (five males and five females). This makes a total of 900 utterances. The acquisition and parametrization of these utterances were similar to the first corpus with two differences: the Cepstrum coefficients were obtained at a rate of 133.33 vectors per second, and for the symbolic representation, the codebook has 32 entries. The utterances range in duration from 38 to 108 frames.

4.2. Experiments

Two series of experiments were made, one series for the DIG corpus, and the other for the SES corpus. In both cases, the speech data were partitioned according to the "Leaving-One-Out" technique, and five partitions were made. In each one, ten repetitions of the vocabulary uttered by eight speakers were used as the training set, and the rest of the corpus (ten repetitions by two speakers, one male and one female) were used as the test set. With these partitions, 1000 utterances are obtained as the global test set for the corpus DIG, and 900 utterances for the corpus of the SES, and the effective training set was 800 and 720 utterances, for the two corpora, respectively. The learning factor ρ, the momentum rate α, the error threshold for the convergence ε and the number of iterations were fixed through some previous experiments to $\rho = 0.1$, $\alpha = 0.4$ and $\varepsilon = 0.003$ (SES), and $\rho = 0.3$, $\alpha = 0.5$ and $\varepsilon = 0.003$ (DIG) that are reported elsewhere[12]. The convergence criterion in all the experiments was either an error threshold of 0.003 for both corpora or a pre-defined number of epochs, whichever fired first. The error threshold was not actually fired, presumably due to larger differences in pronunciation among the speakers and the minimal differences in the vocabulary (SES). The number of epochs allowed to run each experiment was 2000 for the E-Set word patterns and 1000 for the Digits. This criterion has turned out to give good results and to prevent over-training.

The series of experiments for the DIG corpus was composed of four experiments. In the first experiments (1.1 and 1.2), we used discrete HMM for comparative purposes and correspond to the best results that had been obtained in our laboratory with 8 and 30 states, respectively[13]. The network used for the rest of experiments was a fully-connected network with 10 units in the hidden layer and 10 units in the output layer, one unit for each word-category to discriminate. The number of input units depends on the experiment. First, in experiment 1.3, the utterances were centered over the input layer, and the number of input units was fixed to 275 (25 frames x 11 parameters), that is the average length of the utterances that were used to train. In experiment 1.4 the TS strategy was used to feed the input layer, reducing the number of input units to 110 (10 frames x 11 parameters). The different parameters of the experiments performed with the DIG corpus are given below:

Exp 1.1: The model was discrete HMM of 8 states with skip transitions. The number of model parameters was 1400 (20 for transitions and 120 for symbols by each model). The number of training iterations of the Baum-Welch algorithm was 10.

Exp 1.2: Similar to Exp 1.1, but the number of states was fixed to 30. The number of parameters of the models was 5400 (90 for transitions and 450 for symbols by each model).

Exp 1.3: The model was a MLP with 275 input nodes (25 frames x 11 parameters), 20 hidden nodes and 10 output nodes. The number of parameters of the model (connecting links) was 5730, and the number of training iterations of the Back-Error Propagation algorithm was 1000. The input patterns were centered to the input layer and filled with silences if the length of the input pattern was shorter than the number of input nodes.

Exp 1.4: Similar to Exp 1.3, but the number of input nodes was fixed to 110 (10 frames x 11 parameters). The number of connecting links was 2430. TS was used to fit the input pattern to the input layer.

The experiments for the SES corpus were composed of five experiments. As in the first corpus, the first experiment 2.1 corresponds to the best result with discrete HMM that had been achieved in our laboratory with 20 states. In following experiments, the architecture of the MLP is similar to the one used in experiments with the DIG corpus. The hidden layer has 20 units and the output layer has 9 units (nine words in the E-Set). In the experiment with centered samples (experiment 2.2), the input layer has 550 units (50 frames x 11 parameters), that is smaller than the average length of the utterances, but because the discriminate information of the SES words is in their middle part, we could use less input units. After this experiment with MLP, TS was used (experiments 2.3 to 2.5) varying the number of input nodes (10x11, 20x11, and 30x11 input units). As above, there is a list of the experiments performed with the SES corpus with their parameters:

Exp 2.1: The model was discrete HMM of 20 states with skip transitions. The number of model parameters was 6111 (39 for transitions and 640 for of symbols by each model). The number of iterations of the Baum-Welch algorithm was 10.

Exp 2.2: The model was MLP with 550 input nodes, 20 hidden nodes and 9 output nodes (50 frames x 11 parameters). The number of connecting links was 11209, and the number of iterations of the Back-Error Propagation algorithm was 2000. The input patterns were centered to the input layer and filled with silences if the length of the input pattern was shorter than the the number of input nodes, and deleted the initial and final parts if the length of the input pattern was greater than the number of input nodes.

Exp 2.3: Similar to Exp 2.2, but the number of input nodes was fixed to 110 (10 frames x 11 parameters). The number of connecting links was 2409. TS was used to fit the input pattern to the input layer.

Exp 2.4: Similar to Exp 2.3, but the number of input nodes was fixed to 220 (20 frames x 11 parameters). The number of connecting links was 4609.

Exp 2.5: Similar to Exp 2.3, but the number of input nodes was fixed to 330 (30 frames x 11 parameters). The number of connecting links was 6809.

4.3. Results

The results of the experiments described in section 4.2 are grouped into tables according to the class of experiment. Table 1 depicts the results obtained for the DIG corpus from experiments 1.1 to 1.4.

Table 1: Results of the experiments with the DIG corpus (Number of Errors by partition and % Recognition Rate in total).

Exp	Model	P 1	P 2	P 3	P 4	P 5	%Rec.
1.1	HMM with 8 states	6	4	1	1	1	98.70
1.2	HMM with 30 states	0	0	0	0	2	99.80
1.3	MLP-Centered with 25x11 input units	0	4	0	10	2	98.40
1.4	MLP-TS with 10x11 input units	1	1	0	0	0	99.80

The results of these experiments show that MLP with TS presents a higher recognition rate than conventional MLP, and equivalent to HMM.

The following table deals only with the SES corpus. In table 2, the results of Hidden Markov Models, conventional MLP and the application of the TS with different numbers of input nodes are compared.

Table 2: Results of the experiments with the SES corpus and TS (Number of Errors by partition and % Recognition Rate in total).

Exp	Model	P 1	P 2	P 3	P 4	P 5	%Rec.
2.1	HMM with 20 states	41	39	44	58	43	75.00
2.2	MLP-Centered with 50x11 input units	30	35	50	27	35	80.34
2.3	MLP-TS with 10x11 input units	32	40	46	33	48	77.89
2.4	MLP-TS with 20x11 input units	30	27	34	33	38	82.00
2.5	MLP-TS with 30x11 input units	42	29	44	30	46	78.56

The results of these experiments show that MLP with TS presents a higher recognition rate than conventional MLP or even higher than HMM.

5. Conclusions

Two series of experiments demonstrating the use of MLP in IWR tasks are presented in this paper. The main goal of these experiments was to reduce the computational costs which are associated with the learning and recognition processes in MLP without a degradation of the performance. The second goal was to represent the temporal nature of the speech in the static classification approach of MLP. TS is the technique that has been used to achieve both goals. A third goal was the study of the adequacy of the MLP for two different Spanish speaker-independent IWR tasks. The easiest task was with the Spanish Digits (DIG), and the other one was with the most confusable subset from the Spanish alphabet: the E-set (SES).

From all these experiments, the main conclusions are: 1) For an easy task, such as DIG, the use of TS reduces the computational costs 60% with an increase of 1.4% in the recognition rate with respect to the conventional use of MLP. The same performance is achieved with HMM of 30 states with almost the same number of parameters as the conventional MLP. The performance of HMM with 8 states is significantly worse although the number of parameters to learn is very low. 2) For the difficult task (SES), the use of TS reduces the computational cost almost 60% with an increase of 2% in performance with respect to the conventional MLP, and a reduction of 25% in the number of parameters with respect to the HMM technique with 20 states, but with an increase of 9.3% in the recognition rate. These results correspond to the best results obtained by varying the number of input nodes.

We can conclude that TS is an important technique for obtaining significant reduction in the computational costs with MLP, and also offers some improvements in the recognition rate due to a better representation of the temporal nature of speech than in the conventional approach.

6. References

1. R. P. Lippmann (1989). Review of Neural Networks for Speech Recognition. *Neural Computation*, **1**. pp. 1-38.
2. Burr (1988). Experiments on Neural Net Recognition of Spoken and Written Text. *IEEE Trans. on ASSP*, **36** (7). pp. 1162-1168.
3. S. M. Peeling and R. K. Moore (1988). Isolated Digit Recognition Experiments using the Multi-Layer Perceptron. *Speech Communication*, **7**. pp. 403-409.
4. D. E. Rumelhart, G. E. Hinton and R. J. Williams (1986). Learning Internal Representations by Error Propagation. In *Parallel Distributed Processing: Explorations in the Microstructure of Cognition*. Rumelhart, D. E. and McClelland, J. L. (Eds.). Cambridge, MA: MIT Press. pp. 318-362.

5. H. Hackbarth and M. Immendörfer (1990). Speaker-Dependent Isolated Word Recognition by Artificial Neural Networks. *Verba 90*. pp. 91-98.

6. A. Krause and H. Hackbarth (1989). Scaly Artificial Neural Networks for Speaker-Independent Recognition of Isolated Words. *ICASSP 89*. pp. 21-24.

7. H. Sakoe, R. Isotani, K. Yoshida, K. Iso and T. Watanabe (1989). Speaker-Independent Word Recognition using Dynamic Programming Neural Networks. *IEEE Int. Conference on ASSP*. pp. 29-32.

8. M. H. Kuhn and H. H. Tomaschewski (1983). Improvements in Isolated Word Recognition. *IEEE Trans. on ASSP*, **31** (1). pp. 157-167.

9. R. Pieraccini and R. Billi (1983). Experimental Comparison among Data Compression Techniques in Isolated Word Recognition. *ICASSP 83*, Boston. pp. 1025-1028.

10. R. Pieraccini (1984). Pattern Compression in Isolated Word Recognition. *Signal Processing*, **7** (1). pp. 1-15.

11. P. Demichelis, L. Fissore, P. Laface, G. Micca and E. Piccolo (1989). On the Use of Neural Networks for Speaker Independent Isolated Word Recognition. *ICASSP 89*. pp. 314-317.

12. C. Puchol and F. Casacuberta (1990). Reconocimiento de Palabras Aisladas mediante Redes Neuronales. *IV Simposium Nacional de Reconocimiento de Formas y Análisis de Imágenes*, Granada. pp. 127-134.

13. F. Casacuberta (1991). Modelos de Markov Ocultos y Reconocimiento de Palabras Aisladas. *Universidad Politécnica de Valencia*. DSIC-II/2/91.

ON THE IMPROVEMENT OF THE HIDDEN MARKOV MODELS TRAINING FOR SPEECH RECOGNITION

A. Bonafonte, E. Lleida, J. B. Mariño, E. Monte
A. Moreno, A. Nevot and M. Vall-llosera

Department Signal Theory and Communications
Universidad Poltécnica de Cataluña, Barcelona, Spain

ABSTRACT

This paper describes three kinds of techniques that improve the training of the Hidden Markov Models (HMM) applied to speech recognition. First, the representation of the signal by means of regressive parameters is studied. Then, a comparative study of different methods of smoothing the observation probabilities is presented. These techniques are shown to have a great importance when the number of samples to infer the model is small. Afterwards, an algorithm that improves the discrimination ability of the HMM's is proposed. This method has been called corrective training algorithm. It updates the HMM's out of a list of confusable words which has previously been built. Some results are presented so that the importance of each method can be evaluated.

1.- Introduction

In the last decades, with the development of the digital signal processing theory and of systems which can treat digital information, some tasks, as automatic pattern recognition, considered exclusive of the human being have been faced from this perspective. This impulse in pattern recognition was reinforced in the case of speech recognition, by the North American ARPA SUR project at the beginning of the seventies.

A pattern recognition system has two different stages: learning and classifying stages. There is a previous one present either in the learning or in the classifying stages which is the selection of signal features. In some cases, the chosen parameters are the values of the signal itself with a slight preprocessing such as a noise filtering. This process is much more complex in speech because it should eliminate its great redundancy. Only the information useful for recognition should be preserved.

The desired features of a parameterization stage are:

* Discrimination: with a proper mesure, the cost between two parameter vectors should be related with the subjective similarity of the represented sounds.

* Representation efficiency: a great compactation of the information is desired.

* Computational efficiency: the cost in time of the previous stage cannot be too high because the cost of the whole process would be prohibitive.

The learning system can be implemented in two different ways. In the first one, the designer has enough knowledge of the patterns in order to give a set of rules to identify each one. This method has been adopted by most of the vision systems. In speech recognition, the so called phonetic classifiers are derived from this idea. However, this method is hard or impossible to apply either because it is not perfectly known how our mind works in recognising patterns, or because the number of patterns to be recognised is too high. It would be desirable to have an automatic method to train the recognition system. The designer proposes a parametric model for each pattern to be recognised and the system estimates the value of the parameters according to a training set which is a group of samples of each one of the classes to be recognised. In speech recognition the patterns are the phonetic units (word, phoneme, triphoneme...) and the samples are the different utterances of the units.

The first intuitive idea is to choose as model the parameters of a sample. When recognising, the test parameters are compared with the model ones and the recogniser assigns to the test the class whose model gives minimum cost. In speech, this idea derived in the well-known method of template matching. In this method, a dynamic programming algorithm is needed to adapt the duration of the test and the reference templates.

A difficulty appears when 1) a great variability of the items belonging to a class exists and 2) the similarity of the different classes is considerable. Then, the parameters of a particular sample are not significant enough. This is the case of speech where the same phonetic unit is different depending on the speaker, intonation, stress... A solution adopted is to collect a pattern book for each class. The items of the books are selected from a set of samples by means of a clustering process so that they represent well the whole class. Note that the more complete the book is, the more storage capacity and computational time are required.

A more elaborated solution is to propose a general model where the parameters can be adapted to represent a particular class. When a greater number of samples of a class is available, a better estimation of the parameters can be accomplished. Nevertheless, the number of parameters remains fixed. One of the most extended models to recognise speech is the Hidden Markov Model (HMM)[14]. A HMM is composed of two interrelated mechanisms: 1) An underlying Markov chain having a finite number of states and 2) a probability density function (pdf) associated with each state. This paper deals with the discrete version were the characteristic vectors are vector quantified so that a finite (and small) number of labels are the possible inputs to the model. The pdf is a discrete one: its values are the probabilities of observing the different labels from the state. Although there is not an analytic method to estimate the best parameters of the model to represent the training set, Baum proposed an iterating algorithm, a maximum likelihood approach, that has been proved to converge. The use of this kind of models has yielded systems that work fairly well[2,7]. However, to model the great variability of speech, these models need a slightly high number of parameters, therefore, a large amount of samples are required in the learning to obtain a reliable estimation. When such number of samples is not available, there exist techniques to infer the model from a small training set. Such techniques are known as smoothing of the observation probabilities and are based on the criterion that two "similar" samples should have similar acceptation by the models. The use of these methods are indispensable when the models cannot be trained enough.

The goal of either the Baum algorithm or the smoothing techniques is that each model should represent correctly its own class. However, in recognition applications, it is more desirable to have model discrimination than model representation. It is not enough that a model characterises all the elements of its class but it should also be able to reject samples of the other classes. There is not a method for incorporating negative samples to the training, nevertheless corrective training can be used in order to increase the model discrimination.

In this chapter, we are going to present some experiences related with the commented topics in the field of automatic speech recognition. The different techniques have been tested either in a continuous or in an isolated speech application. Section 2 is devoted to a method that makes more profit of any parameterization. Different techniques of smoothing the probabilities of a HMM are presented in the section 3. In 4, a corrective training algorithm is proposed. Afterwards some results are presented and the improvements are discussed. At last some conclusions about the performance of the methods are drawn out.

2.- On the Use of Regressive Parameters

The classical treatment of the speech before obtaining the features is as follows: the signal is filtered by an antialiasing low-pass filter and sampled; then the signal is isolated by and end-point algorithm; afterwards it is segmented into frames which have a duration of about 20-30 ms, because in this interval speech is considered being stationary; a window is applied so that spectral distortion is minimised and finally the spectrum is estimated. The most extended estimation method is AR spectral estimate, closely related to linear prediction coding. The distance chosen depends on the representation of the spectrum: the Itakura-Saito measure is suitable to quantify the similarity between vectors of the predictor coefficients while the euclidean distance is appropriated when a cepstral representation is adopted[5]. Some researchers transform these coefficients according to non-uniform scales related to perceptive models[16]. Others look for parameters and distances robust to noise[10,11]. The purpose of this section is not to study the different parameterization methods but 1) see how not only the instantaneous parameters but also their derivative are useful to the recognition process and 2) show how the use of the energy difference improves the recognition results.

In order to calculate the first derivative of the cepstral coefficients, some results coming from numerical series analysis are needed. The first order finite difference is intrinsically noisy[4]. A simple method is to consider an odd number of values to calculate the line that better fits the points (linear regression) and to assign its slope to the derivative of the central point. Naming $c_1(1) \ldots c_m(n)$ to the n cepstral coefficients of the m-th frame, the derivative of the coefficient $c_m(k)$ can be approximated as

$$c'_m(k) = \frac{\sum_{L}^{i=-L} i\, c_{m-i}(k)}{\sum_{L}^{i=-L} i^2} \tag{1}$$

Although the use of the frame energy has improved the results of some isolated speech recognition systems, some difficulties have appeared with continuous speech. The cause of these difficulties is the absence of a proper normalisation. Such normalisation is needed because obviously, the information does not depend on factors as the microphone closeness, the amplifier gain or the loudness of the utterance. In isolated words each utterance is scaled to the maximum of the word, but the extension to continuous speech is not trivial because the intensity of phonetic units can vary depending on their situation on the sentences. A dynamic normalisation has been tried out where the energy is normalised according to a window whose length is the mean duration of the phonetic units, but the results have not been quite satisfactory. The use of the energy derivative eliminate the normalisation need because the additive constants do not affect to the differences; note that the energy is considered in decibels due to the logarithmic response of the human ear. Thus, the energy difference is estimated as in the cepstral case

$$E'_m = \frac{\sum\limits_{L}^{i=-L} i\, c_{m-i}}{\sum\limits_{L}^{i=-L} i^2} \qquad (2)$$

The information per rate has been drastically increased. Before we had a n-feature vector while now a 2n+1-feature vector is considered. However, a disadvantage exists because of the vector quantization. Discrete HMM's use a finite (and small) number of labels or symbols. Then, vector quantization is used to assign a label to each input vector. If the vector size is increased while the number of symbols remains fixed, the quantization error becomes relevant. Nevertheless, an increment of the number of labels is not always possible because the number of HMM parameters is approximately proportional to that of labels, and therefore, to the needed training. In fig. 1 a qualitative curve of the quantization error and the uncertainty of parameters estimation are shown as a function of the codebook size. It is expected that the optimum VQ size will be on the neighbourhood of the crossing point of the two curves.

As the vector size increases, the distortion introduced by the codebook is higher and the optimum VQ dimension has more distortion and more uncertainty in the estimation.

If the simplifying hypothesis of independence between cepstrum, cepstrum derivative and energy difference is accepted, and a generalised HMM is adopted so that three symbols can be observed each time, three codebooks can be used. Then, the codebook distortion does not increase, and although the model has triple number of parameters, the uncertainty is the same because three labels are obtained of each frame. The prize to pay is that more memory is required to storage these parameters, and the computational cost to calculate how a model fits a test signal also increases.

Fig. 2 shows the block diagram to obtain the observation vector, which is a previous step to train the model or to recognising the test signal.

206

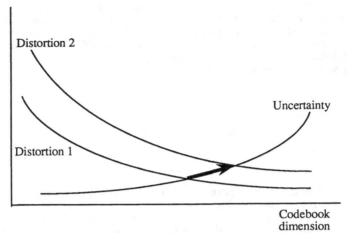

Fig. 1 Vector distortion and uncertainty in the estimation as a function of the codebook dimension.

3.- Smoothing Techniques

In the recent years, HMM modeling of the speech has advanced considerably. However, a common drawback of these systems is the need of a large amount of training data. Usually, a sufficient amount of training data is not available, so the estimation of the HMM parameters is not reliable. One of the most popular solutions to the problem of the undertraining is the smoothing techniques. In these techniques, the probability of an unobserved spectrum is estimated by means of the probability of those observed spectra which have same "relation" with the unobserved spectrum. The definition of this relation makes the difference between the set of smoothing techniques.

The common element of the smoothing techniques is the smoothing matrix T. In discrete HMM, each state 's' has a discrete probability density function (pdf) associated which gives the probability that a symbol (spectrum) k_i will be observed in this state. In fact three pdf coexist in each state to represent the cepstrum and the derivative of the spectrum and of the power. However, due to the independence assumption, no loss of generality occur considering a simple observation per frame. The pdf can be written as a vector

$$P_o(s) = [p(k_1/s), p(k_2/s),.......,p(k_N/s)] \qquad (3)$$

being
   k_i : label i
   s   : state to which the pdf $P_o(s)$ is associated
   N : number of labels

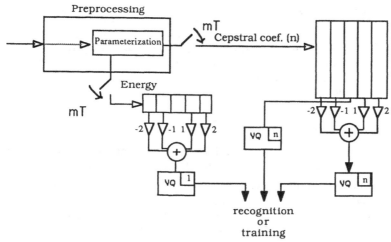

Fig. 2. Block diagram showing how the observation vector is obtained.

Supposing that all the observable spectra are related to each other, this relation could be expressed as a conditional probability $p(k_j/k_i)$ of observe the symbol k_j assuming that the symbol k_i has been observed. Thus, the elements of the smoothing matrix T are defined as

$$T_{ij} = p[k_j/k_i] \qquad (4)$$

The new smoothed observation probability vector is obtained as

$$P_{sm}(s) = P_o(s) * T \qquad (5)$$

The estimation of the smoothing matrix gives the difference between the smoothing techniques. We have divided the techniques by means of two criteria: the distance criterion and the mutual-ocurrence criterion. We have tried three methods for estimating the smoothing matrix by means of the distance criterion and two methods for the mutual-ocurrence criterion.

208

3.1. Distance Criterion

This criterion establishes the smoothing matrix using the similarity between pairs of symbols (codewords of the codebook).

Parzen Method:

Parzen estimation assumes that the true probability density varies slowly in space[15]. Thus, symbols that are close according to some distance measure should also have similar probability densities. The Parzen estimation defines a window function which is used for interpolation, with each symbol contributing to the estimate in accordance with its distance from the symbol to be estimated[3]. Proposed by Schwartz[15], we have tried the window function defined as

$$e^{-(d^2/\sigma^2)\alpha} \tag{6}$$

Thus, starting from a distance matrix with the distance between each pair of symbols, the distance is replaced by the window function value α controls the shape of the window. If α is 1, the window si proportional to a Gaussian window. As α becomes greater than 1, the window becomes flatter, and as a becomes less than 1, the window becomes more pointed. The last step is to normalise each row of the matrix so that the sum of the probabilities equals 1.

Mutual distance method

This technique, proposed by Sugawara et al[17], is a simplification of the Parzen method. Thus, given a symbol k_i which probability has to be estimated, the nearest n symbols are selected. Let the k-th nearest symbol be $n_i(k)$ $0 \le k \le n$. Then, the smoothing matrix is computed according to a given window function $f(k)$

If $j=n_i(k)$ then $T_{ij}= f(k)$

otherwise $T_{ij}=0$ \tag{7}

Suggested by Sugawara et al., we set n=5, f(0)=0.9 and f(k)=0.02 for $1 \le k \le 5$.

Correlation method

This method computes the elements of the smoothing matrix using directly the correlation between pairs of symbols. Thus, the T_{ij} element of the smoothing matrix is computed as

$$T_{ij} = \frac{k_i\, k_j}{|k_i|\, |k_j|} \qquad (8)$$

where k_n represent the codeword associated to symbol k_n.
Afterwards, the rows of the matrix are normalised so that the sum of each row equals 1.

3.2. Mutual-occurrence Criterion

This criterion establishes the relation between symbols as a function of its probability of occurrence at similar contexts. If the occurrence of a symbol k_i in a word is frequently accompanied by the occurrence of another symbol k_j, then, there is a high probability of mutual-ocurrence between both symbols and it must be expressed by a high value of the element T_{ij} of the smoothing matrix. The different between methods is in the measure of the mutual-occurrence.

Correspondence method

This method, proposed by Sugawara et al[17], estimate the probabilities counting the number of times that two symbols are aligned against each other in dynamic programming (DP) matching between utterances of the same word. The process is as follow

For each word do
    For each pair of utterances do
        Align the utterances using DP matching
        Accumulate the number of occurrences of label pairs along the optimum path
    End
End
Normalise the number of occurrences of label pairs to get the elements of the smoothing matrix:

$$T_{ij} = \frac{T_{ij}}{\sum_j T_{ij}} \qquad (9)$$

Co-ocurrence method

This method, proposed by K.F. Lee et al[8], measures the likelihood that two symbols will occur in similar context. Thus, the co-occurrence probability of symbol i given symbol j is defined as

210

$$T_{ij} = P(k_i / k_j) = \frac{\sum\limits_{p=1}^{NP} \sum\limits_{s=1}^{NS(p)} p(k_i/p,s)p(k_j/p,s)p(s)p(p)}{\sum\limits_{n=1}^{NC} \sum\limits_{p=1}^{NP} \sum\limits_{s=1}^{NS(p)} p(k_n/p,s)p(k_j/p,s)p(s)p(p)} \qquad (10)$$

where NP is the number of recognition units, NS(p) is the number of states for the recognition unit 'p', NC is the number of codewords in the codebook, and $p(k_i/p,s)$ is the output probability of codeword k_i for state s in the recognition unit p.

Combining Models

Usually, the smoothed pdf may be too smoothed and give poor results. Therefore, the smoothed pdf is combined with the original pdf by means of a linear combination[15]:

$$P_{Final}(s) = w(s) P_0(s) + (1-w(s))P_{sm}(s) \qquad (11)$$

There are different ways of computing w(s). Schwartz et al[15] proposes to compute w(s) as a function of the number of training tokens ($N_T(s)$) of the model

$$w(s) = \min [0.99, 0.5\log_{10}N_T(s)] \qquad (12)$$

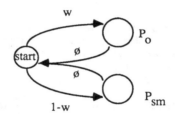

Fig. 3. Interpretation of deleted interpolation algorithm with a model with of states. There is a probability w of going from the starting state to the state corresponding to the original pdf, an a null transition from the original pdf to the starting state. Idem with a probability of 1-w for the smoothed pdf.

Another way of computing w(s) is by means of the deleted interpolation algorithm[6]. In this case, the weight is independent of the state (w(s)=w). Figure 3 shows an interpretation of the combination process as a Markov model. Therefore, the weight w can be computed as the transition probabilities in the Baum-Welch algorithm.

Deleted interpolation algorithm can be used for combining smoothed pdfs by different methods to get a new smoothed pdf.

$$P_{Final}(s) = \beta_1 P_{sm1}(s) + \beta_2 P_{sm2}(s) + ... + \beta_N P_{smN}(s) \qquad (13)$$

Each weight β_i is found by the recursive estimation algorithm

$$\beta_i^{n+1} = \frac{1}{K} \sum_{k=1}^{K} \frac{\beta_i^n \, p(O^k/SM_i)}{\sum_{j=1}^{N} \beta_j^n \, p(O^k/SM_j)} \qquad (14)$$

where K is the number of utterances used for the deleted interpolation estimation, β_i^n is the value of the weight in the n-th step and $p(O^k/SM_i)$ is the probability that the k-th utterance were produced by the i-th smoothed model.

4.- The Corrective Training of HMM

One of the problems when training the HMM is that the criterion for the training is the maximisation of the likelihood of one model. Nevertheless, that is not the best criteria, because during the recognition phase, several models will be evaluated in parallel. Thus, a much better training scheme would be to maximise the probability of one model while simultaneously minimising the probability of all the others.

Several techniques have been proposed in order to implement a discriminative training like the MMI[13] and the Corrective Training[1,9,18]. We propose the use of the Corrective Training in order to obtain more robust models. In this method all the models are first trained by means of the maximum likelihood estimation, and then several recognitions are made in order to obtain a list of acoustically confusable words based on recognition mistakes and near misses (i.e.: the probabilities of the recognised word and the first best are very similar). Once one has this list, the model of the word that has been mistaken or has been a near miss is modified in order to lower the probability that this word generates a mistake (or another near miss) and increase the probability of the word that is mistaken by another. When this modification has been done, another list of acoustically confusable words is obtained and the processes is repeated until there are no more mistakes or there is no improvement. This method was proposed for recognising isolated words. Another method was proposed for connected word recognition[8], where the list of acoustically confusable units were obtained by means of DTW. In this section we are going to discuss only the corrective training when doing the recognition of isolated words.

4.1. The Algorithm

The algorithm that we are going to present perform the corrective training on the probability of emission matrix, and on the transition matrix. While Merialdo[13] aplied the corrective training algorithm only on the emission matrix, our method also allows the training of the transition matrix in a straight forward manner.

First of all we will define two magnitudes: $\gamma_t(i)$ and $\xi_t(i,j)$ which are:

$$\gamma_t(i) = P(q_t = s_i \,/\, O, \lambda) \qquad (15)$$

This is, the probability of being at the state s_i at the moment t given the observation O and the model λ. The other magnitude is the following:

$$\xi_t(i,j) = P(q_t = s_i, q_{t+1} = s_j \,/\, O, \lambda) \qquad (16)$$

which is the probability of being at the state s_i at the moment t and doing a transition to the state s_j at the moment $t+1$ given the observation O and the model λ.

There is a relationship between the two magnitudes which is that the sum of all the possible transitions from i is the probability $\gamma_t(i)$: (note that N is the number of states of the model):

$$\gamma_t(i) = \sum_{j=1}^{N} \xi_t(i,j) \qquad (17)$$

Once we have these two magnitudes, one can find the expression of the probabilities of emission of observations and of transition between states.

The probability of transition from the state i to the state j will be:

$$a_{i,j} = \frac{\displaystyle\sum_{t=1}^{T-1} \xi_t(i,j)}{\displaystyle\sum_{j=1}^{T-1} \gamma_t(i)} \qquad (18)$$

and the probability of emission of the symbol **k** at the state **j** is the following:

$$p[k/s_j] = \frac{\sum\limits_{\substack{t=1 \\ \text{if emission=k}}}^{T-1} \gamma_t\,(i,j)}{\sum\limits_{j=1}^{T-1} \gamma_t(i)} \tag{19}$$

The last two magnitudes can be calculated by means of another variable which we will call $c_{i,j}{}^w\,(k)$. It represent the relative joint frequency of observing the symbol **k** at state **i** just before of making a transition to state **j** for the word **w** (which is the model which we want to train). This variable can be computed as follows:

$$c_{i,j}{}^w\,(k) = \sum\limits_{\substack{t=1 \\ \text{if emission=k}}}^{T} \xi_t\,(i,j) \tag{20}$$

The variable $c_{i,j}{}^w\,(k)$ can be seen as a count and is used in order to update the probabilities defined in Eq. 18 and Eq. 19:

$$a_{i,j} = \frac{\sum\limits_{k} c_{i,j}{}^w\,(k)}{\sum\limits_{i}\sum\limits_{j}\sum\limits_{k} c_{i,j}{}^w(k)} \tag{21}$$

$$p[k/s_j] = \frac{\sum\limits_{i} c_{i,j}{}^w\,(k)}{\sum\limits_{k}\sum\limits_{j} c_{i,j}{}^w\,(k)} \tag{22}$$

The corrective training will be done on the variables $c_{i,j}{}^w\,(k)$ because they are related with the frequency of observation of the symbol **k** when training the model. A correction on this variable as a consequence of a mistake will supply additional information that is not found when training. The lack of training information might generate a biass on the values of the model that might cause some of the mistakes. The discriminative nature of this method rises from the fact that the correction on the variable **c** is done when a mistake or near miss is found. If the cost of recognising an utterance **O** is similar or greater using the correct model **w** than using another model ω then

$c_{i,j}^{w}(k)$: probabilities calculated using the model w and symbols **O**, and

$c_{i,j}^{\omega}(k)$: probabilities calculated using the model ω and symbols **O**
are estimated and the following equations are applied:

For the correct model **w**:

$$\bar{c}_{i,j}^{\mathbf{w}}(k) = c_{i,j}^{\mathbf{w}}(k) + \alpha\,(\,c_{i,j}^{w}(k) - c_{i,j}^{\omega}(k)) \tag{23}$$

For the model where a mistake has been done ω:

$$\bar{c}_{i,j}^{\omega}(k) = c_{i,j}^{\omega}(k) + \alpha\,(\,c_{i,j}^{\omega}(k) - c_{i,j}^{w}(k)) \tag{24}$$

The variable α is a positive constant lower than one which is decremented at each iteration of the corrective training. Therefore, each time a list of confusable words is obtained decreases the perturbation introduced in the emission and transition probabilities.

5.-Experimental Results

Two applications have been selected to test the validity of the above methods:

1) Recognition of the Spanish numbers from zero to one thousand. Our system has been called RAMSES, which is the Spanish acronym for "automatic recognition by means of demisyllables". A description of the system can be found in[12].

2) Recognition of the Catalan digits with an isolated speech version of RAMSES.

For both applications, the data base consisted of ten speakers: four women and six men.

5.1. Use of regressive features

In figure 4 we show a preliminary experiment on isolated word recognition done on a multi-speaker basis. In this experiment it is shown that the use of the differential parameters improves the recognition rate. This results encouraged us to do more ambitious experiments, such as is the case of continuous speech recognition.

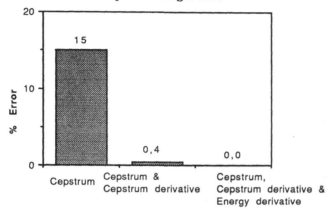

Fig. 4. Results with the different informations for the task of the catalan digits recognition.

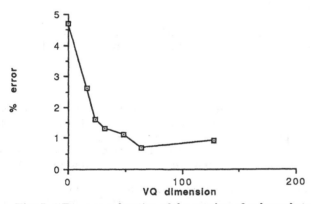

Fig. 5. %Error as a function of the number of codewords to quantify the information of cepstrum derivative. The number used to quantify the cepstrum remains fixed and equals 64 codewords.

In figure 5 we show the improvement that is obtained by introducing the cepstral variation. We compare the recognition results for different dimensions of the codebook used to quantify this information (the dimension of the cepstral codebook is held constant and equal to 64). It can be seen that as we improve the quantification, the recognition rate increases.

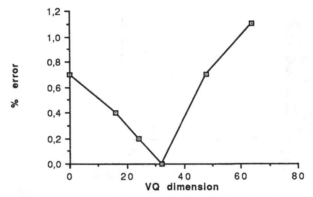

Fig. 6. %Error as function of the number of codewords to quantify the energy information. The number used to quantify either the cepstrum or the cepstrum derivative is 64 codewords.

The effect of the quantification of the energy derivative can be seen on figure 6, here due to the fact that the energy is represented by means of only one coefficient, the quantification error is lower. As it was commented on section II, the curve has one minima which is located for 32 codebooks. As it could be expected this minima is lower than in the case of differential cepstrum.

5.2. Use of smoothing techniques

In order to test the properties of the smoothing algorithms, some of the experiments that have been devised consisted on training poorly the models (only one sample for each speaker), then doing the smoothing of the observation probabilities, and finally doing the recognition experiment on a multi-speaker environment. Only spectral information has been used.

Figure 7 compares the recognition rate of several smoothing techniques, with and without using deleted interpolation. The smoothing techniques improve the recognition rate on all cases.Note that the mutual-ocurrence methods usually work better than the distance criteria although their computational cost is greater. To combine the original and smoothed models also improve the accuracy but note that additional data is needed to estimate the ponderation factor.

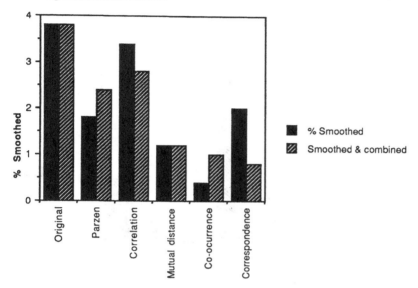

Fig. 7. Results with the different techniques to smooth HMM's in the application of isolated speech.

If the models are not so poorly trained mutual-occurrence methods should be applied. This can be observed in figure 8 where the models are trained with eight speakers in order to recognise the continuous speech application. This allows us to study how these techniques work in a speaker independent situation where regressive features were used. The error rate of the speakers who did not train the system is 3.3, when the models are smoothed by the co-occurrence algorithm. This is and significant improvement when compared with the original models which give a 6.0 score. It should be noted that the distance methods, in particular the correlation one, only in situations where the data base is very small should be used.

5.3. Use of corrective training algorithm

As the goal of this algorithm is to improve the recognition rate in a task of isolated speech, it seems suitable to the digits application. Nine speakers have trained the HMM's. The corrective training has been accomplished with the utterances of the same speakers. The other one has been used to test the system. To illustrate the convergence of the algorithm we have plot (fig. 9) the error rate versus the iteration number. Note how the method converge not only for the speakers who have trained the system but also for the speaker that is not in the training database. The final value is well below the initial one.

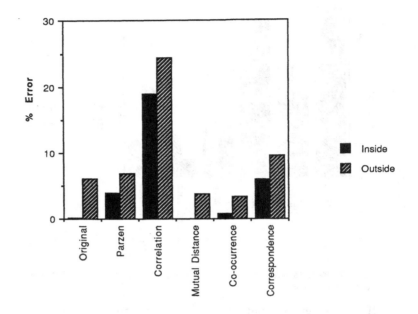

Fig. 8. Results with the different techniques to smooth HMM's in the application.of continuous speech.

Being the error so low, we have performed an "artificial" experiment consisting in recognising the demisyllables of the continuous speech application in an isolated way. This has been possible because the date base has been hand segmented and labeled. The results shown in fig. 10 are similar to the obtained in the previous experiment. We have to say that although the models recognise better the demisyllables it does not work in when recognising continuous speech. A justification might be that the list of confusable words is mainly devoted to errors which are not allowed by the grammar. An extension of the algorithm is needed so that the list of confusable words is obtained when recognising in the continuous speech application.

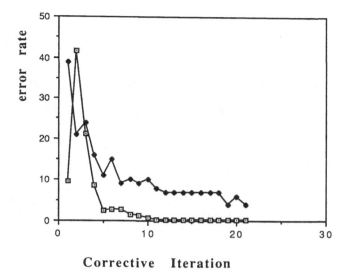

Fig. 9. Using corrective training to recognise catalan digits. The upper curve are the mistakes on speakers outside the training database, the lower curve are the mistakes for speakers inside the traning database.

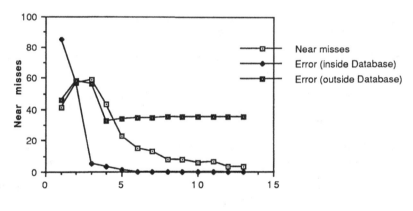

Fig. 10. Using corrective training to recognise demisyllables in an isolated speech way. Errors for speakers in the data base and outside the database.

6.- Conclusions

In this chapter, some techniques to obtain a better performance of speech recognition systems have been reviewed. The use of the derivative of the cepstrum and of the energy has been shown improve significantly the recognition rate. Therefore, some authors have recently proposed the use of higher derivatives[18]. However, this new informations need the same training requirements that using only the cepstrum. Where these requirements are not satisfied some methods to smooth the observation probabilities of the HMM's provide a solution to this drawback. The methods based on a distance criterion are simpler than the methods based on a mutual-ocurrence criterion. Nevertheless, as they smooth "too much" the HMM, they should only be applied in situations of extremely poor training. In other situations the mutual-ocurrence methods are preferred .At the end, a corrective training algorithm has been proposed to face on the problem of HMM's discrimination. The test experiments have show the validity of the method in an isolated speech application.

7.-References

1. L.R.Bahl, P.F. Brown,P.V.Souza, R.L.Mercer. "A New Algorithm for the Estimation of Hidden Markov Model Parameters". Proc. ICASSP-88.

2. Y.L.Chow wt al "BYBLOS: The BBN Continuous Speech Recognition System" ICASSP-87, IEEE.

3. R. duda, P. Hart, Pattern Classification and Scene Analysis, John Wiley & Sons, 1973.

4. S.Furui, "Speaker-Independent Isolated Word Recognition Using Dynamic Features of Speech Spectrum". Trans on ASSP, vol 34, n 1, Feb 1986.

5. R.Gray, A.Buzo, A.Gray,Y.Matsuyama."Distortion Measures for Speech Processing" Trans on ASSP, vol 28, n 4. Aug 1980

6. F. Jelinek, R.L. Mercer, "Interpolated estimation of Markov source parameters from sparse data", Pattern Recognition in Practice, pp 381-397, Amsterdan 1980.

7. K.F.Lee et al "The SPHINX Speech Recognition System" ICASSP-89, IEEE

8. K.F. Lee, H.W. Hon, "Speaker-independent phone recognition using hidden Markov models", Trans on ASSP. vol 37, n 11, Nov, 1989

9. K.F. Lee and S. Mahajan. "Corrective and Reinforcement Learning for Speaker Independent Continuous Speech Recognition". Eurospeech 89. Paris.

10. D.Mansour and BH.Juang. "A Family of Distortion Measures Based upon Projection Operation for Robust Speech Recognition" IEEE Trans. on ASSP,Vol 37, n 11, Nov 1989, pp 1659-71

11. D.Mansour and BH.Juang."The Short-Time Modified Coherence Representation and its Application for Noisy Speech Recognition" IEEE Trans. on ASSP,Vol 37, n 6, Jun 1989, pp 795-804

12. J.B.Mariño et al. "Recognition Of Numbers by Using Demisyllables and Hidden Markov Models" Proc EUSIPCO-90.

13. B.Merialdo, "Phonetic Recognition using Hidden Markov Models and Maximum Mutual Information Training". Proc. ICASSP-88.

14. L.R.Rabiner. "A Tutorial on Hidden Markov Models and Selected Applications is Speec Recognition" Proc. of the IEEE; Feb. 1989

15. R. Schwartz, O. Kimball, F. Kubala, M. Feng, Y. Chow, C. Barry, J. Makhoul, "Robust smoothing methods for discrete hidden Markov models", Proc. ICASSP-89, pp. 548-551, 1989

16. S. Bavis and P.Mermelstein."Comparison of Parametric Representations for Monosyllabic Word Recognition in Continuous Spoken Sentences", IEEE Trans. on ASSP,Vol 28, n 4, Aug. 1980, pp 357-366.

17. K. Sugawara, M. Nishimura, K. Toshioka, M. Okochi, T. Kaneko, " Isolated word recognition using hidden Markov models", Proc. ICASSP-85, pp. 1-4, Tampa 1985.

18. M. Vall-llossera, E.Monte, J.B. Mariño. "Estimación de los modelos ocultos de Markov mediante la técnica de Entrenamiento correctivo". IV Simposium Nacional de Reconocimiento de Formas y Análisis de Imágenes. Granada 1990.

19. J.G. Wilpon. "Improvements in Connected Digit Recognition Using Higher Order Spectral Features". Proc. ICASSP-91.

APPLICATIONS IN IMAGE ANALYSIS AND COMPUTER VISION

ANALYSIS OF GAMMAGRAPHIC IMAGES BY MATHEMATICAL MORPHOLOGY

A. Dupuy
Labo. Image, Ecole Nationale Supérieure des Télécommunications de Paris, 46 rue Barrault, 75634 Paris Cedex 13, France

J. Serrat, J. Vitria
Department d'Informàtica, Universitat Autònoma de Barcelona, 08193 Bellaterra,Spain
and
J. Pladellorens
Escola Universitària d'Optica, Universitat Politècnica de Catalunya, Colom 1, 08222 Terrassa, Spain

ABSTRACT

In this paper we present a method for the automatic analysis of heart grammagraphic image sequences. The final objective is to delineate the left ventricle contour in order to compute its volume. First, a restoration process is performed by a Wiener filter. Then, each image of the sequence is partitioned in local maxima influence zones, a concept derived from Mathematical Morphology. One of them which can be identified by using position criteria contains the whole left ventricle (and other areas). A subsequent process, based also on morphological operations extracts its contour.

1. Introduction

Gammagraphic images allow us to obtain some parameters which are useful in the diagnosis of heart diseases. Each gammagraphic study of a patient is a sequence of 16 to 20 images of the heart at different times of the cardiac cycle. Typical sizes of these images are 64 by 64 pixels and 128 grey levels (figure 1). Despite their low resolution this modality presents the advantages of being non-invasive and of providing dynamic information of the heart functioning. In particular the measurement of the ejection fraction from systole and diastole left-ventricular volumes is a rutinary procedure.

The manual outline of left ventricle contours demands considerable skill and training. Even then, results are subjective and not very reproducible. Hence, an automatic (but adjustable) method for the analysis of this kind of image is of great interest. In this article we describe such a method which is composed of three phases : image restoration (section 2), partition of the resulting image in local maxima influence zones and extraction of the left ventricle contour (section 4), in addition to the treatment of a special case (section 5). Finally, we discuss the implementation and results in section 6. Apart from restoration, our method is based on morphological transforms,

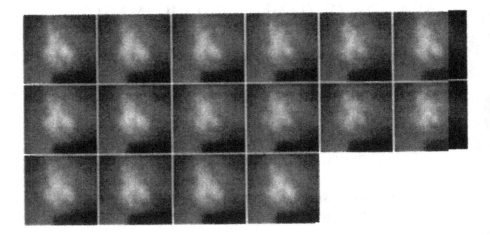

Figure 1: sequence of non-restored original images

which we shall show are very effective in this class of images. Hence, we include a brief introduction to mathematical morphology (section 3).

2. Restoration

Scintigraphic images are characterized by a low signal-to-noise ratio inherent in their formation process. Moreover, gammacameras produce a considerable effect of dispersion. In the past, several filtering schemes e.g. the median filter[1] have been tested in order to remove noise. However, restoration by Wiener filter was shown to be more suitable, due to its ability to invert the gammacamera dispersion in presence of noise[2] (figure 2). The transfer function of the Wiener filter is :

$$W(u,v) = \frac{H^*(u,v)}{|H(u,v)|^2 + (S_n/S_f)} \tag{1}$$

where $H(u,v)$ is the Fourier transform of the gammacamera point spread function $h(x,y)$, $H(u,v)^*$ its conjugate, S_n the noise power spectrum and S_f the (original) image power spectrum. h –the dispersion effect– is approximated by a bidimensional, symmetric gaussian function with σ obtained from the gammacamera characteristics. If we assume a poissonian noise distribution we can use the results of Goodman and Belsher[3] to simplify the image and noise power spectrum ratio :

$$S_f = \frac{S_g - S_n}{|H(u,v)|^2} \tag{2}$$

where S_g is the power spectrum oh the degraded image g and S_n is constant and equal to the mean of g.

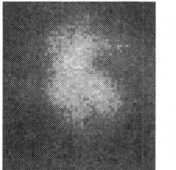 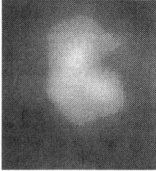

Figure 2: original and restored image

3. A Review of Mathematical Morphology

There are different general approaches to image processing and analysis depending on the adopted image model : a sampled and quantized two dimensional signal, a random field, etc. In mathematical morphology, images, both binary and grey scale, are seen as one or more sets of points in a space[4]. Morphological operations are based on the geometrical relationships among points of such sets. As Serra has pointed out, mathematical morphology is the application of lattice theory to the spatial structures[4]. A pyramid of more complex and powerful operations are built[4,5] from set union, intersection, difference, complementation and two basic transformations – erosion and dilation–.

Let us consider a set of points X not especially connected, in an euclidean space E. Its translation according to a vector h, and its symmetric set according to the origin are defined as

$$
\begin{aligned}
X_h &= \{x \in E, x - h \in X\} & (3) \\
\check{X} &= \{-x,\, x \in X\} & (4)
\end{aligned}
$$

Given two sets $X, B \subset E$, the erosion and dilation of X by B are defined as

$$
X \ominus \check{B} = \{x,\, \forall b \in \check{B},\ x + b \in X\} = \bigcap_{b \in \check{B}} (X + b) \tag{5}
$$

$$X \oplus \check{B} = \{x + b, \; x \in X, b \in \check{B}\} = \bigcup_{b \in \check{B}} (X + b) \tag{6}$$

B is a special set, the structuring element, which acts like a parameter of morphological transformations. Its shape and origin position have a decisive influence on the result.

The next level of operations is formed by the opening and closing, denoted by X_B and X^B respectively, and defined as

$$X_B = (X \ominus \check{B}) \oplus B \tag{7}$$
$$X^B = (X \oplus \check{B}) \ominus B \tag{8}$$

Now, we shall expose two more operations, thinning and thickening, where the structuring element T must be composed of two sets, $T = \{T^1, T^2\}$. Thinning and thickening are defined respectively as

$$X \bigcirc T = X \setminus [(X \ominus T^1) \setminus (X \oplus T^2)] \tag{9}$$
$$X \odot T = X \bigcup [(X \ominus T^1) \setminus (X \oplus T^2)] \tag{10}$$

Usually, the two former operations are not applied in a unique direction but, in order to achieve the same effect in all directions, the structuring element T is rotated. Let $\{T\}$ be the sequence $T_1, \ldots T_n$ of different structuring elements obtained by successive rotation of T. Then we shall express

$$X \bigcirc \{T\} = (\ldots (X \bigcirc T_1) \bigcirc T_2) \ldots) \bigcirc T_n \tag{11}$$

and similarly in the case of thickening. Finally, any operation ψ on a set X can be performed conditionally on another set Y, in the following way :

$$\psi(X) \; ; \; Y = \psi(X) \bigcap Y \tag{12}$$

As we can see, morphologic operations go in pairs, each being, in some way, opposite to the other. This is because any transformation ψ has associated with another transformation ψ^*, called its dual, with the following property :

$$\psi^*(X) = [\, \psi(X^c) \,]^c \tag{13}$$

Morphologic transforms can be classified according to several properties. The four most important are the following :

- ψ is *increasing* if $X \subset Y \Longrightarrow \psi(X) \subset \psi(Y) \;\; \forall X, Y \in \wp(E)$ (parts of E)

- ψ is *anti-extensive* if $\psi(X) \subset X, \;\; \forall X \in \wp(E)$

- ψ is *idempotent* when $\psi[\psi(X)] = \psi(X) \;\; \forall X \in \wp(E)$

- ψ defined in the plane is *homotopic* when it maintains the number of regions and pores of X, and their hierarchical inclusion relationships (the homotopic tree).

Thinning and thickening can be made homotopic by selecting an appropiate structuring element T. In a digital image, T depends also on the type of grid (square or hexagonal). None of them is idempotent, but if we define the sequential thinning as the thinning of a set by the infinite sequence $\{T_i\} = T_1, T_2, \ldots, T_n, T_1, \ldots T_n, \ldots$ then $X \bigcirc \{T_i\}$ definitely is.

The operations we have seen defined on sets of a space E are immediately extended to binary, discrete images considering X, Y, B and T as sets of points at grey level 1 over a background at level 0. However, they can be easily extended to grey level images too[6]. One such image is considered a set, called umbra or subgraph, defined as $f = \{(x, y, z) \mid z \leq f(x, y)\}$. Then, it can be seen that dilation and erosion become

$$f \ominus B = inf[f(x - i, y - j) - B(i, j)] \qquad (14)$$
$$f \oplus B = sup[f(x - i, y - j) + B(i, j)] \qquad (15)$$

where B is a set of a three-dimensional space. If B is flat, i.e $B(i, j)$ is only 0 or 1, erosion and dilation are simply the local minimum and maximum respectively.

4. Left Ventricle Segmentation

A number of methods for extracting the left ventricle region have been proposed : global and adaptive thresholding[7,8,9], edge detection by different gradient approximations[10], optimal contour following by dynamic programming[11], or knowledge-based systems which combines these image processing techniques with knowledge about the gammagraphic images domain[12,13,14]. The variety of methods illustrates the difficulty of the problem and the fact that none of them seems to be sufficiently perfect to be considered as the standard method.

In order to explain the segmentation algorithm, we consider a grey scale image as a topographic surface or relief. Then, local maxima correspond to summits and local minima to sinks. We want to ascribe to these points their influence regions, which will be hills in the maxima and watersheds in the minima. We shall see that the partition of the filtered image in maxima influence regions allows us to delimit a region containing the whole left ventricle.

Let us suppose that it is raining on our topographic relief. When the water gets to the surface it goes down the highest slope path until it gets to a minimum or to a sink where it stops. The watershed associated with a local minimum is the set of points from which the path with a highest slope gets to the considered local minimum. The set of points from which arise several paths of maximum slope to different sinks is called a divide. By duality, the regions of influence of the local maxima of f are the watersheds of $-f$ [5].

230

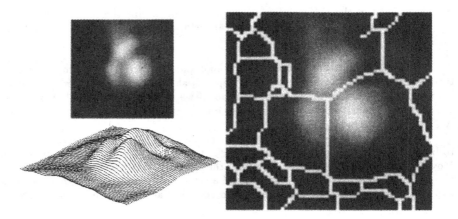

Figure 3: a) isoplot of a filtered image, b) boundaries of its local maxima influence regions

From this point of view, in our restored images the left ventricle appears as a gentle hill with a maximum of high grey level (figure 3a). It is separated by a saddle and two quite elevated valleys, from another mountain corresponding to the other cardiac cavities, rich in blood. The proximity of these two structures and their weak separation constitute the main difficulty in segmenting the left ventricle. Nevertheless, image partition in regions of local maxima influence will separate in an optimal way both structures (figure 3b).

The process of segmentation follows three steps: a) calculation of the influence regions of local maxima, b) selection of the region corresponding to the left ventricle, and c) extraction, inside this region, of the ventricle contour.

4.1. Regions of Influence of Local Maxima

We have implemented a parallel algorithm in order to obtain such regions. Although all the images of a sequence are simultaneously processed, we shall describe it as a single image or frame.

Let be $X_i, i = 1 \ldots n$ the different *levels* of an image f, where n is the maximum grey value of f :

$$X_i = \{p \mid f(p) \geq i\} \quad i = 0 \ldots n \tag{16}$$

Our algorithm processes each level of the image, from X_n to X_0. At each level X_i, it performs an homotopic thickening of the partial result Y_{i-1} obtained up to the moment, conditional to X_i. Then, Z_i, the maxima which appear just at the current level, are added to the result (figure 4). It is necessary to use an homotopic thickening in order to keep the different regions of influence Y_i separate. In consequence, the algorithm is :

$$
\begin{aligned}
Y_0 &:= X_n \\
\text{for } i &:= 1 \text{ to } n \\
&\quad Z_i := X_{n-i} \setminus (Y_{i-1} \oplus \{B\} \ ; \ X_{n-i}) \\
&\quad Y_i := (Y_{i-1} \odot \{T\} \ ; \ X_{n-i}) \cup Z_i
\end{aligned}
\tag{17}
$$

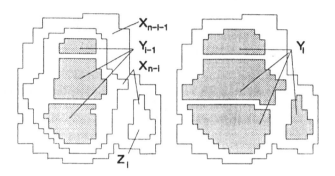

Figure 4: one intermediate step of the algorithm

In practice it is not necessary to perform thickening or dilation by an infinite sequence of structuring elements $\{T\}$ and $\{B\}$. By $(Y_{i-1} \oplus \{B\} \ ; \ X_{n-i})$ and $(Y_{i-1} \odot \{T\} \ ; \ X_i)$ we only mean that it is necessary to achieve the idempotence of these operations on the current image. Considering the difference of size between Y_{i-1} and X_{n-i}, sequences of 20 elements are sufficient.

At the end, Y_n is a binary image which contains the zones of influence of the maxima at 1 and the border between them at 0. In figure 3b we can see the result complemented, i.e $(Y_n)^c$, added to the filtered image.

4.2. Selection of the Left Ventricle Influence Region

The gravity centre (x_g, y_g) of the restored image f (again one of the sequence frames) is calculated as :

$$
x_g = \frac{\sum_{i=1}^m \sum_{j=1}^m i \, f(i,j)}{\sum_{i=1}^m \sum_{j=1}^m f(i,j)}
$$

$$y_g = \frac{\sum_{i=1}^{m} \sum_{j=1}^{m} j \, f(i,j)}{\sum_{i=1}^{m} \sum_{j=1}^{m} f(i,j)} \tag{18}$$

m being the number of files and columns. There usually appear two bright zones in an image, one corresponding to the left ventricle and the other one to the right ventricle plus cavities joined to it due to the angle of image acquisition (lateral oblique projection). Hence, the gravity centre is located between these two zones. Moreover, in order to identify the region which contains the left ventricle, we shall make the assumption that this region shows an elevated maximum located at the bottom right part with respect to the gravity centre.

Local maxima are calculated as those image points which do not vary in a dilation with a 3x3 planar structuring element C, and whose intensity is greater than half of the maximum grey level n. Among them, we select as possible summits of the left ventricle those located down on the right of the gravity centre (x_g, y_g).

4.3. Extraction of the Left Ventricle Contour

As we see in figures 3a and 7, the whole selected region of influence region does not correspond to the left ventricle. We must choose the elevated part, i.e points at high grey level, plus the points at low intensity but where the mountain slope begins to be pronounced, i.e., with a high gradient. Hence, we shall take as points of the left ventricle those having :

- a grey level higher than a certain threshold value t_1 which is sufficiently elevated so to select only left ventricle points (region R_1).

- a gradient magnitude which overcomes another threshold value t_2 (region R_2). In order to avoid the inclusion of points belonging to structures other than the ventricle, these points must be near R_1. Therefore, we condition R_2 on $(R_1 \oplus B)$ (figure 7).

The gradient, like all other segmentation steps, is a morphological operation. Given a continuous function f, it can be seen[5] that

$$\text{grad } f = \lim_{\lambda \to 0} \frac{(f \oplus \lambda B) - (f \ominus \lambda B)}{2} \tag{19}$$

In grey level, discrete images, the gradient is usually computed as

$$\text{grad } f = (f \oplus B) - (f \ominus B) \tag{20}$$

B being a small, symmetric structuring element in order to achieve an isotropic gradient. However, the optimal size of the structuring element so as to detect a given contour, depends on its width or spatial extension. As we can see in figure 5, an element of size 3 is well suited to an ideal step contour but not to a ramp contour with a width that is greater than 3. In this case, the gradient magnitude does not correspond to the total height variation.

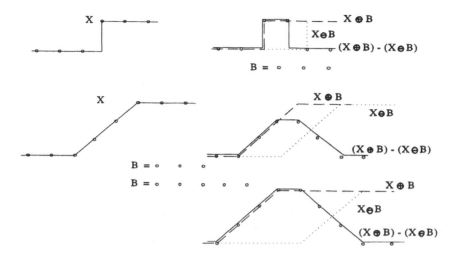

Figure 5: one-dimensional gradient with structuring elements of different size

Taking into account the width of the left ventricle contour the gradient is calculated by using the structuring element of figure 6.

t_1 and t_2 are the only parameters of our method, and we shall use them to minimize the difference between the results that provide it and those given by radiologists. t_1 was fixed to 84 over 128 intensity levels. Next, we evaluated several values for t_2, the gradient threshold. The highest correspondence with results of human experts, in terms of total counts (sum of grey levels for all points inside the selected region), was obtained for t_2 equal to 33. Note that this measurement is suitable for a comparison of the final result of the method, i.e volume of left ventricle. However, it does not show the similarity between the extracted contour and the contour outlined manually by the expert, because points at the ventricle border have a low grey level. Nevertheless, there is a high degree of correspondence between them.

Once we joined the two resulting sets of points, we have a region R which often presents an irregular contour, or small pores of few pixels. In order to eliminate these features, we apply a closing operation followed by an opening. The first fills the holes and the second eliminates the small protrusions. The closing structuring element must be small enough to preserve the shape of the segmented region —an excessive smoothing would distort it, making the final shape similar to the structuring element— but at the same time it must be able to fill the possible pores. We chose the same element B which was used for computing the morphologic gradient. The

234

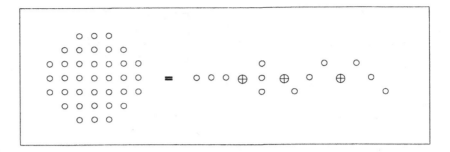

Figure 6: structuring element B for gradient image computation

opening however, must be performed by a smaller structuring element in order to preserve ventricle regions smaller than B, a frequent situation in some patients in systole. Hence the opening uses the 3x3 structuring element C (figure 7).

According to Eq. 12, 16 and 7, the segmentation of the left ventricle region V from its maxima influence region can be summarized as :

$$R = X_{t1} \bigcup ([(f \oplus B) - (f \ominus B)]_{t2} \cap (X_{t1} \oplus B))$$ (21)
$$V = (R^B)_C$$ (22)

5. A Special Case

However, a certain situation may arise in some sequences and needs additional treatment : the absence of a maximum associated with the left ventricle. Sometimes, the systole frame and those close to it, may not have a local maximum for the left ventricle. This is due to the fact that the aforementioned ventricle appears not as a separate mountain, but as a reinforcement of the right ventricle. Possible causes are an unfavourable angle of vision, or the fact that the left ventricle has a very low volume. Obviously, without a maximum we shall not have a region of influence which contains the ventricle and we shall not be able to proceed. To solve the problem, we shall take advantage of the fact that the left ventricle regions of influence do not differ much in a frame from its neighbours, thereby allowing us to use the zone of influence of the nearest frame with a maximum. Once this has been done, the process continues as usual.

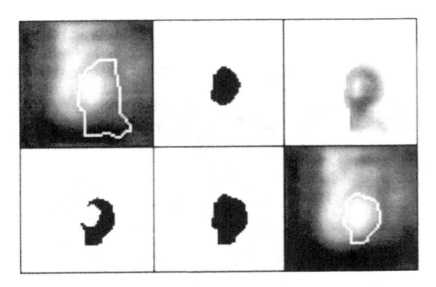

Figure 7: a) a single frame with its selected zone of influence boundary, b) R_1, c) gradient image, d) $R_2 \bigcap (R_1 \oplus B)$, e) $R_1 \bigcup (R_2 \bigcap (R_1 \oplus B))$, f) final contour after filtering by closing-opening

6. Discussion

In this article we present a new method to segment the left ventricle of heart scintigraphic images by using mathematical morphology techniques. From a set odf very simple operations this approach to image processing and analysis creates new transforms that allow to find complex image features like local maxima regions of influence or homotopic thinning and thickening.

Our method has been implemented on a VICOM/VDP system which is able to perform a set of basic morphological operations in parallel over all the points of an image. Therefore, by putting the whole sequence in a sole 256x512 pixels image, we can realize the major part of the process (extraction of local maxima zones of influence and of regions R_1, R_2 and V) simultaneously.

The bottle neck of our method is the computation of the regions of influence. The algorithm, despite being the mere implementation of the definition of this concept, is not the fastest because of the great number of levels used. The time spent for each level is 10 seconds. A possible solution to decrease its computational cost is to skip two or three levels each time instead to one level, obtaining similar results in most cases.

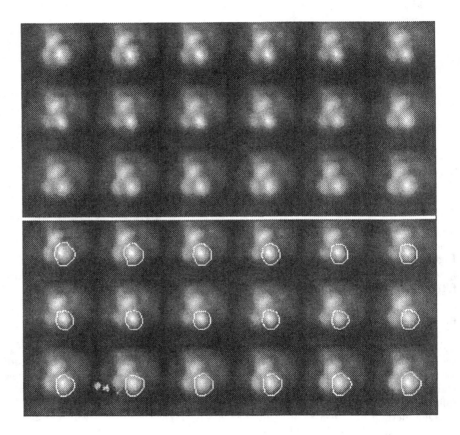

Figure 8: examples of segmented left-ventricular regions

The contours obtained are considered good by the experts and there is also an excellent correlation between the total counts obtained by the experts analysis and those obtained by this automatic method.

References

1. F. Deconinck and R. Luypaert, "Desing and evaluation of median filters for scintigraphic image filtering", *Proc. First Int. Symp. on Medical Imaging and Image Interpretation* (1982) p. 20-23.

2. M. A. King et al. "A Wiener filter for nuclear medicine images", *Med. Physics* **10** (1983) p. 876-880.

3. J. W. Goodman and J. F. Belsher, "Fundamental limitations in linear invariant restoration of atmospherically degraded images", *Proc. SPIE* **75** (1976) p. 141-154.

4. J. Serra, "Introduction to Mathematical Morphology", *Computer Vision, Graphics and Image Processing* **35** (1986) p. 283-305.

5. J. Serra, *Image Analysis and Mathematical Morphology*, (Academic Press, 1982).

6. S. R. Stenberg, "Grayscale morphology", *Computer Vision, Graphics and Image Processing* **35** (1986) p. 333-355.

7. W. Chang et al. "Methods for detection of left ventricle edges", *Seminars in Nuclear Medicine* **10** (1980) p. 39-53.

8. H. Bunke, "Smoothing threshold and contour extraction in images from gated blood pool studies", *Proc. First Int. Symp. on Medical Imaging and Image Interpretation* (1982) p. 146-151.

9. J. A. K. Blokland, A. M. Vossepoel and E. K. J. Pauwels, "Movement of left ventricule centre of mass", *Proc. Int. Symp. on Medical Imaging and Icons* (1984) p. 282-287.

10. E. G. Hawman et al. "Digital boundary detection techniques for the analysis of gated cardiologic scintigrams", *Optical Engineering* **20** (1981) p. 719-725.

11. Bunke et al. "Artificial intelligence and image understanding methods in a system for the automatic diagnostic evaluation off Tc-99 gated blood pool studies", *Proc. Int. Symp. on Medical Imaging and Icons* (1984) p. 417-423.

12. J. Reiber, "Esats: an expert system for the quantitative analysis of thallium-201 scintigrams", *Proc. SPIE Advances in Image Processing* **804** (1987) p. 116-122.

13. G. Sagerer, "Automatic interpretation of medical image sequences", *Pattern Recognition Letters* **8** (1988) p. 87-99.

14. J. Duncan, "Knowledge direct left ventricule boundary detection in equilibrium radionucleide angiocardiography", *IEEE Transactions on Medical Imaging* **6** (1987) p. 325-336.

AUTOMATIC RECOGNITION OF PLATE NUMBERS

M. A. Arregui   and   J. A. Mitxelena

Sistemas Sensoriales y Visión Artificial, IKERLAN
Apdo 146, 20500 Mondragon, Gipuzkoa, Spain

ABSTRACT

This article covers some general aspects of the study and implementation of a system able to identify Spanish number plates automatically by means of machine vision. Possible uses to which it may be put include controlling entry to car-parks, restricted areas, motorways, etc...

Basically the process works by locating the number plate on an image of the vehicle, so as then to carry out a series of morphological treatments with the aim of cleaning the plate and then reading the characters that are seen.

The aim is for the recognition of the number plates to take place in as short a time as possible and with maximum exactitude.

1. Introduction

This paper presents an automatic recognition system for Spanish vehicles. It is based on machine vision and primarily, uses mathematical morphology techniques to prepare the plate for the recognition of the characters it contains.

As the rear number plates of Spanish vehicles may not only be of two different sizes and shapes (110 x 500 mm. and 200 x 280 mm.) but fitted in different places as well, it was decided to carry out the recognition process on the front plates as these are always of the same size and shape (110 x 500 mm.) and are located in the central part of the vehicle. The characters are printed in matt black on a white background.

Basically the aim is to have the vehicle drive along a lane, detect its presence, acquire an image, prepare the image for its later recognition and finally, to verify the characters recognized.

While on the subject, we feel it is necessary to mention certain factors which should be taken into account as they play a vital part in the recognition process. These are the light conditions, dirt and foreign elements on the number plates and the physical layout of the different elements which make up the system.

Consequently, the process consists of the following stages:

- Setting of the camera parameters for local light conditions.
- Vehicle detection.
- Image acquisition.
- Search for the number plate.
- Cleaning of the number plate.
- Characters recognition.
- Verification.

The following equipment and devices were used to carry out the task:

- EXPERT vision equipment.
- Matrix CCD camera with a resolution of 510 x 492 pixels. It comes fitted with a video signal gain control (CCIR) which is programmable, this enables the dynamic signal range to be adapted to the local light conditions.
- Halogen/Flash lamps. These were required both to light up the number plate as well as to make up for the difference between the setting lighting and that of the number plate itself during the day.
- Ultrasonic sensors. These enable ultrasonic waves to be received in order to detect the presence of objects or for the measurement of distances.

Even though this kind of sensor was used, it does not rule out the possibility of using other devices such as infrared or laser devices to achieve the same purpose.

2. Physical Layout

Before explaining each step which makes up the automatic recognition of number plates, we will describe the physical layout of each of the functional elements of the system.

In order to obtain a good picture, the camera and the number plate should be face to face. A possible way of achieving this would be to place camera in a specially prepared hole or gap in the access lane itself. The camera would be set at such an angle that its range of vision in height would be enough to see the number plate perfectly at all times (see Fig. 1).

Figure 1

Another important aspect is the width of the range of vision; the vehicle may arrive out of line with the access lane and, if the range of vision is too narrow, the camera may not be able to get a total view of the number plate.

On the other hand, if it were too wide, the image of the number plate would be reduced thereby reducing the the size of the characters, which would make recognition difficult.

The distance between the camera and the vehicle must not be too rigid. A certain margin should be allowed without it having an undue effect on the size of the number plate in the image. To achieve this, the camera should be placed as far away as possible. However, should two vehicles arrive one after the other, what could happen is that the first vehicle may obstruct the acquisition of the image of the second vehicle by getting in the range of vision of the camera. In short, a compromise must be reached on camera-vehicle distance and the variation in the dimensions of the number plate and then impose some kind of restriction to make sure the application does what it is supposed to.

The solution we propose consists of having a vehicle come along a lane of approx. 2.50 m. wide, a lane similar to those used in motorway toll approaches. A camera is placed about 5 m from the vehicle with a field of vision of 1.60 m. (25mm lens). This solution provides a suitable compromise between the lane width, the field of vision and the size of the characters. Using this layout, the number plate will always be within the range of the camera no matter how the vehicle is lined up with respect to the lane.

As can be seen in Figure 2, the field of vision of 1.60 m. is enough to be able to see the number plate completely in all possible cases. The minimum vehicle width has been taken to be 1.50 m.

242

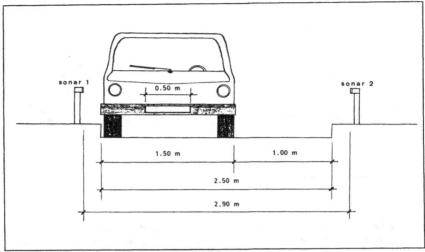

Figure 2

The maximum width in which the number plate can be found.
   2.50 m. - (2 x 0.50 m.)   = 1.50 m.
   1.60 m. (field of vision) > 1.50 m.   (1)

The time factor plays an important role in this application and the amount of image data to be handled should be minimized; i.e. all work will be carried out using windows.

The images captured using a resolution of 256x256 pixels did not offer a high enough quality and consequently images were taken with a resolution of 512x512.

Working in the initial treatment stage with 512x512 pixels images means an excessive computing load. This load can be greatly reduced however, if the number plate can be framed in a smaller-sized window. To answer this problem, the system should be equipped with some kind of device which limits the number plate zone.

The window which will frame the number plate can be perfectly fixed by placing ultrasonic devices on either side of the lane. These devices show the distance from each to the vehicle and having previously established the lane width, the frame can be perfectly fixed.

Sensors are therefore placed 0.20 m. from the edge of the lane (see Fig.2).

Finally, we shall deal with the subject of illumination and its placement. Should the vehicle be stationary or moving at a low speed, a series of halogen lamps placed on either side of the access lane will be sufficient. These lamps should provide suitable illumination of the bottom part of the car while at the same time not having an intense effect on the driver.

If they are placed on the lane itself, they will be installed in the same way as the camera.

It should be taken into account that the operation may be carried out at night, the illumination provided by the lamps should therefore be intense.

If the vehicle should be moving at a considerable speed, this type of illumination would be of no use and a flash would have to be installed. The image would be taken the moment the flash went off so that the movement would not produce a distortion on the image.

See Figure 3 for a plan of the physical layout of the system.

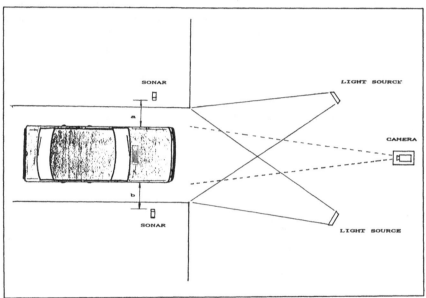

Figure 3

3. Setting For Local Lighting Conditions

The levels of brightness in the local lighting conditions will vary constantly and be of a very diverse nature (sunny day, dull day, morning, evening, night, ...). Rapid changes may even come about due to the existence of clouds on sunny days. In order

244

to deal with these changes in brightness, we need to modify both the opening of the lens diaphragm (autoiris) and the High and Low reference points defined on the EXPERT, which in turn activate the gain and the offset of the camera. The state of the number plate (dirt on the plate, a new or an old plate, ...) also requires that an adjustment to these variables be carried out.

What we have aimed at is that the large adjustments should be made by means of changing the diaphragm opening, and that the fine adjustments should be carried out by varying the aforementioned High and Low reference points.

In the case of inside a building where these changes in the local lighting conditions are not produced, the problem is negligible. Nevertheless, a stroboscope light device (flash) offers the best results as it greatly reduces the effects of sunlight.

On a typical histogram of the the area of the number plate, two peaks, more or less pronounced, can be seen to exist. These correspond to the characters (the smallest and situated to the left, as they are the darkest characters) and the background of the number plate (the largest peak situated on the right, as the background is light).

Once this point has been reached, what we want is that in the histogram, the zone corresponding to the characters is moved to values nearer to 0 grey level and that corresponding to the background of the number plate towards saturation level (63). This stretching of the histogram is achieved by varying the High and Low reference points. In figure 4 the desired effect may be seen.

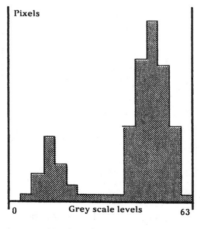

Number plate histogram

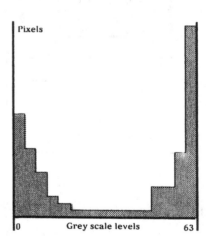

Stretching of the histogram

Figure 4

The zones corresponding to the characters and the background have now been clearly differentiated. As a result, if we place a binary threshold in the region of grey level 32, we will have the characters perfectly differentiated on a white plate background.

4. Vehicle Detection

As has already been mentioned, the elements which will detect the presence of a vehicle as well as its position relative to the lane, are two ultrasonic sensors placed on either side of the lane and whose operating range has been set to between 0.20 and 1.20 m., extendible to 1.40 m.

In order to configure the detection system, an ultrasonic-computer interface developed in IKERLAN has been used. Its functions are as follows:

- Generate pulses every 10 msc.
- Measurement of the time taken between sending the pulse to the reception of the corresponding echo.
- Transmission via series line to the computer of a value proportional to the said time.

The detection process is carried out in the following way: one of the sensors is constantly checking to see whether a vehicle has entered the field of action. When this happens, the interface sends the data on the time to the EXPERT computer which transforms them into distance. The computer then sends a signal (through a parallel output) to switch a relay and start the second ultrasonic sensor working. This second sensor then carries out the same operation as the first and in this way the system has full knowledge of the position of the vehicle with respect to the lane.

5. Image Acquisition

Once the vehicle is detected, the system is now in a position for the camera to take a picture. This has already been calibrated due to the fact that the program can cope with dimensional measurements. The image is acquired with a resolution of 512x512 pixels and with an hexagonal grid (more effective for later morphological treatment).

The video signal is held in the EXPERT image memory with the aforementioned space resolution and with a brightness resolution of 64 levels of grey (fig.5).

246

Figure 5. Original Image (512x512 pixels)

As already explained, working with windows is advisable in order to make the process as quick as possible as this results in a smaller computing load. For this reason, the area of the number plate has been framed in a window of 256x256 pixels over the original image. To do so, a window whose first and last line parameters remain unalterable has been used and only the columns (first and last) may vary depending on the result of the detection mentioned in the previous section (fig. 6).

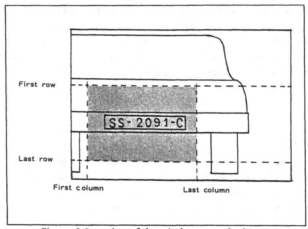

Figure 6. Location of the window over the image.

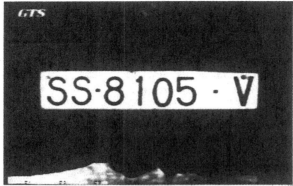

Figure 7. 256x256 pixel window

The formula for calculating the first column of the window is as follows:

$$Pc = \left((D1 + \frac{290 - D1 - D2}{2} - 65) \cdot \; 3.25 \right) - 128$$

where:

D1	= Distance between left sensor and vehicle (cm.)
D2	= Distance between right sensor and vehicle (cm.)
1 cm.	= 3.25 pixels (calibrated)
65 cm.	= distance between sensor and start of field of vision
290 cm.	= distance between sensors

6.   Search For Number Plate

The next stage involves finding, within the 256x256 pixels window, the area corresponding to the number plate. To do so, the image is treated by means of binary morphology based on erosion and dilatation operations on the white areas by analyzing the proximity of each pixel. Before these operations are carried out, the image must be binarized, that is to say, the grey levels must be transformed into black and white. A threshold should therefore be chosen with which grey level values greater than that of the threshold are converted to level 63 (white) and those the same or

248

smaller are converted to 0 (black). The morphological treatment consists of an hexagonal closing. The aim of this is to make the characters (in black) disappear thus leaving a white rectangular shape corresponding to the number plate. After that, an hexagonal opening is made in order to eliminate small white areas. This is due to the fact that since later on contours of the image are going to be extracted and the parameters of each of them (area, perimeter, ..) checked, if some of the contours are eliminated, the calculation time will be greatly reduced (see Fig. 8 and 9).

In short, these operations are to try and isolate an area with characteristics similar to those of the rectangle of the number plate.

Figure 8. Binary morphology. Hexagonal closing

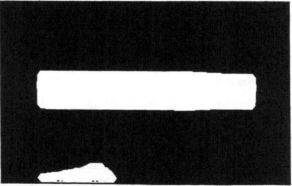

Figure 9. Binary morphology. Hexagonal opening

To carry out a recognition of a rectangle similar to that of the number plate, contours of the previous binary image are extracted and a series of parameters such as the perimeter, area, compactness [(area/perimeter^2)] and the centre of gravity of each of them are calculated. Given that the extreme value of each of the parameters has already been fixed, if one of the contours tested falls within the margins, this contour will be that corresponding to the number plate. In this case, a small working window containing the number plate will be set up over the initial image (fig. 10).

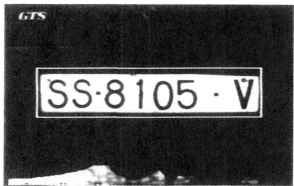

Figure 10. Working window over 256x256 pixel image

If no contour corresponding to the number plate is found, an attempt to find some characters from the number plate will be made and a working window 256 pixels wide and slightly higher than the characters themselves will be later set up. All the characters on the number plate will be located within this.

To do so, a masking operation is carried out between the binary image obtained during the previous process (closing + opening) and the initial one. The image obtained is then binarized and contours are once again extracted (the characters now also appear) and finally the bounding boxes from each contour are calculated. These boxes will have particular dimensions should the contours inscribed within them be characters from the number plate.

This second situation may come about if the vehicle in question is white or similar, owing to the fact that the background of the number plate and the rest of the vehicle are of a similar level of brightness.

7. Cleaning Of The Number Plate

The state the number plate is a determining factor when carrying out a recognition process on its characters. There may be foreign elements such as rivets, stains, scratches, it may even be bent and twisted, contain partially erased characters, etc. which make it very difficult to read. For this reason, a cleaning process needs to be carried out prior to recognition to get rid of anything which may spoil the task.

To try to reconstruct partially erased characters is a complicated and time-consuming task which is why this aspect has not been dealt with in this study. Number plates which have any of their characters in this state will not be read correctly.

First of all, in this phase, a closing of the initial image (only in the window) is made in grey levels, followed by a subtraction between the two images, which allows small dark areas corresponding to the characters to be recovered and a part of those not belonging to the same to be removed. the dark detail (e.g. characters) will appear light on a black background given that the result of the subtraction is always positive (see fig. 11).

Figure 11. Grey scale morphology

The image is then binarized and, if the number plate is found, the actual cleaning of the number plate is now ready to be carried out.

However, when the number plate still has not been found but a window has been set up over the image,in the place where the image itself will later be included (second case in the previous section), the first and last character of the number plate will be accurately identified and a window which only included the number plate will later be set up. To do so, contours of the image are extracted and bounding boxes are obtained.

Now that the number plate has been perfectly framed within a window of the image (for both of the aforementioned cases), the contours of the characters are gently cleaned by means of a triangular opening morphological treatment. Next, the edges of the characters are cleaned by skeletonising and trimming.

Finally, those dark areas on the original image which do not correspond to the characters are removed. These could be dashes, rivets, stains and number plate edges. The figures 12 and 13 show the results of the cleaning process.

Figure 12

Figure 13

8. Character Recognition And Verification

Once the cleaning phase has finished, we move into the character recognition of the number plate using a commercial OCR based on structural analysis of the segmented characters.

During the first phase, the OCR separates each of the characters and calculates their bounding boxes. It then standardizes them in 16x16 pixel window and treats them using structural characteristics.

This software imposes restrictions as far as the minimum size of the characters to be recognized is concerned and the process we have just described complies with these.

In order for the OCR to operate correctly, the image should show black characters on a white plate background. As our previous images contained white characters on a black background, a duplication process with inversion has to be carried out beforehand (see fig. 14).

Figure 14

The OCR can be programmed to search for either letters or digits, and in any order desired. In the case in hand, however, we only know that Spanish number plates begin and end with a letter and the rest of the characters are previously unknown. We have therefore programmed the OCR to search for any character without specifying its type. The OCR will supply the recognized characters and if any have not been recognized, it will point them out showing their position.

At the present time, the number plates of Spanish vehicles fall into two different types (old: prior to 1985 and new: after 1985), and they consist of six, seven or eight characters, containing four digits one after the other in the middle. Given the peculiarities of these number plates, verification will use them to carry out the recognition process in the simplest manner possible. This verification will enable us to deal with certain ambiguities such as the similarity between the characters 0 and O, or the likeness between the 1 and the I in both types.

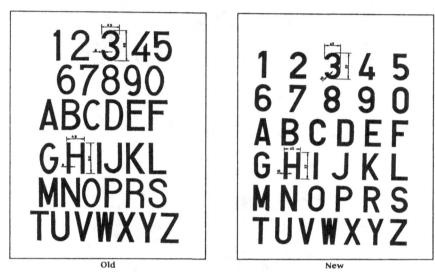

Old   New

Figure 15. Number plate character types

If the number plate contains six characters, it will be checked the first and last character are letters and the rest are digits. When the number of characters is eight the same will be done for the first two and the last two. Finally, when there are seven, it is deduced whether the two letters are at the beginning or at the end by analyzing the separation between characters.

Previous figures show the process followed for a registration number whose plate is located after the opening and closing operations. On the other hand, in figures 16-23 it can be seen that none of the contours correspond to the number plate so the end characters have had to be found to define the window which contains the number.

Figure 16. Original image

Figure 17. 256x256 window

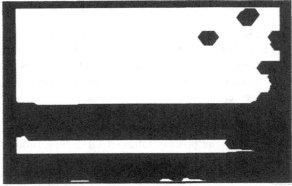

Figure 18. Closing

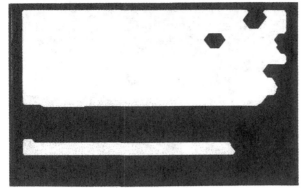

Figure 19. Opening

Figure 20. Grey scale morphology

Figure 21. Binarization and working window

256

Figure 22. Complete cleaning of the plate

Figure 23. Recognition

9. Results

Given that there are several aspects which have a bearing on the overall result of the recognition process, each one will be dealt with independently.

All the tests were carried out in conditions of natural light, and with additional illumination consisting of halogen lamps. The speed of the vehicles was low due to the fact that because stroboscope light was not used, unwanted distortions might have come about at high speeds.

With the use of this intense artificial light aimed at the area of the number plate, image acquisition was satisfactory in 95% of the cases. Problems during the capture of images were produced by the existence of number plates which were not flat, abnormal orientation of the plate or the effects of sun and shade on the plate. This last problem would not come about in areas which are partially or totally enclosed. The use of stroboscope light would also be the most suitable for lessening the effects of natural light.

Locating the number plate using an image correctly acquired may bring about two situations:

- The plate is on a dark background. This happens in the majority of vehicles and localization takes place without problems in a time under 0.5 secs.

- The plate is on a light background. In all cases the horizontal edges of the plate can be distinguished without any trouble. The vertical edges, however, are sometimes problematic. This is fundamentally due to rivets or stains which mix the characters at the ends with the edge of the plate. The time taken with task may reach 0.9 secs.

Taking both situations into account. localization of the number plate is achieved in 90% of cases.

The last aspect to be considered is character recognition in its own right. The mistakes produced and the reasons for them are as follows:

- Confusion or non-identification of the character due to:
  Part of the character missing
  Dirt build-ups
  Rivets situated at critical points

- The appearance of a false character at one of the two ends due to inaccurate localization of the plate.

- Loss of a character at one of the ends due to its nearness to the edge or because of inaccurate localization of the plate.

The time taken to carry out the recognition process ranges between 0.35 and 0.6 secs. depending on the size and number of characters to be recognized.

258

Bearing in mind all the aforementioned aspects, it can be concluded that reliability of the system lies in the region of 80%, with a total variable processing time of between 0.9 and 1.6 secs.

10. References

1. J. Serra, *Image Analysis and Mathematical Morphology* (Acad. Press, New York, 1982).
2. MVA/SME, *Machine Vision: Capabilities for Industry* (1986).
3. P.W. Verbeek and H.A. Vrooman, *Low-level image processing by max-min filters* (Signal Processing, 1988) p. 249.

A NEW HYBRID CODING METHOD FOR VIDEOCONFERENCING APPLICATIONS AND ISDN

J. Zamora, S. Sallent
Department of Applied Mathematics and Telematics
ETSIT - UPC P.O. Box 30002, Barcelona, Spain

and

L. Torres, P. Muñoz
Department of Signal Theory and Communications
ETSIT - UPC P.O. Box 30002, Barcelona, Spain

ABSTRACT

This paper presents a new hybrid coding method for low bit-rate videoconferencing transmission over ISDN. The use of both predictive and transform coding techniques along with motion compensation allows to obtain bit-rates suitable for ISDN applications. To that extend, a new quad tree based segmentation technique to detect stationary and moving parts of an image is introduced. On the other hand, to fully exploit the statistical properties of the signal to be encoded, an adaptive predictor is designed as well as a transform coding scheme to encode the prediction error. A buffer design that provides constant bit-rate is also introduced. Good visual results are obtained in the range of m x 64 Kbits/s, m = 1,2,3,... .

1. Introduction

A video conferencing system is defined as a system that provides a mean to transmit moving images in real time from participants in a conference or in a meeting. The single person-camara (SPC) system is the most commonly used video conferencing system[1] . This type of system uses a single camera to capture a view of conference participants and the resulting video signal is transmitted to the other end where it is displayed on one or more monitors. This system is suitable for situations where the number of participants per conference site is limited to one to three. The system provides visual presence of all conference participants all the time.

This work has been supported by IBM under Study Contract TC-740 and partially by PRONTIC grant 105/88 of the Spanish Goverment.

In this paper we present a videoconferencing scheme based on person to person communications (videotelephony) which is still a more restrictive case of the SPC system. In our scheme all the images to be transmitted will be of the model defined as "head and shoulders"[2].

During many years, the videoconferencing systems did not experience a big development due to the fact that analog communication systems are not very effective except for short distances. With the increasing use of digital communication links, videoconferencing systems have gained a wider acceptance. The standardization effort actually in progress for ISDN networks, has paved the way to a variety of multiple coding techniques especially suited for videoconferencing applications.

On the other hand, the easy implementation of digital systems does not come free. In comparison with a digitized speech signal at 64 Kb/s, straightforward digitization of image sequences requieres approximately 100 Mb/s. It is then clear, that to fully exploit the advantages provided by the new communication channels at bit rates of m x 64 Kb/s, m= 1,2,3 ..., efficient compression techniques are in order. If high compression rates at good visual quality are developed and new VLSI techniques are introduced that allow to implement in real time the new coding schemes, videoconferencing and videophone systems may become one of the most popular visual communications applications.

2. Coding Schemes

The main compression schemes are fundamentally based on three different techniques, predictive methods transform methods and hybrid methods. In order to have a self contained paper, the basic principles of the three techniques are briefly introduced below. This introduction follows very closely that of Netravali and Limb [3].

2.1 Predictive Methods

In basic predictive coding systems, a prediction of the sample to be encoded is made from previously coded information that has been transmitted. The error resulting from the subtraction of the prediction from the actual value of the sample is quantized into a set of discrete amplitude levels. These levels are represented as binary words of either fixed or variable word length and sent to the channel coder for transmission. Thus, the predictive coder has three basic components: 1) predictor, 2) quantizer, 3) code assigner. Depending upon the number of levels of the quantizer, a distinction is often made between Delta Modulation (DM, two levels) and Differential Pulse Code Modulation, more than two levels). Although DM has been used extensively in encoding other waveforms (e.g. speech), it has not found great use in encoding pictures. Consequently, only DPCM systems will be considered.

In its simplest form, DPCM uses the coded value of the horizontally previous pel as the prediction. However, more sophisticated predictors use the previous line (two-dimensional predictor) as well as previous frame of information (interframe predictor).

As it will be shown in the paper, our system uses two different predictive systems, particularly, an interfield predictor without motion compensation and a interfield predictor with motion compensation.

2.2 Transform Methods

In transform coding, an image is divided into subimages and then each of these subimages is transformed into a set of more independent coefficients. The coefficients are then quantized and coded for transmission. At the receiver, the received bits are decoded into transform coefficients. An inverse transform is applied to recover intensities of picture elements. Much of the compression is a result of dropping coefficients from the transmission that are small and coarsely quantizing the others as required by the picture quality. Important parameters that determine the performance of a transform coder are: size and shape of the subimages, type of transformation used, selection of the coefficients to be transmitted and quantization of them, and the bit assigner which assigns a binary word for each of the quantizer outputs. Transforms methods can be made adaptive by: adapting the transform to the statistics of the data, by selecting more or less coefficients depending on the contents of the image and by designing adaptive quantizers. Examples of transforms are: the Karhunen-Loeve, the Discrete Fourier the Discrete Cosine and the Hadamard transforms. The Discrete Cosine transform is becoming a standard in many coding schemes applications.

In our scheme, the Discrete Cosine transform is used to code the prediction error in order to further remove redundancy after the predictive stage.

2.3 Hybrid Methods

Transform coding schemes are inherently more complex in terms of both storage of data and number of operations per pel. Although the use of large block sizes removes statistical redundancy quite effectively, it has two distinct disadvantages: 1) it requires storage of large amounts of data both at the transmitter and the receiver, and consequently produces a delay in transmission, and 2) the accuracy with which different regions of the image need to be coded may vary widely within the block, and this makes adaptive coding (e.g., quantization) more difficult to accomplish. Hybrid coding is a partial answer to this problem. In hybrid coding, we consider small blocks, evaluate the coefficients, and perform DPCM of the coefficients using coefficients of the previously transmitted blocks as predictors. It has been shown that the theoretical and practical performance of hybrid coders is excellent.

3. Hybrid Coder

The coder and decoder we have implemented is shown in figure 3.1.a, 3.1.b.

The encoding algorithm uses a hybrid technique combining predictive and transform schemes. An adaptive prediction loop of transform discrete cosine transform coefficients of the original sequence to be encoded is used. The quantized coefficients are encoded through variable length coding. To further decrease the bit-rate, temporal subsampling has been done on the original image. Motion compensation has been introduced to take advantage of the reliable motion estimator that has been developed. At the decoder side, the inverse discrete cosine transform is applied to the the received coefficients and the corresponding predictive decoder is used to recover the pixels in the spatial/temporal domain. Simulations on buffer occupancy in order to obtain fixed transmission rates have also been performed. In the paragraphs to follow, a description of the encoder and the decoder is provided.

3.1 Filtering and Sampling

The spectrum of most of the videoconference sequences to be encoded, contains very low activity in the temporal domain, so it is possible to apply a temporal subsampling in order to further compress the original sequences. This subsampling consists of eliminating n images out of m (m>n) such that from 25 images/s the new sequence has 25/(n+1) images/seq. This subsampling can be generalized to spatial/temporal sampling lattices[4]. In order to avoid aliasing in the sampled spectrum due to the subsampling process, spatial/temporal low-pass filtering should be performed prior to sampling. However, videoconference images possess very low spectral contain in the temporal domain, and in our case no prior filtering was needed.

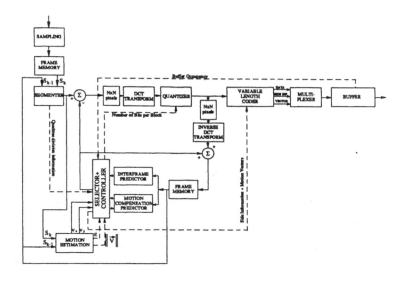

Figure 3.1.a Implemented Coder

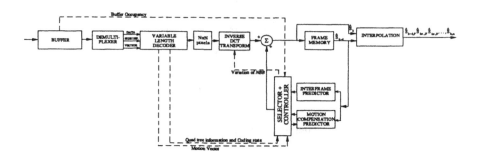

Figure 3.1.b Implemented Decoder

264

3.2 Segmentation Stage

The goal of this stage is to segment every image of the sequence in stationary parts and moving parts in order to take advantage of the high redundancy present in stationary parts of moving images. Once this segmentation is done, only moving parts of the image need to be sent. This technique is known as conditional replenishement.

Our image segmentation is based on a recursive quadtree division of the image. The actual image to be encoded S_i is pixel to pixel compared against S_{i-1} in order to detect what we call active pixels. A pixel is labeled active if the luminance difference between its value in image S_i and image S_{i-1} is above some specified pixel threshold U_y. If the number of active pixels within a block (initially all the pixels) is above some specified block threshold U_b , the block is labeled as an active block. All the blocks that habe been labelled actice blocks, are quad-tree divided and the same method is applied iteratively. The process continues until a so called static block or a minimum block size of 8 x 8 has been found. In the first case the block is not encoded and in the second the block is encoded. This process is shown in figure 3.2.

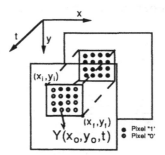

Figura 3.2 Segmentation process

The following expressions summarize the method

$$\text{Act}_{pix} (x_o, y_o, i) = \begin{cases} 1 & \text{if} \quad |Y(x_o, y_o, i) - Y(x_o, y_o, i-1)| \geq U_y \\ 0 & \text{otherwise} \end{cases}$$

(3.1)

$$\text{Block} \left([(x_i, y_i);(x_f, y_f)], i \right) = \begin{cases} \text{active} & \text{if } \sum_{x_i}^{x_f} \sum_{y_i}^{y_f} \text{Act}_{pix}(x,y,i) \cdot \alpha(x,y) \geq U_b(M) \\ \\ \text{stationary} & \text{else} \end{cases} \tag{3.2}$$

$$M = x_f - x_i = y_f - y_i \in \{256, 128, 64, 32, 16, 8\}$$

$Y(x,y,i)$ luminance of pixel **(x,y)** from frame **i**

The block threshold U_b varies according to the block size and the position of the pixel within the image. The image is a priori divided in three activity zones based on both a statistical study of the segmentation process and the head and shoulders model. Depending on to which zone a pixel belongs to, a more or less restrictive value of U_b is selected, giving more weight to those belonging to zone 3, i.e., eyes, mouth, etc. and less to those belonging to zone 1, i.e., background. This classification of the image in three zones eliminates background noise, isolated pixels changes, etc. The classification is shown in figure 3.3.

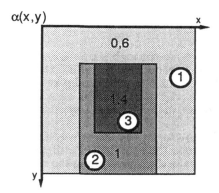

Figura 3.3 Zonal weighting

3.3 Motion estimation

A motion compensation algorithm based on block matching[5] is applied to all blocks that have been labeled as active. The algorithm gives an estimation of the direction in which the block has moved with respect to the previous image. Due to the fact that these algorithms are mainly designed for translation pure motion and do not have into account changes of luminance, zooms, and other types of motions, the error being done in the estimation has to be calculated. The two-dimensional logarithmic search[6] is used to obtain the estimation of the motion vector. The error is obtained by using the MAD criteria (Mean of the Absolute Differences) defined as

$$\varepsilon = \text{mad}\ (x, y) = \frac{1}{M \times M} \sum_{x_i}^{x_f} \sum_{y_i}^{y_f} |Y(x, y, i) - Y(x, y, i - 1)| \tag{3.3.1}$$

The estimation error ε and the magnitude of the motion vector $\|\vec{v}\|$ will allow to select the adequate prediction mode.

3.4 Prediction System

The prediction system consists of two different selection modes using interfield prediction, one with motion compensation and another without motion compensation. One or the other is selected depending on ε and $\|\vec{v}\|$. If $\|\vec{v}\|$ is different than zero and ε is small, prediction with motion compensation is selected. In all other cases simple interfield prediction is selected.

3.4.1 Interfield Prediction

The prediction is done through a linear combination of the pixels of the previous image. The prediction coeffcients are selected inversely proportional to the distance of the predicted pixel.

3.4.2 Interfield Prediction with Motion Compensation

The prediction is done in the same way as above but using motion compensation. That means that the interfield prediction is done with the pixels of the previous image displaced along the direction of the motion.

3.5 Block Transform

The prediction error of the transmitted blocks are transformed using the Discrete Cosine Transform (DCT). The general definition of a 2D transform is:

$$v(k,l) = \sum_{m,n=0}^{N-1} \sum u(m,n) a_{k,l}(m,n) \qquad 0 \le k,l \le N-1$$

$$u(m,n) = \sum_{k,l=0}^{N-1} \sum v(k,l) a^*_{k,l}(m,n) \qquad 0 \le m,n \le N-1 \tag{3.5.1}$$

where $u(m,n)$ is a bidimensional sequence and $\{a_{k,l}(m,n)\}$ is the image transform. The DCT is a separable transform defined as:

$$C(k,n) = \begin{cases} \dfrac{1}{\sqrt{N}} & k = 0,\ 0 \leq n \leq N - 1 \\[3mm] \sqrt{\dfrac{2}{N}} & 1 \leq k \leq N - 1,\ 0 \leq n \leq N - 1 \end{cases}$$

(3.5.2)

The DCT, although suboptimum in the minimum square error sense, has proven to be one of the best transform in terms of ease of implementation and compaction properties. It has become a world standard in image compression techniques.

Each one of the transform coefficients is separately quantized. The number of bits assigned to each coefficient depends on the value of its variance. It can be shown[7] that the optimum assignment is done by

$$b_{uv} = \frac{1}{2} \log_2 \left(\frac{\sigma^2_{uv}}{\theta} \right)$$

(3.5.3)

where b_{uv} is the number of bits assigned to coefficient (u,v), σ^2_{uv} is the variance of the coefficient and θ is some value that is adjusted such that the total number of bits b_{uv} gives the number of bits assigned to that specific block. Since it has been shown that the transform coefficients approximately follow a Laplacian statistic, the obtained coefficients are quantized using Laplacian quantizers.

After quantization, the coefficients, the side information and the motion vectors are coded using a Huffman variable length code. All this information is then multiplexed and sent to a buffer that guarantees a fixed transmission rate. In order to avoid an empty or full buffer, the buffer informs, through a feedback loop, the controller stage to change the segmentation stage thresholds and/or the quantizer parameters to have a constant bit-rate.

3.6 Selection and Control of the Buffer

The coding scheme we present is adaptive in two different ways. One implies that the parameters of the coder are changed (by the so called Selector) in order to exploit the local characteristics of the sequence to be

268

coded, and the other adapts the bit-rate (by the so called Controller) to the channel requirement of fixed transmission rate.

3.6.1 Controller

In order to access a fixed transmission rate channel, a buffer is needed to smooth the activity peaks of the sequence. The problem of *undeflow/overflow* of the buffer is avoided by using a coding state diagram. The coder will switch to one or to another state depending on the buffer occupancy. Figure 3.6.1 shows the coding state diagram that has been implemented. In our simulations we have used six different coding states named M_{-1}, M_0, M_1, M_2, M_3 and M_4.

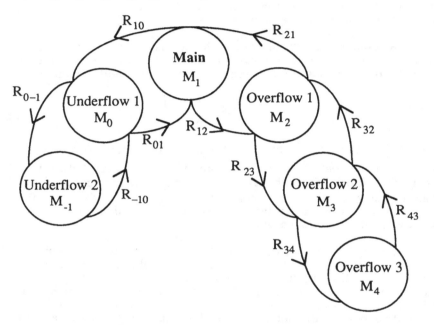

Figure 3.4 Coding state diagram

Three different types of coding states have been implemented : 1) the underflow states (underflow 1 and underflow 2) represented by M_{-1} and M_0, 2) the main working state (M_1) and 3) the overflow states represented by M_3 and M_4. The switching between coding states is done through the transitions R_{ij}/R_{ji}. These transitions are controlled by the occupancy states of the buffer.

If the buffer tends to becomes empty (low activity sequence) the scheme will switch to the underflow coding states. These states increase the bit rate by sending more pixels than necessary (low selective segmentation) or by representing with bigger accuracy the transmitted pixels (more quantization levels). If the buffer tends to become full (high activity sequence) the scheme will switch to the overflow coding states which work in the opposite form.

3.6.2 Selector

All the coding states are composed of several coding substates in order to obtain a better adaptation to the local characteristics of the images. To that end, a predictor bank has been designed in such a way that the more adequate predictor, according to some predefined switching function, is chosen depending on the image characteristics. The switching funcion is controlled by the magnitude of the motion vector $\|\vec{v}\|$ and the error associated to the estimation of such a vector. The two-dimensional logarithmic search is used to obtain the estimation of the motion vector and the error is obtained by using the MAD criteria (Mean of the Absolute Differences) as has been explained in 3.3.1. The switching function $f_{HIB}(\|\vec{v}\|,\varepsilon)$ is defined according to:

$$f_{HIB}(\|\vec{v}\|,\varepsilon) = \begin{cases} \text{Interframe} & \|\vec{v}\| = 0 \text{ and } 0 \le \varepsilon < e_2 \\[2mm] \text{Repeated block.} & mod_1 \le \|\vec{v}\| < mod_2 \text{ and } 0 \le \varepsilon < e_1 \\[2mm] \text{MotionCompensation} & \begin{cases} mod_1 \le \|\vec{v}\| < mod_2 \text{ and } e_1 \le \varepsilon < e_2 \\ \quad\quad o \\ mod_2 \le \|\vec{v}\| < mod_3 \text{ and } 0 \le \varepsilon < e_2 \\ \quad\quad o \\ 0 \le \|\vec{v}\| < mod_3 \text{ and } e_2 \le \varepsilon < \infty \\ \quad\quad o \\ mod_3 \le \|\vec{v}\| < \infty \text{ and } 0 \le \varepsilon < \infty \end{cases} \end{cases}$$

$$(3.6.1)$$

3.7 Buffer

The buffer smoothes the data flow changes due to the different characteristics of the input image. In order to well design the buffer capacity C_B, two factors have to be taken into account. The bigger the buffer capacity the smoother the data flow will be thus avoiding overflow problems. However, as the videoconference service must happen in real time, the delay cannot exceed of 0.5 sec. round-trip. Then, C_B must satisfy the following relationship

270

$$2\Delta = \frac{2C_B}{V_n} \leq 0,5 \text{ sec.} \Rightarrow C_B \leq 0,25 \cdot V_n \tag{3.7.1}$$

For the coder to work properly, what means to be most of the time in the main coding state M_1, the average bit-rate of the multiplex should approach the transmission rate of the channel. To achieve this, the buffer is divided into the different coding states, each state separated by flags which indicate the transitions between the states. The objective of this flags is to maintain the buffer in the main coding state as long as possible. To avoid oscillations between the coding states, some hysteresis is given to the transitions. Good results are obtained if the hysteresis is given a value of 0.25 % of C_B. Figure 3.7.1 shows the buffer and the different flags defined to indicate the transitions between the states.

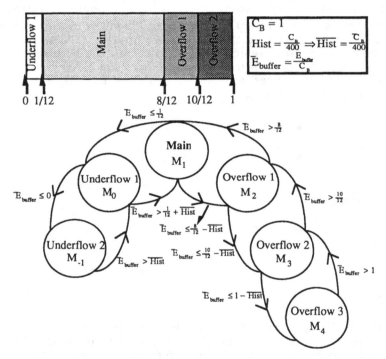

Figure 3.5 Flags and buffer transitions

The buffers of the coder and decoder are exactly the same, what means that except for the channel delay, the evolution of the buffer occupancy is the same at both ends. This implies that side information concerning the change of coding states does not need to be transmitted as the decoder will be able to follow all the changes produced at the coder.

4. Results

In order to completely check and evaluate the performance of the proposed coder, a variety of tests and measures have been realized. The tests have been divided in quality measures and compression measures. The first give an idea of how similar the coded and original sequences are, while the second provide a relationship between the information contained in the original sequence and the necessary for transmission. Generally, both types of measures are closely related. Only black and white images have been tested, but it is believed that the same results may be applied to color images. Figure 4.1 shows the different tests and measures.

$$
\text{Type of Measures} \begin{cases} \text{Quality Measures} \begin{cases} \text{Objective (SNR)} \\ \text{Subjective} \end{cases} \\ \\ \text{Compression Measures} \begin{cases} \text{Transmission rate} \begin{cases} \dfrac{V_{cod}(t)}{V_{cod}} \end{cases} \\ \text{Entropy } (H(X)) \\ \text{Compression Factor (F.C.)} \end{cases} \end{cases}
$$

Figure 4.1 Types of measures and tests realized to evaluate performance

Only results with the very well known image sequence Miss America are presented, although similar results have been obtained for the sequences Trevor and Walter. Two different transmission rates have been simulated, one corresponding to a channel of 384Kbits/s what means a compression of about 40, and the other corresponding to a channel of 64Kbits/s what means a compression of about 200. Signal to noise ratio, transmission speed for different images of the sequence, visual results of the encoded image and the segmentation obtained of the original images are given for both transmission rates.

4.1 384Kbits/s Channel

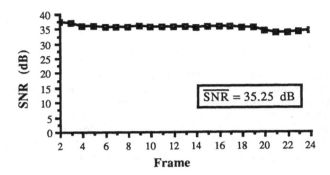

Figure 4.2 SNR of the first 24 encoded images

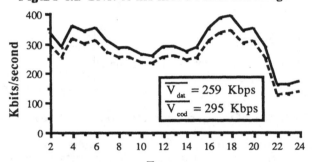

Figure 4.3 Transmission rate of the first encoded 24 images

H1dat(X)	H2dat(X)	H3dat(X)	H4dat(X)	H5dat(X)	H6dat(X)	H7dat(X)
0'000	1'991	0'000	3'7312	0'000	0'000	0'000

Table 4.1 Entropy of the quantized channels (NBB bits)

$H_{div}(X)$ (bits/symb.output)	$H_{mov}(X)$ (bits/symb)	% (side.inf) (bits/symb)	F.C.
1'9360	2'4630	12'31 %	44'35

Table 4.2 Overall performance

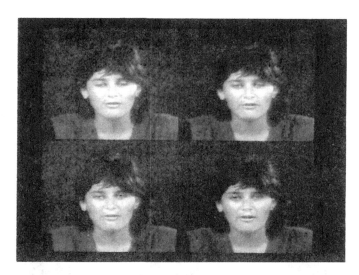

Figure 4.4 Original sequence Miss America (frames 9 - 12)

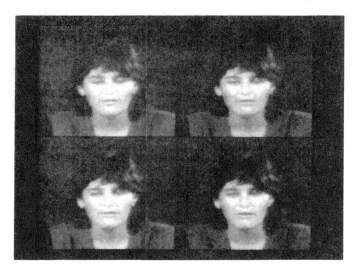

Figure 4.5 Coded Miss America at 384 Kbits/s (frames 9 - 12)

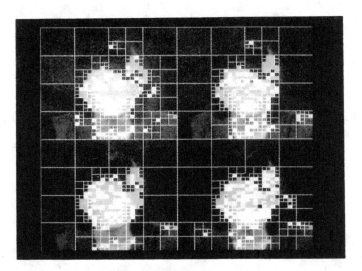

Figure 4.6 Segmentation of frames 9 - 12

4.2 64Kbits/s Channel

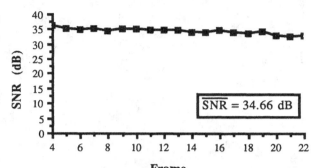

Figure 4.2 SNR of the first 24 encoded images

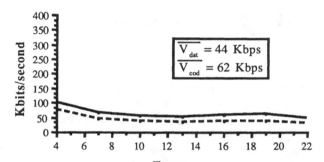

Figure 4.7 Transmission rate of the first encoded 24 images

H1dat(X)	H2dat(X)	H3dat(X)	H4dat(X)	H5dat(X)	H6dat(X)	H7dat(X)
0'000	1'980	0'000	0'000	0'000	0'000	0'000

Table 4.3 Entropy of the quantized channels (NBB bits)

$H_{div}(X)$	$H_{mov}(X)$	% (side.inf)	F.C.
(bits/symb.output)	(bits/symb)	(bits/symb)	
1'720	2'970	30'04 %	208'59

Table 4.4 Overall performance

276

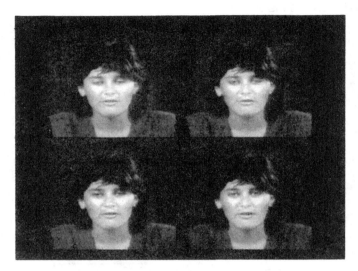

Figure 4.8 Original sequence Miss America (frames 9 - 12)

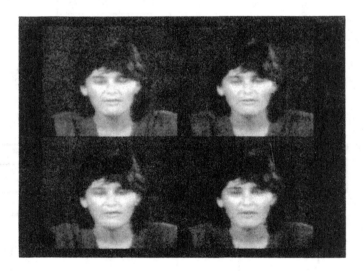

Figure 4.9 Coded Miss America at 64 Kbits/s (frames 9 - 12)

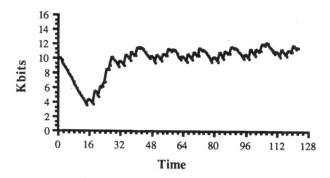

Figure 4.10 Buffer occupancy

From the above results the following conclusions can be drawn:

1. For transmission channels of 384 Kbits/s, no temporal subsampling is done, i.e., the full sequence of 25 images is coded every second.

2. The optimum parameters of the selector are those that make the coder to work mainly in the motion compensation state. This state is the best matched to the characteristics of the videoconference sequences.

3. The percentage of side information used is constant, as long as the subsampling factor is not very high.

4. The entropy of the data, segmentation information and motion vectors do not experience big changes for both transmission rates.

5. As less coefficients are selected (lower transmission rate), more low pass effect is appreciated in the encoded images.

6. For other videoconference images, similar results are obtained.

5. Conclusions

A new hybrid videoconference coding system has been presented. The system is based on the "head and shoulders model" and presents good visual results in the 64 - 384 Kbits/s range. Hybrids methods based on predictive and transform techniques are used. Motion compensation is also introduced depending on the estimation motion error and the magnitude of the motion vector. Designs of the buffer to accommodate a fixed transmission channel rate have also been introduced.

It has been proven that the new system can be used in low speed transmission channels as may be the case for the basic access of the ISDN.

6. References

[1]   S.Sabri, B.Prasada, *"Video Conferencing Systems"*, Proceedings of the IEEE, Vol 73, NO.4, April 1985.

[2]   R.C.Harkness, *"Video Teleconferencing"*, Digital Communications, SAMS 1986.

[3]   A.W.Netravali, J.O.Limb, *"Picture Coding: A Review""*, Proceedings of the IEEE, Vol. 69, NO.3, March 1980.

[4]   E.Dubois, *"The Sampling and Reconstruction of Time-Varying Imagery with Application in Video Systems"*, Proceedings of the IEEE, Vol.73, NO.4, April 1985.

[5]   A.Netravali, J.D.Robbins, *"Motion-Compensated Television Coding: Part I"*, The Bell System Technical Journal, Vol. 53, NO.3, March 1979.

[6]   J.O.Limb, J.A.Murphy, *"Estimating the Velocity of Moving Images in TV Signals"*, Computerr Graphics and Image Processing, March 1980.

[7]   N.S.Jayant, P.Noll, *Digital Coding of Waveforms*, Prentice-Hall, New York 1984.

ARTIFICIAL VISION APPLIED TO THE GUIDANCE OF AN AUTONOMOUS ROBOT

M. Mazo

Dpto. Tecnología Electrónica, Universidad de Alcalá
28871 Alcalá de Henares, Madrid, Spain

and

D. Maravall

Dpto. Inteligencia Artificial
Universidad Politécnica de Madrid
28660 Boadilla del Monte , Madrid, Spain

ABSTRACT

The general problems and solutions concerning the visual guidance of a mobile robot whose main purpose is to follow a line on the floor are described. After briefly commenting the general ideas behind the visual feedback and control of the robot, the paper presents the algorithms implemented to automatically analyze in real time the scenes viewed by the robot and the corresponding computation of the control variables needed for its guidance. These algorithms have been developed in the authors' laboratories.

1. Introduction

In these days there is an enormous, immense effort put on work and research aiming at the implementation of machines endowed with considerable capacity of self-decision and autonomy. In this respect, mobile robots present a tremendous challenge because they integrate the different aspects concerning machine perception, decision and action. The mobile robots will help to solve some of the most difficult problems in Artificial Intelligence like the programming of common sense reasoning and the way of learning through sensory experiences.

Up to now the mobile robots used in industry employ guidance techniques limited to (a) underground cables (the well-known filo-guided charts with a widespread use), (b) optical or magnetic tracks (painted lines detected by optical sensors or lines of metallic mass recognized by magnetic detectors) and (c) chemical tracks (based on ultraviolet rays).

The research efforts concerning mobile robots are nowadays centered on systems without any underground infrastructure. These mobile robots will therefore be able to operate in environments with unexpected obtacles and their trajectories will be easily modified, allowing the optimization in real time of robots trajectories and tasks.

Some of the current developments in the industrial sector are directed to the tracking of computer-stored trajectories. The possible deviations of the robot from

280

the ideal trajectory can be computed by means of several methods: (a) using triangulation with infrared sensors, (b) with inertial navigation (gyroscopes and accelerometers) and (c) using computer vision algorithms and visual navigation signs. Through the combination of several of these techniques the mobile robot can estimate its "true" position at every instant of time and subsequently correct its trajectory when necessary.

Due to the complexity of the environments in which usually the mobile robots have to operate, we believe that the research must be directed towards the coordination of several sensors: ultrasounds, infrared and vision in particular. Computer vision is the most powerful sensory information for the mobile robot, not only for its guidance (which endows the robot with a great autonomy) but for implementing another tasks like object recognition, identification of places etc.

In this paper we expound some of the problems concerning the guidance and control of a mobile robot based on the concept of visual feedback. We have developed for this purpose a prototype of autonomous vehicle which is able of following all kind of trajectories at speeds of 1.5 m/s. In Figure 1 is shown the configuration of the vehicle, which consists mainly of: mobile robot structure, black and white video camera, the computer with an image digitizer and the electronic board to control the servomotors of the vehicle and to communicate with the image processor. For the sake of notation we will refer to this prototype from now on by AVGAV (Autonomous Vehicle Guided by Artificial Vision).

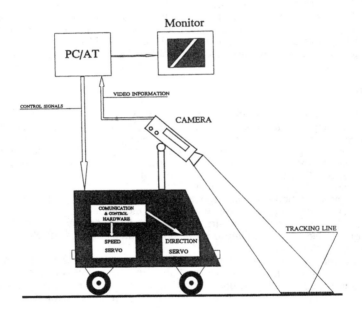

Figure 1. Configuration of the mobile robot.

2. Control Based on Visual Feedback

Visual feedback differs from other types of control systems in the fact that some or all the signals appearing in the system are of a "visible" nature. Obviously, the mobile robot guided by computer vision enters this control category.

The implementation of control algorithms for a mobile robot using artificial vision creates important problems due to the non-linear nature of the robot dynamics, the complexity and time-consuming characteristics of the image processing involved and the uncertainty inherent to the environment.

The objective of the visual feedback is to eliminate the environment uncertainty, but the information provided by the vision system is not complete regarding the surroundings of the robot because it is limited by the field of vision of the camera. For this reason, the vehicle control must be based on measurements of its position relative to the trajectory to be followed (tracking line).

The idea for our prototype, AVGAV, is to operate in completely unknown environments by following a trajectory defined by a painted line on the floor, using to this aim the visual feedback provided by the vision system. The physical variables to be controlled (Figure 2) are the following.

1. Angle θ formed by the longitudinal axis of the vehicle, which is lined up with the on-board camera, and the tracking line (TL).

2. Distance x between the middle point of the TL and the robot longitudinal axis.

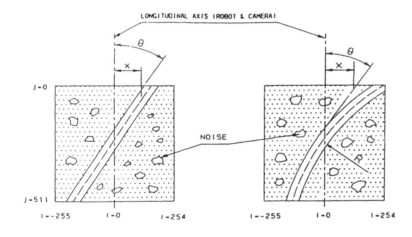

Figure 2. Control variables used by the visual feedback.

282

The justification for the use of two control variables is that both of them are needed for steady movement of the robot, without oscillations, and for a good alignment with the TL. In Figure 3 are displayed two situations in which it is advisable the use of both control variables. In the situation depicted in Figure 3   if only the control variable x were used the robot would turn in principle to the left and inmediately afterwards it would turn to the right; which would mean an oscillatory, undesirable trajectory of the robot.

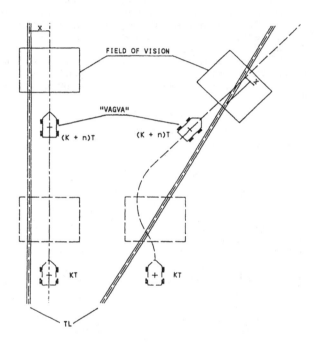

Figure 3. Examples of deficient line tracking when using a single control variable.

Another important point in the robot's guidance is the distance between the vehicle and the point at which the variables x and θ are computed. The type of the trajectory the robot have to follow depends strongly on the value of that distance. For straight trajectories this distance should correspond to the farthest points from the camera, while for curved trajectories the distance must correspond to the nearest points. Figure 4 represents two situations where this distance is not suitably chosen and therefore the vehicle moves incorrectly.

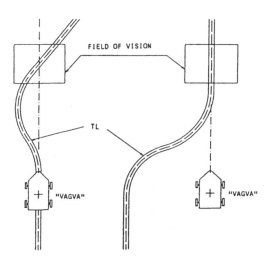

Figure 4. Influence of the distance between the robot and the points in which θ and x are computed (field of vision).

Finally, in order to accomplish the conditions $x(t) = 0$ and $\theta(t) = 0$, which is obviosly the global objective of the robot's guidance, a control loop based on visual feedback has been implemented, as shown in Figure 5. In this figure the control variable vector $\vec{u}(t)$, is formed by the turn angle applied to the directrice wheels and the speed applied to the driving wheels.

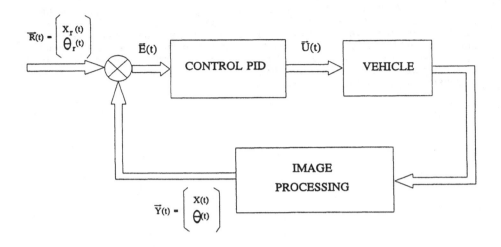

Figure 5. Block diagram of the control loop with visual feedback for the robot´s guidance.

3. Identification of the Vehicle Dynamics

If in the control loop of Figure 5 the vehicle transference function $Y(s)/U(s)$ was known, well-stablished optimal control techniques could be applied.

Unfortunately, the dynamics of AVGAV is unknown and variable in time (because of different speeds, accelerations, loads etc.). For this reason adaptive control in real time is absolutely necessary for the vehicle guidance: the controller law must change accordingly with the plant´s changes which must be detected by some identification procedure.

With this objective in mind, we have implemented an identification model in real time (Maravall, 1987; Mazo, 1988) based on Taylor´s series development of the variables to be controlled. This approach is quite different from the usual one based on approximations to physical and mathematical models of the plant to be controlled. Our approach has proved to be successful in the guidance of the robot and we believe it could be of interest in another control systems.

Using the Taylor's series development approach, the dynamics of the variables θ and x for a generic sampling instant $t = kT$ are described by the equations

$$\theta[(k+1)T] = \theta[kT] + T\dot{\theta}[kT] + \frac{1}{2!}T^2\ddot{\theta}[kT] + \ldots + \frac{1}{n!}T^n\theta^{(n)}[kT] + \ldots$$

$$X[(k+1)T] = X[kT] + T\dot{X}[kT] + \frac{1}{2!}T^2\ddot{X}[kT] + \ldots + \frac{1}{n!}T^n X^{(n}[kT] + \ldots \qquad (1)$$

These equations provide with the real dynamics of the two variables. Nevertheless, the problem consists on the fact that the successive derivatives of both variables cannot be computed with enough accuracy.

By approximating

$$\dot{\theta}[kT] \approx \frac{\theta[kT] - \theta[(k-1)T]}{T}$$

$$\ddot{\theta}[kT] \approx \frac{\dot{\theta}[kT] - \dot{\theta}[(k-1)T]}{T}$$
. . . .

$$\dot{X}[kT] \approx \frac{X[kT] - X[(k-1)T]}{T} \qquad (2)$$

$$\ddot{X}[kT] \qquad \frac{\dot{X}[kT] - \dot{X}[(k-1)T]}{T}$$
. . . .

then the dynamics of θ and X, without any reference to the particular sampling instance, would be given by

$$\theta(k+1) = W_{\theta 1}\,\theta(k) + W_{\theta 2}\,\theta(k-1) + \ldots + W_{\theta N}\,\theta(k-N+1) + \ldots$$

$$X(k+1) = W_{x1}\,X(k) + W_{x2}\,X(k-1) + \ldots + W_{xN}\,\theta(k-N+1) + \ldots \qquad (3)$$

For our prototype we have limited the Taylor's development to the fourth element, obtaining the following MA equations

286

$$\theta\,(k+1) \;=\; W_{\theta 1}\,\theta(k) \;+\; W_{\theta 2}\,\theta(k-1) \;+\; W_{\theta 3}\,\theta\,(k-2) \;+\; W_{\theta 4}\,\theta\,(k-3) \qquad (4)$$
$$X\,(k+1) \;=\; W_{x1}\,X(k) \;+\; W_{x2}\,X(k-1) \;+\; W_{x3}\,X(k-2) \;+\; W_{x4}\,X\,(k-3)$$

The $W_{\theta 1},$ $W_{\theta 2}$, $W_{\theta 3}$, $W_{\theta 4}$, W_{x1}, W_{x2}, W_{x3}, W_{x4} coefficients that define the mobile robot dynamics can be computed in real time by means of well-known estimation techniques. For out prototype we have employed the recursive mean least squares algorithm.

Once the system's coefficients have been estimated, the next step is the corresponding tuning of the control algorithm. For the mobile robot, a control algorithm incorporating the three components: proportional, integral and derivative (PID) has been successfully applied. This self-tuning PID has proved to be extremely robust considering the extreme variations appearing in the robot's dynamics. The block-diagram of this control algorithm is displayed in Figure 6.

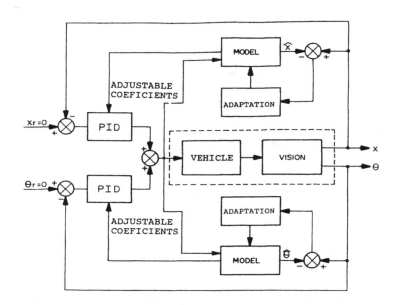

Figure 6. Block diagram of the control system applied to the AVGAV.

4. Computation of the Control Variables Using Visual Information

The information concerning the trajectory that the robot must follow is obtained through the video camera lined up with the longitudinal axis of the robot. This information, as stated below, is summarized in the variables x and θ.

The computation of x and θ may be implemented using different strategies, but there are always two important aspects (usually opposite each other) to be taken into consideration: high immunity from noise and low computing times. The first condition is vital for obtaining a reliable information of the control variables even under hostile situations: brightness, floor intensities similar to the TL etc. The second condition allows small sampling periods and therefore more robust control algorithms and the capacity of higher robot's speeds as well.

The computer vision algorithm implemented in AVGAV (Marzo, 1988) begins by a priori fixing a number m of rows of the frame image to be analyzed. These m lines correspond, within the field of vision, to points in the floor equidistant over the longitudinal axis of the vehicle. So, once the camera position is fixed and calling L the scene length "seen" by the camera, i.e. the image frame, the lines (j) candidate to be analyzed correspond to the points on the longitudinal axis that are separated by a distance L/m.

The computation of the intensity threshold (THR) that permits to discriminate points of the floor from the TL is based on the histogram of the first row or column analyzed. Because it is not expected an important change of the intensities pattern of the TL and its environment, i.e. the floor, within a single frame image and with the purpose of reducing the processing time as much as possible, the threshold value is maintained for each frame. This value is updated for the next frame using the same method.

The search starts by the inferior row j_0 in the image frame, see Figure 7, that is the nearest zone to the robot. If no crossing point of the TL is detected within this lowest row, the first and the last column of the image frame are analyzed to check whether or no there are crossings points of these extreme columns with the TL. Once detected the crossing the analysis is centered on the candidate rows that are placed above the row to which belongs the middle point of the segment formed by the TL with the corresponding column. When no crossings are detected after examining the row j_0 and the first and the last columns, the conclusion is that there is no TL within the frame or that the TL is interrupted.

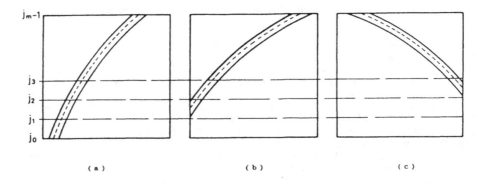

Figure 7. Different situations appearing in the search of the TL.

In order to avoid the effect of possible noises such as pixels corresponding to the floor with similar intensities than those of the TL and to simultaneously reduce the time processing, instead of analyzing all the pixels of each row the following procedure has been applied.

In the first place and only when the vehicle is started the two first middle points of the TL are obtained after analyzing the pixels of two rows, which is the case depicted in Figure 7(a), or the pixels of one row and one column, that corresponds to the situations appearing in Figure 7(b) and (c). Using these two points the column order i of the middle point of the TL corresponding to the next row to analyze is predicted.

With that coordinate the row analysis is centered on the corresponding column until the two edges of the TL are found and therefore its middle point is computed. The column order, which defines the coordinate of the corresponding pixel together with its row, for a generic row j is given by

$$ipm = \frac{\sum i \, f(i)}{N} \qquad (5)$$

where:

$$f(i) = 0, \text{ if intensity (i)} < THR$$

$$f(i) = 1, \text{ if intensity } (i) > THR$$

$$N = \text{sum of all pixels with } f(i) = 1$$

With this approach it can easily be seen that the noise effect is reduced and at the same time the image processing speed is increased. When the number of pixels analyzed on the right and on the left of the predicted point is higher than a prespecified value and there is no TL's middle point detected, then the conclusion is that there does not exist TL in the frame analyzed or the noise present does not permit to detect its edges.

The prediction algorithm is based on the hypothesis that the predicted point is over the segment linking the two last TL's middle points computed; i.e.

$$i_n = A\ i_{n-1} + B\ i_{n-2} \qquad\qquad (6)$$

where

$$A = \frac{j_n - j_{n-2}}{j_{n-1} - j_{n-2}} \quad ; \qquad B = \frac{j_n - j_{n-1}}{j_{n-2} - j_{n-1}}$$

This hypothesis comes from the fact that if the AVGAV moves always on straight sections of the TL then the prediction will be accurate, unless there are errors on the preceding points. For the case in which there are turns m can be determined as a function of L and the maximum curvature of TL in order to obtain an accurate prediction. In Figure 8 it is shown an example in which the pixels with intensities equal or higher than the TL do not affect the TL's middle point when using prediction.

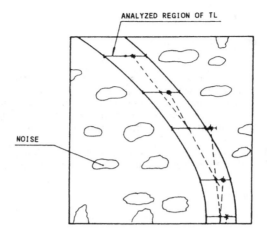

Figure 8. Example of the prediction algorithm.

      For the prediction of the control variables x and θ it was taken into account the possibility of errors in the estimation of the TL´s middle point. These errors come usually from local variations in the TL´s width, which are produced by the irregularities of the TL itself, by the presence of brightness in some sections of the TL´s environment, by regions near the TL with similar intensity levels, by spots over the TL, by very sharp turns etc. etc.

      These errors are not very important in the measurement of x, but they are extremely influential on θ.

      For that reason the computation of θ in the image frame's region of interest must not be based on the points obtained through the image processing but on the middle points of successive segments. Mathematically speaking this means that θ can be considered as the angle formed by the AVGAV´s longitudinal axis and the straight line

$$j = j_{m0} + \frac{j_{m1} - j_{m0}}{i_{m1} - i_{m0}} \ (i - i_{m0}) \qquad (7)$$

where

$$j_{m0} = \frac{1}{2^{n-1}} \sum_{h=0}^{n-1} \binom{n-1}{h} \ j(h); \quad j_{m1} = \frac{1}{2^{n-1}} \sum_{n=0}^{n-1} \binom{n-1}{h} \ j(h+1)$$

$$i_{m0} = \frac{1}{2^{n-1}} \sum_{n=0}^{n-1} \binom{n-1}{h} i(h); \quad i_{m-1} = \frac{1}{2^{n-1}} \sum_{n=0}^{n-1} \binom{n-1}{h} i(h+1)$$

and n is the number of middle points obtained by the image analysis.

Afterwards, in order to avoid abrupt changes that can appear in the estimation of θ, a low pass filter was applied.

Finally, let us say that the vision algorithm detects when there is a risk of losing the TL and when this happens the algorithm is able to recuperate the TL.

5. Optimum Width of the Tracking Line (TL)

An important and influential parameter design in the guidance of the AVGAV is the TL´s width, which must be big enough to allow an easy, direct identification and, at the same time, must not trascend the limits imposed by the field of vision.

Obviously, the optimum width must minimize the identification error, which depends on the sensor characteristics (camera plus image digitizer) and the geometrical arrangement of the camera including possible errors of its position (Mazo, 1988). Starting from the camera model shown in Figure 9, it can be proved that the image coordinates, x_i and z_i, of a generic point as a fuction of its absolute coordinates (x,y,z) are given by

$$x_i = f \frac{x \cos \alpha + y \sin \alpha}{-x \cos \phi \sin \alpha + y \cos \alpha \cos \phi - z_0 \sin \phi}$$

(8)

$$y_i = f \frac{x \sin \alpha \sin \phi - y \sin \phi \cos \alpha - z_0 \cos \phi}{-x \cos \phi \sin \alpha + y \cos \alpha \cos \phi - z_0 \sin \phi}$$

Where α and ϕ are the pan and roll angles, respectively. f is the focal distance.

292

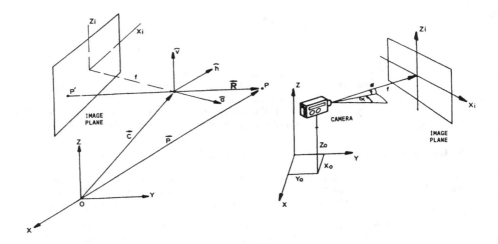

Figure 9. Camera model and computation of the image coordinates.

Using these equations it is easy to obtain the minimum width of the TL, W_{min}, that happens to be

$$W_{min} = \frac{b \ (y_{max} \cos \phi - z_0 \sin \phi)}{f} \ I \qquad (9)$$

where

- b is the minimum number of pixels estimated for the TL's width in the image frame

- I: pixel's length

- y_{max} : maximum distance of the field of vision

The maximum width of the TL is estimated considering that in the worst case it cannot completely cover the field of vision.

Finally, it can be shown using the above equations that the error obtained in the computation of the TL width, considering all the possible variations of the camera position (variations of ϕ, α and z_0) diminishes with the increment of the TL width.

Conclusions

We have described the problems and solutions concerning the visual guidance of a mobile robot whose main purpose is to follow a tracking line on the floor, with highly noisy backgrounds. After briefly commenting the general ideas behind the visual feedback and control of the robot, we have presented the algorithms implemented to automatically analyze in real time (determined by the specification of industrial speeds for the mobile robot; i.e. about 1.5 m/s) the scenes presented to the robot and the corresponding computation of the control variables needed for its guidance. These algorithms have been successfully implemented on a mobile robot designed and built in the author's laboratories.

References

1. Maravall, D. "Identification and Control of a Vehicle Guided by Computer Vision" (in Spanish). Group of Advanced Control and Artificial Vision. Polytechnical University of Madrid. Madrid, 1987.

2. Mazo, M. "Contribution to the Control and Guidance of an Autonomous Vehicle with Visual Feedback" (in Spanish). Ph. D. Dissertation. Polytechnical University of Madrid. Madrid, 1988.

3. Kuan, D. et al. "Autonomous Robotics Vehicle Road Following". IEEE Trans. Pattern Analysis and Machine Intelligence, Vol. 10, No. 5, Sept. 1988.

4. Weiss, L.E. et al. "Adaptive Control of Robots Using Visual Feedback". The Robotics Institute, Carnegie-Mellon University. Pittsburgh, 1986.